D1521085

Consensus and beyond

The development of Labour Party strategy since the second world war

FOR MY PARENTS

Alan Warde

Consensus and beyond

The development of Labour Party
strategy since the second world war

MANCHESTER UNIVERSITY PRESS

Published by Manchester University Press
Oxford Road, Manchester M13 9PL

British Library cataloguing in publication data

Warde, Alan
    Consensus and beyond.
    1. Labour Party (Great Britain) — History
    I. Title
    324.24107'09   JN1129.L32

    ISBN 0-7190-0849-2

Printed in Great Britain by
Biddles Ltd, Guildford, Surrey

Contents

Acknowledgements

Many people have helped me to write this book. I would like to thank my friends in the Sociology Department at Leeds University, especially Zygmunt Bauman who supervised the writing of its previous incarnation. I appreciate deeply the valuable advice and criticism that I have received from Nick Abercrombie, Robert McKenzie, Lewis Minkin, Patrick Seyd, John Urry and Peter Worsley, all of whom persevered to read drafts of the manuscript right to the end. My gratitude to Nancy Warde is greater than ever; if I could write as quickly, or think as precisely as she types, then the book would have been complete before most of the events had occurred. Most of all I want to thank my friends Lee Comer and Doug McEachern who, together, are responsible for the better features of the book, from the good ideas, to the studied absence of split infinitives, to the fact that it was ever finished. I made the mistakes, but by accident. I would also like to thank the staff of the libraries of the Labour Party, Leeds University and Lancaster University.

Alan Warde
Lancaster

List of abbreviations

AEU	Amalgamated Engineering Union (later AUEW, Amalgamated Union of Engineering Workers)
CBI	Confederation of British Industry
CDS	Campaign for Democratic Socialism
CLP	Constituency Labour Party
CLPD	Campaign for Labour Party Democracy
CND	Campaign for Nuclear Disarmament
EEC	European Economic Community
ILP	Independent Labour Party
IMF	International Monetary Fund
LPCR	Annual Report of the Labour Party Conference
NATO	North Atlantic Treaty Organization
NEB	National Enterprise Board
NEC	National Executive Committee
NEDC	National Economic Development Council
NUM	National Union of Miners
NUR	National Union of Railwaymen
OECD	Organization for Economic Co-operation and Development
PLP	Parliamentary Labour Party
SDA	Social Democratic Alliance
SDF	Social Democratic Federation
TGWU	Transport & General Workers Union
TUC	Trades Union Congress
USDAW	Union of Shop, Distributive & Allied Workers
VFS	Victory for Socialism

Introduction

The British Labour Party has always been divided. Whilst initially a creature of the trade union movement, seeking repeal of restrictive legislation,
other groups involved in its formation conceived it to be the institution
through which a socialist commonwealth, of whatever kind, might be built
in Britain. These two notions of the purpose of the party, dominant
during the first two decades of the twentieth century, still persist. The
subsequent demise of the Liberal Party complicated further the political
alliance of Labour as it became the political instrument of the vast majority of people of radical sympathy. After 1920 the Labour Party grew
to be an organization sheltering a mixture of trade unionists, socialists,
radical—liberals and humanitarians, whose divergent interests and aspirations frequently brought them into conflict with one another. This book
is about the dynamics of such conflict, its outcomes and its impact on
British society in the period after the second world war.

It is odd, given their frequency, that disputes within the Party per-
petually evoke surprise among political commentators. Whenever the Party
publicly disagrees about its future an elaborate, almost ritualized, set of
reactions follow. Regardless of the issue, someone will condemn the
argument as an arcane and indulgent, quasi-theological, inquiry; another
will contend that it is irresponsible, since there are more important things
to be done; a third will predict the imminent disintegration of the Party;
and a fourth will claim that it is nothing more than a screen concealing
personal ambitions and sinister motivations. But despite the regularity
with which this litany is recited, and although it may sometimes express
partial truths, it obscures the systematic basis of intra-party cleavage.
Internal conflict is neither unusual nor eradicable.

The big, public disputes which so regularly divide the Party continue to
centre on whether a socialist society is desirable, attainable or viable. True,
there are other sources of division within the Party which affect the way

it acts and cause resentment: the oligarchical tendencies of organization separate elite from mass membership; and distinctions enshrined in the party constitution, between unions and Constituency Labour Parties (CLPs) in Conference, between Parliamentary Labour Party (PLP) and Conference, and between cabinet and back-benchers within the PLP, define potential lines of conflict. However, even grievances arising from such apparently institutional fissures are usually grounded in contrary views of ultimate ends. For example, the dispute which monopolized attention in late 1980 and resulted in the formation of the Social Democratic Party concerned, *prima facie*, the constitutional powers of various committees and officers of the party. New procedures for electing the party leader, adopted at the special conference at Wembley in January 1981, provided the ostensible public reason for the most concerted set of resignations from the PLP since the Independent Labour Party seceded in 1932. The culmination of a decade of struggle for control over the formulation of party policy, the split related less to internal procedure, will to power or patronage than to calculations about the quality of social change which the Labour Party should promote. It was no accident that the arguments about proper democratic customs were accompanied by rather more copious, if nebulous, declarations about future political orientations.[1]

For the groups involved, even internal procedures are directly related to their hopes and fears about the future structure of society. The left, posed with the 'gradualist dilemma' of achieving a socialist transformation by parliamentary means, calculates that the best chance of success lies in insisting that Labour governments implement programmes formulated by partisan Conference and its agents. Espousing what political scientists call the 'democratic elitist' model of politics − which maintains that the reality of democratic systems is that electors choose, at regular intervals, between competing party programmes − the left has selected the easiest, and perhaps the only, available means whereby an elected government might both adopt and implement a socialist programme. The right, by contrast, employs a 'plebiscitarian' model of politics according to which MPs are responsible not to party membership or organization but to the individual constituents who elect them. This model, sedimented in certain antiquated myths of the British constitution, focuses on individual voters who, by definition, are heterogeneous. MPs are thereby released from obligation to those collective interests which, typically, have provided the rationale for competition between parties for the popular vote but which are perceived now as the major threat to the social system preferred by the right. The model thus serves to conceal the principal structural antagonisms between classes and functional interest groups which while recurrently provoking political crises are only indirectly transmitted through the electoral system. Whether or not a realignment of British political parties results, it should be remembered that, although both sets of contestants traded claims to conformity with established democratic doctrines, the dispute revolved around basic political strategy.

If intra-party conflict is about ultimate ends then it is necessary to examine the ideologies expressed by political actors, an exercise which has become very unfashionable of late. The derision to which political argument has been subjected in the past thirty years is a cumulative effect of both contemporary political ideas and institutional pressures. It was conceived in the 1950s that Western societies had reached a point in their development where such a strong consensus existed among the populace that substantial disagreement about political goals no longer obtained. This belief was rapidly succeeded by a general cult of expertise whereby political decisions, for example about economic policy, could be referred to informed professional advisers and administrators rather than being subjected to political debate. Both these tendencies were given considerable institutional support by the expanded power of the executive arms of the state. These developments marked a sharp devaluation of political ideas and political vision; competing views of a desirable future were dismissed as anachronistic and ineffectual. With the passage of time these conceptions have themselves been seen to contain normative prescriptions for the future, albeit a future rather like the present. But ideology has not thereby been rehabilitated. Ideological disagreements are still predominantly trivialized, reduced to the personal motivations of ambitious politicians.[2] Yet to the extent that party government is effective in Britain (i.e. that governments can and do implement *party* policies, even when they are contrary to the recommendations and interests of powerful private and state organizations), ideological disputes are determinant.

It is unfortunate that ideological diversity within the Party has been distilled into the hoary imagery of a left—right continuum. While serviceable enough in everyday usage, the distinction becomes a liability in precise, historical analysis. One of its failings is that it imposes non-existent continuities, by neglecting to specify the content of alternative strategies and philosophies at stake. Hence the fact that the right has been, variously, socialist, utilitarian, and liberal, with distinct and important consequences for British politics, is lost from view. This mistake is compounded by attending too exclusively to the question of why the Labour Party has proved an ineffective vehicle of socialism, a habit which tends to distinguish only along the axis socialism/non-socialism. A second defect is that the language of left and right implies that there must also be a centre. It is one of the more pervasive illusions of contemporary politics which suggests that as the programmatic statements of the two main parties polarize they vacate the middle ground which is the terrain of majority opinion. It is equally misleading to deem any group in the Labour Party which seeks compromise positions in disputes as 'centrists'. For example, the distinctiveness of Wilson's politics of the 'technological revolution' in the mid 1960s was missed when, because it afforded a basis for unity within the Party, it was deigned to be a centrist coup. A final deficiency of the image is its inability to locate the trade union interest in Labour politics. Patterns of intra-party conflict make it apparent that the interests of the trade unions are of paramount importance in determining the outcome of power struggles. But union decisions to support different factions in the Party are less reflections about ideological niceties, and more calculations about their members' interests. Such motivations hardly fit a left—right continuum of ideological convictions; and nor do they always benefit the same side.

The two decades of bipartisan politics after 1950 created several illusions about permanent changes in the British political system. The idea of the centre, which had some substance in that specific period of inter-party consensus, exaggerated the decline of party government. Without doubt, the autonomy of parties with respect to the state has declined in the twentieth century, but it has still mattered which party won elections. What have been obscured, though, are changes in the role of parties. Offe has argued that as the state expanded its range of competence in this period, it pre-empted and absorbed activities formerly undertaken by parliament and party government.[3] However, the state apparatus is inherently incapable of providing justifications for its own activities. Accordingly, compensating for the potential deficit in legitimation has become the main function of parliament and the parties. Legitimation is not solely accomplished by the direct transmission of ideological messages: the proper use of parliamentary procedures is usually sufficient to bestow legitimacy on a government command regardless of its content; the provision of just, or generous, welfare services is also a means by which social arrangements are legitimated. And even when legitimacy is secured through the transmission of ideology there are many channels other than the political system — the mass media, educational establishments, etc. But it remains a remarkable feature of post-war Britain that it was largely a Labour Party ideology which created and sustained the dominant form of legitimation, the post-war 'consensus'. The term 'consensus' has a variety of meanings.[4] I use it to refer to a system of beliefs, moral values, and social aspirations, held in common by the majority of powerful political agents and institutions, and imputed by them to most citizens.[5] The period after 1950 was characterized by such an ethical agreement among elites, including the greater parts of the major political parties, state and public agencies, and the 'peak organizations' of capital and labour. This formidable consensus was the basis for a bipartisan political formula which specified the general direction of government policy between 1950 and 1970. When, for various reasons, that consensus faltered, it was again the Labour Party which attempted to provide an alternative formula, the Social Contract, for the maintenance of harmony and consent.

It was not inevitable that the Party should have become such a staunch prop of consensus politics. By the same token that the Party may positively engage in legitimating the social order, it can also contest dominant legitimations. Arguably, a continued democratic socialist presence in the Party was necessary for Labour involvement in the project of social stabilization in the period. Panitch observed that the Party performs a dual role, as both a working class and an integrative party.[6] He implied that the Party's capacity to act as an integrative party was dependent upon its class base, even though the imperatives associated with each role contradict one another. It would seem that to maintain that dual role depends upon a real, if tenuous, possibility that the Party might put its class function before its integrative one. As an effect of the 'mobilization of bias', intra-party dispute about such priorities has become one of the few channels, receiving mainstream media transmission, for opposition to hegemonic beliefs. Whatever their defects, Labour projects for socialism remain important foci of social dissent and alternative conceptions of society.

The Labour Party is, perhaps, subject to more contradictory constraints than any other major institution in Britain. Its working-class base, its associations with the trade unions, and its socialist traditions, push it to act as a party of social opposition. Pulling it towards social affirmation, however, are its role as a party of government managing a major unit in the international economic system, its electoral calculations, its parliamentarism, and its fondness for ideologies of social unity. These contrary pressures are themselves often internally contradictory. But though many analysts of the Labour Party, liberal and marxist alike, have observed that it acts in a contradictory society, they rarely notice that it embodies those contradictions. Too often it is concluded that the Party resolves them unambiguously, in favour of 'reformism', 'integration', 'parliamentarism', etc. Whereas, in fact, these contradictions are endlessly reproduced, for they are irresolvable given the structural constraints within which it does, often by choice, act. For even though the Party in the post-war era came closer than ever before to opting entirely for integrative politics, it never remotely approached a situation in which it could disavow its class base.

Concentrating on contradictions revolving around domestic economic production, plebiscitarian representation and social legitimation, I have considered the Labour Party as an institution of interest aggregation.

Despite growing intervention by government, state and corporate organizations, political parties remain the principal agency for developing political arrangements which arbitrate between antagonistic collective interests. Levels of social conflict bear witness to the success of parties in managing the relationship between private interests and popular consent.

Chapter 1 provides the theoretical framework of the analysis. A method of understanding intra-party division, deriving from distinctions between 'pure' types of strategy available to social democratic parties, is constructed.

Chapter 2 sketches in the basic social structure of, and the social forces operating in, the post-war Welfare State. The institutional arrangements bequeathed by the Attlee governments generated a specific set of social trends and, equally, a limited set of political possibilities. Characteristic patterns of economic relations, political legitimations, and modes of conflict resolution of the post-war settlement are described in some detail since they provide the structural parameters of Labour Party strategies. Without such a background the historical specificity of Labour practice after the war cannot be determined.

In the course of intra-party conflict different strategies developed. With the exception of Chapter 6, the remaining chapters examine their ideological foundations, the context of their emergence, their internal contradictions, and the social consequences of their implementation. The analysis of these strategies is set against the more general thesis concerning the Party's role in the creation, development and demise of consensus politics.

Chapters 3–5 examine strategies in the period of consensus. Consensus politics was largely the effect of a widespread elite adoption of the 'Social Reformism' pursued by the group more usually known as the Revisionists (Gaitskell, Crosland, Jenkins, *et al.*). This strategy represented both a coherent response to the uncertainty about Labour's future role after the implementation of its inter-war programme and an ideal social legitimation for the post-war Welfare State. The philosophy of Social Reform was able to provide the bipartisan basis for consensus politics, in part because it was derived from the British liberal tradition to which other fractions of the elite could subscribe. At the same time it satisfied a sufficient section of the labour movement, especially the trade union interest, which was content with critical social egalitarianism as a complement to its own unregulated bargaining activities in the industrial sphere. The dominance of that strategy, which was temporarily successful in containing structural social conflict, rapidly extended the affirmative tendencies of the Party. The main alternative to Social Reform, a leftist Fundamentalism, while provoking bitter disputes, was an ineffectual defence of the Party's oppositional role. After an exploratory period of cautious support for the Welfare State settlement, Fundamentalism reverted to propagating the basic tenets of inter-war socialism. Its appeal was limited and, despite some victories within the labour movement, remained a marginal challenge to the ruling political formula. Mild recession, dissatisfaction with Britain's economic performance in comparative international perspective, a malaise in public life, and a degree of despair about Labour's electoral prospects, presaged a significant change in both Labour strategy and the dominant political formula. The form of the consensus was appreciably altered by the Wilson governments after 1964 which operated with a very different conception of the political process and of Labour's part in it. But when the major corporate organizations refused to act as if there was a 'national' economic interest which surpassed their class interests, and when other social movements of the extra-parliamentary left, women, students, and nationalists, demonstrated disaffection, the fragility of the settlement was apparent, and the need to provide an alternative source of consent became imperative.

Whereas the Labour government of the late 1960s had found it difficult to maintain popular support and legitimacy, its Conservative successor found it impossible. Chapter 6 examines, briefly, the social, economic and political tendencies which led to the ultimate disintegration of the consensus. The fiscal crisis of the state, legitimation problems, and the resurgence of class conflict, disrupted political equilibrium. The various reactions to the new circumstances of the 1970s are explored in the remaining chapters.

One major consequence of the 'crisis tendencies' of the 1970s was the absolute collapse of the strategy of Social Reform. During the Wilson governments, 1964—70, the Social Reformists had co-operated in the technocratic project of creating a New Britain and, indeed, their prior construction of the consensus provided an invaluable, if implicit, ideological prop for the governments. But in the early 1970s Social Reform withered, confounded by the stringent limitation of state expenditure on social policies, the patent absense of that voluntary consensus which, supposedly, had superseded class conflict, and the apparent failure of Keynesian techniques of economic management. In its place the Labour Party developed the Social Contract. A substitute for consensus, this was a political formula which sought social peace on the strength of collaboration outside parliamentary channels with the principal functional interests in society — business and unions. The strategy, implemented after 1974, was a mild, and specific, variant of corporatism. Though the implications of the Social Contract were ambiguous, the government sought to operate it without any innovations in the basic institutional structure of the Welfare State. For a while remarkably successful in re-storing consent, it proved a precarious arrangement, less tolerable to the Party than earlier leadership strategies. As consensus politics gave way to overt, if urbane, class politics, a coherent democratic socialist strategy emerged for the first time since 1945. Having defended, rather negatively, the interests of the working class through the late 1960s and early 1970s, the Tribune Group seized the opportunity to exploit political discontent within the labour movement to gain support for an oppositional strategy.

Study of the development of strategies cannot produce conclusive pre-dictions about the Party's future. It does, however, provide a re-interpretation of the trajectory of the Party since the war and an indi-cation of the permanence of the constraints which make the Party such a curious institution.

1 Strategy and intra-party division in the Labour Party

This Congress having regard to its decisions in former years, and with a view to securing better representation of the interests of labour in the House of Commons, hereby instructs the Parliamentary Committee to invite the co-operation of all co-operative, socialistic, trade union and other working organizations to jointly co-operate on lines mutually agreed upon, in convening a special congress of representatives from such of the above-named organizations as may be willing to devise ways and means for securing the return of an increased number of Labour members to the next Parliament. (Motion passed by the Trades Union Congress, 1899.)[1]

Throughout the eighty years of its existence the Labour Party has sought in vain for that revered situation where 'all co-operative, socialistic, trade union and other working organizations' can 'jointly co-operate on lines mutually agreed upon'. This chapter attempts to create a conceptual framework to explain why this is the case, and to emphasize the social bases of the problems of securing co-operation. It is argued that the trajectory of the Labour Party can best be understood by relating broad ideological differences between antagonistic groupings within the Party to general types of strategy available to a social-democratic Labour Party in specific historical situations. Some clarification of the concepts of faction and strategy are necessary to establish connections between the internal affairs of the party and the external social context within which it operates.

'Segments' and intra-party division

Intra-party division in the Labour Party has frequently been recognized as significant. It is conventional to assert that the Labour Party originated as a coalition of various socialist groups and the trade union interest and that mediation between the heterogeneous groups, the ILP, the SDF, the

Fabian Society and the trade unionists, each with distinctively different interests and ideologies, posed considerable problems.[2] It is less common to see the inter-war period in these terms, mostly, it would seem, because of the general acceptance of Beer's thesis of the 'Socialist Generation'.[3] This thesis is beginning to be challenged through studies of various left-wing movements of the era[4] and through an emerging scepticism that the 1930s was the 'golden age of British socialism'.[5] The evidence would suggest that many of the divisions of the 1950s were present, if submerged, in the 1930s: there was not a great deal in common between Strachey, Laski, Tawney, Dalton, Jay, Morrison and Attlee. Despite the continued existence of internal cleavage in the Party after the second world war it has been little analysed.

There have been two broad approaches to the question of division in the post-war period, one minimizing it, the other examining it rather unsystematically. The first approach was espoused by both American political scientists and British left-wing commentators. American political science in the 1950s and 1960s, under the influence of the 'End-of-Ideology' thesis, expressed surprise at the *cohesion* of British parties, especially Labour.[6] It was asserted that Labour was practising consensus politics and that only a residual fracture remained, between a group still employing ideological conceptions — traditional, anachronistic socialism — and a dominant, pragmatic corps.[7] Some British socialist commentators, addressing themselves to the question of whether socialists should remain in the Labour Party, identified an even more pragmatic and accommodatory Labour Party, monolithic except for the continued presence of a misguided group of socialists.[8] Their explanation of Labour Party practice focused on the debilitating effects of the British political system and culture; social transformation through parliamentary politics, they contended, was impossible.

The second approach, that of most British interpreters, accepted that the manifest internal variances in the Party were significant. The way in which cleavage was characterized, though, was superficial. They tended either to adopt a simple left—right dichotomy based on ideological differences,[9] or to look for institutionalized divisions between, for example, leaders and backbenchers,[10] sponsorship groups,[11] or the Parliamentary and the Constituency Labour Parties.[12] While all these lines of fracture are useful in understanding aspects of Party alignments they do seem inadequate for a comprehensive understanding of party cohesion and cleavage.

What might, at first sight, seem paradoxical, that the Labour Party was both remarkably cohesive and multiply divided, was resolved by Rose.[13] He argued that commentators had overlooked the fact that parties play several roles, each with a different rationale. Parties are not only electoral institutions, concerned with mobilizing majority support among voters, but they also act as governments, oppositions and organizations. *Qua* government there are many groups and interests outside the party which have to be accommodated, leading to conflict on the basis of 'transparent differences between previous party policy and the policy of the party as government'; *qua* opposition, when party pressures predominate, disagreement arises over future electoral strategies and policy formulations; *qua* organization the party demonstrated 'perhaps the greatest degree of cohesiveness' based on the solidarity of party employees.[14] This observation, that contradictory pressures for both cohesion and division operate simultaneously, is important because it partly explains why the Party remains intact despite the permanent presence of antagonistic factions. Having explicitly recognized the Party's role as a bureaucratic organization, as distributor of patronage, as an electoral machine, and moreover, as a rationally chosen instrument for the pursuit of the aspirations of the various groupings within the Party, its continuity through time and its capacity to embrace groups with contrary ideologies become less problematic. Support for the Party and internal conflict co-exist in such a way that it is not necessary to underrate either: the Party may be divided over programmes and practices without being on the verge of disintegration. Indeed Rose made a key point about the study of intra-party division in British politics in arguing that 'the surface cohesion of British political parties reflects an equilibrium between forces pulling in different directions, not a unity obtained by a single united thrust'.[15] From this perspective he argued that re-alignments within and over party boundaries have proved to be more important in policy transformation than have elections. Nevertheless, neither he nor anyone else has satisfactorily solved the problems of explaining the logic behind that 'equilibrium of forces' operating within British political parties.

Existing studies of factionalism have been devoted mostly to arguing about definitions and constructing typologies. The technical literature includes distinctions between: ideological and interest factions;[16] faction, tendency and non-alignment:[17] and factions and splinters.[18] It also contains typologies of the possible *raisons d'être* of faction formation: for example, Zariski claimed that factions could be based on shared values, strategic conceptions, 'affinity based on common material interests, common origins, or common functions', or on personal or local cliques.[19] Though all may have their uses, they have a common defect, that they fail to explain the rationale behind intra-party division. The predominant impression is that cleavage is a pathological condition, a deviation from some ideal party unity, engineered by organized cabals. But in fact, cleavage is a perfectly normal state of affairs, particularly in a two-party system, and is most often only loosely co-ordinated. The main reason for the infelicities of existing analyses seems to be the preference for using simple empirical indicators of internal division rather than embarking on the less precise, but ultimately more informative, task of explaining the systematic causes of disagreement. The major empirical studies in the British literature have used, almost exclusively, the criterion of individual MPs either voting against, or signing Early Day Motions critical of, their own party's leadership.[20] Such occurrences tend to be aggregated over time and then correlated with the social characteristics and organizational affiliations of the individual MPs concerned. This sort of inquiry has firmly demonstrated the absence of unanimity in the Labour Party, and the impossibility of characterizing it in terms of homogeneous and organized left and right, but it has prevented any meaningful patterns of division emerging. The concentration of attention on individuals who dissent on a wide range of specific issues is unfortunate. Critiques of the 'decision-making' approach to the distribution of power apply just as cogently to intra-party division,[21] dissentient voting may be the most spectacular and easily accessible evidence for internal disagreement, but it is a limited explanatory device, which often fails to explain even the political rationale behind cleavage, and never relates division to social process and social antagonisms. If the significance of cleavage and alliance within parties is to be grasped it must be related to the prevailing balance between antagonistic social interests. In order to do this it is necessary to operate with rather different concepts at a level of abstraction where preoccupations with individual acts are of lesser importance. One concept I shall use is that of *segment*, referring to a group which shares a common political strategy; then, by examining and distinguishing between strategies in terms of their social effects and their capacity for advancing particular social interests, it becomes possible to relate intra-party divisions to the balance of social forces as a whole. One consequence of this is that it is not always easy to describe unambiguously the place of each and every individual in the scenario; but this is a minor price to pay for a general explanation.

Strategies

The term 'strategy' is usually employed in a taken-for-granted and self-explanatory way. Yet it is one of the few terms in political discourse which carries overtones of an organic relationship between thought and action, theory and practice. The nature of a strategy is dependent on the relations between three major, interdependent, components: an ideology, a form of organization, and a concrete historical situation.

The relevant elements of ideology, for present purposes, are a projection or aspiration towards a future desired state, an analysis of the structure of the extant social order, and the embodiment of a definite social interest. These elements are indivisibly integrated in the sense that the projection is derived from the social analysis of a concretely situated section of the given society, and equally the root-interest is created and mobilized by the projection from a given social condition.

All strategies for collective political action imply the use of some organizational instrument, whether party, trade union or army. In some cases these have to be created for the purpose, although in the case of mid twentieth century Labour politics certain instruments have been inherited intact and remain largely unquestioned; the Parliamentary Labour Party and the national trade union movement are predominantly accepted and unchanging forms of organization for working-class politics.

A particular historical configuration, though at first glance incommensurable with the other two elements, is a crucial third component. The historical configuration might best be considered the objective otherside to the voluntaristic, consciously created, ideological and organizational components. If it is not taken into account all political activity becomes entirely free-floating, and the determinate constraints on the actors are reduced to their own assessments of the given balance of social forces. The relationship between historical situation and ideology and organization is partly a direct one, to the extent that ideologies and organizations can be said to be determined by, or correspond to, a given social structure. Even if this structure cannot be known positively or independently, several social effects cannot be understood without it. The success of a strategy is determined not by its adherents' *assessment* of social forces but by 'real' ones; ideologies, because of their practical intent, are limited by the need to concentrate on a relatively narrow area of social relations. Political organizations themselves, as well as being active agencies, inhere in the given social formation and hence have concrete properties independent of, and often inimical to, the pursuit of their avowed strategy. If all notions of historical situation be abandoned, unanticipated consequences become entirely divorced from conscious action, and strategy becomes assessable only *ex post facto*, in the light of its success in achieving consciously stated goals.

Strategy, then, is a more complex phenomenon than most analysts of factions, concentrating on 'policy parties' and decision-making, can allow for. Competing strategies have more dimensions of differentiation than, for example, Beer can find in ideological differences between Fundamentalists and Revisionists, or McKenzie can uncover by examining institutional channels of decision-making, or Berrington can grasp through analysis of the grouping of individual MPs on polemical issues. There are several distinct strategies available to social-democratic parties. The rationale behind those strategies illuminates the basis for intra-party conflict, and the combinations of them explain the dynamics of conflict in particular cases. It is adherence to these alternative strategies, not the formal organization of groups of stable sets of attitudes *per se*, which permits the identification of fractures in the Labour Party. Clearly this represents a level of abstraction in analysis unusual in studies of the Labour Party, for, being based on the pre-supposition that collective action and consciousness cannot be reduced to the characteristics of individual carriers, empirical referents like voting-behaviour or regular meetings between individuals are not directly confirming evidence. The validity of these propositions however, can only be assessed through their heuristic utility for my analysis.

The principal structural determinants of social-democratic party strategies are the concrete situation of the subordinate classes in modern capitalist societies, and the existence of parliamentary institutions and flexible interest-group associations.

The Labour Party has always affirmed and legitimated certain of the institutions of liberal capitalist society: it has accepted parliamentary methods, the civil and political liberties of individuals, and the rights of all voluntary interest associations to organize — all of which are important components of the dominant culture. Gradually, the range of institutions accorded legitimacy has increased, partly as a result of the experiences of government which have brought the Party into closer contact with state and capitalist organizations; some sections of the Party have even become defenders of the wisdom and neutrality of the civil service, the benefits of the market mechanism and the virtues of profitable private enterprise. On the other hand, social democratic parties continue to face the problem of how to represent the interests of the working class, whether or not they want to use the concept of class and even though their concerns with that class may be little more than historical residues. In Britain, party and socialist traditions, electoral support, and the institutional connections with the trade union movement, all sustain Labour in its role as an oppositional party of the working class. The absence of other major social cleavages which might divert attention away from class divisions, ethnic or religious differences for example, reinforce the centrality of class and class-related issues. Labour Party strategies revolve around attempts to mitigate or abolish the inherent contradictions between affirmation and opposition. The index of this is intra-party division where struggle takes place over ways of resolving these tensions, defining the kind of social interests that the Labour Party ought to promote and the extent of change necessary for such a purpose.

A social interpretation of politics must gravitate around the concept of interests. One way or another, political organization is directed towards furthering specific interests, whether they be individual, group, class, or national interests. Political decisions advance some interests and retard others. But the concept of interest is problematic; often interests are construed as primitive and incorrigible, which is necessary if we are to distinguish true from false needs or to analyse situations where social structures generate interests not perceived by participants. But for purposes of political analysis it is more important to recognize that the interests of groups, classes and institutions change over time, and, moreover, that much ideological debate is precisely about identifying, reconstructing, and even creating, definitions of collective interest. Political solidarity emerges from persuading people about what their interests are, and in the process political entrepreneurs develop strategies which attend to those interests. The kinds of interest which may provide the basis for political mobilization are probably infinite, but in the case of the Labour Party three types have consistently lain behind varieties in Party strategy: these are sectional-occupational, class, and community-based interests. Deriving from structural characteristics of society, all have proved effective in forming consciousness, creating political identity, and inducing solidarity.

(i) Simple sectional interest is easy to comprehend, whether it be that of a pressure group or of a trade union involved in unilateral collective bargaining. Ends are clearly fixed, and the social groups in whose interests demands are advanced are readily identifiable. In the labour movement the principal form of such interests is sectional-occupational, as represented by an individual trade union. Such interests derive from the division of labour and the opposition between employer and employee which originally brought forth the trade union. In Labour Party politics this interest has been represented classically by trade union sponsored MPs who devoted their attention to issues concerning the sponsoring body.[22] Typically it has been supposed that the trade union MPs' only political significance was that they loyally supported the leadership of the Party and provided automatic allies for right-wing intellectuals.[23] This error results from the lack of attention paid to the trade union interest in the PLP because its bearers have taken few initiatives and because the rationale behind its activities has been assumed to be simple: Finer et al., having demonstrated a strong correlation between union sponsorship, ex-working class background and a low level of education, concluded that to understand their attitudes 'one needs go no further than to refer to their occupational composition'.[24] Most trade union leaders would agree with Vic Feather, himself a Labour Party activist, when he defined the role of union representatives:

The job of a trade union leader is to look after the interests of his members, not to serve the purposes of other groups or individuals who see in the unions a pathway to political power... Every political situation should be judged upon its merits, and only from the standpoint of its Members' interests.[25]

However, the precise way in which union members' interests may best be advanced can change over time. Unions have generally preferred that their functions be kept separate from those of the Party, requiring only that the Party intercede in parliament on their behalf under certain, limited circumstances. Richter summed up the reasons for union involvement in the Labour Party:

(a) to retain the alliance as a sort of insurance policy to protect the bargaining system; (b) to enhance their own bureaucratic image and security *vis-a-vis* their memberships; (c) to help assure the continuance of a Labour leadership that would not intrude into the traditional bargaining system.[26]

Trade unions, Richter suggested, intervened mainly to preserve a free collective bargaining system. He asserted that national unions 'abjured political action in a substantive, or programmatic, sense', preferring a simple unionism 'without significant involvement in national economic or policy formation'. The unions do '*not* rely on it (the PLP) either for their conventional bargaining function or for broad social policy purposes'.[27]

Richter's evidence derived from the period 1954—66 and his conclusions now look very dubious given the extensive, direct involvement of the TUC in national politics in the last fifteen years.[28] But there has not been so much change. The TUC remains a confederal organization, a committee for the aggregation of the interests of individual unions, whose authority ultimately rests on its capacity to gain concessions for the memberships of its individual component units. The means of securing concessions is a matter for debate, whether by national political agreement, industry-wide negotiation or shop-floor bargaining. The rationale remains the same: acknowledging a gross simplification, trade union interest amounts to securing improvements in the rewards and working conditions of union members.[29] This continues to have implications for the Labour Party. The trade union interest is a partially independent element in the balance of power in the party. While neither the Trade Union Group of MPs nor individual union delegations in Conference dominate the Party, they do collectively exercise a negative veto power by limiting the alternatives open to the Party.[30] The sectional—occupational interest retains a presence in the determination of Party practice through the operation of the internal balance of power.

(ii) On many occasions, though not so constantly as is often assumed, the Labour Party, or segments of it, have expressed class interest. Certain programmes and lines of action were designed to improve the life-situation of the working class as a whole *vis-a-vis* other classes in society. Most factions of the Party in the inter-war years considered their strategies to be predominantly for the working class. How to identify the working class, and what constitutes working class interests, have always been in dispute, but the general implication is clear: capitalist society, with its particular forms of property ownership, authority structure and value system, generates systematic class divisions which create common interests and opposition among the subordinate classes. Such interests transcend occupational spheres and form a political constituency for the labour movement.

(iii) A third type of interest has predominated in the most recent period, though it has been present throughout the history of the Labour Party, one rooted not in the interest of the working class but in the interest of the public, nation or community. The nation is a focus for identity, realized and reinforced by the very existence of the nation-state. War, international economic competition and imperialist ventures constitute Britain as an entity in rivalry with other nation-states; and the existence of central, national, institutions of government, administration and culture, constitute the nation internally. Many commentators have seen the Labour Party's attachment to national symbolism and interest as the major source of its failings.[31] It is implied that Labour's concern for the national interest is a mystification, disguising the effective and real interests behind proposed courses of action which, in a capitalist society, *ipso facto* will be the interests of the ruling class. The concept of national interest is particularly spurious, and certainly may be used, in direct opposition to the sectional or class interests of labour. But despite its predominantly conservative intimations it may sometimes contain popular, democratic and liberative elements. It is so indefinite that any one particular use of the concept may be totally different from another: in Labour ideology its use ranges from vulgar appeals to patriotism, through liberal egalitarianism, to populist protest. The equating of class interest with progressive policies, and national or public interest with retrogressive activities, is simplistic. Some class-based strategies are defensive, and some non-class-based strategies are transformative. In fact, some varieties of socialism, including rationalist marxisms, are premised on the possibility of their being strategies which foster universal interests. The ILP's ethical socialism prior to 1900, for example, envisaged a universal moral regeneration:[32] socialism offered an egalitarian morality for all, founded on the conviction that socialist ethics in a socialist order represented the

most human and most rational form of social organization. The standpoint was not one of redressing the grievances of the working class by
overthrowing and suppressing another class, but rather it professed that
a new order, egalitarian and harmonious, would be in the best interests
of all people. While this conception was far distant from that of Wilson
or Callaghan it serves to warn against using the nation—class opposition
as a total explanation of Labour Party practice. The reconciliation of class
and universal interests is a perpetual dilemma,[33] one which has occupied
British socialism since its beginnings. While a strategy attending to
national or universal interests will have different implications from one
based on the irreconcilable interests of antagonistic classes, there is a
great danger of over-simplification if concepts of national interest are not
decomposed so that their various applications may be distinguished.

The identification of social interests comprises one dimension for differ-
entiating between strategies. A second axis is one which defines the
quality of social change necessary for the advancement of such social
interests.
    From the point of view of the labour movement and the subordinate
classes in Britain, treating them as a collective historical agency, a difference exists between courses of action which were a structural challenge
to the existing social order and those which accepted the parameters of
that order. The innovations of the early period of the Attlee government
were structural challenges in the sense that they irreversibly changed the
structure of British society independently of, and in a form unwelcome
to, the dominant classes of the time. Labour introduced changes which
the ruling classes had to adapt themselves to, in just the same way that
the formation of the Labour Party itself, while dependent on the legitimized procedures and common values of British parliamentarism, was a
creative development instituted by the trade union representatives of the
working class. Neither of these developments were revolutionary, but in
their own time they entailed *structural change* and were threatening to
established interests and institutions. In contrast, some strategies explicitly founded in working class interest appear unambiguously defensive,
direct responses to external impositions, requiring only *ameliorative*
measures within existing structural parameters. Prices and incomes policies
and industrial relations legislation, intended to alter the framework of
collective bargaining, for example, evoked a reaction principally designed
to defend the established rights of the labour movement. The distinction
between structural-critical and defensive-ameliorative practices is neither
wholly unambiguous in application nor operationally precise: what
represented a critical strategy at one time in particular circumstances
may be defensive at another time in another place; and, further, what

began as a defensive strategy may transform itself into a progressive one should it be recognized that without the introduction of new elements failure would result. For example, the defensive-corporate opposition to the 1971 Industrial Relations Act generated a distinct, if temporary, socialist revival within the labour movement. Similarly, innovations in the industrial sphere, work-ins and workers' co-operatives, were ambiguous, being on the one hand a traditional defensive manoeuvre to protect jobs, and, on the other, presenting a structural challenge to property relations and industrial authority. (This dimension has, note, nothing to do with militancy as such, for courses of action can be aggressive and violent while remaining functionally defensive.) In practice, some segments of the labour movement hope for a social transformation, while others are apparently content with amelioration: the former are committed to transforming the fundamental structures which determine the parameters of everyday experiences — the distribution of effective power, the mode of economic production, the manner of status attribution; the latter aim only to improve the condition of the underprivileged within existing structural forms. These contrasting orientations towards change should not be confused with the difference between promoting class and national interests.

From these distinctions, between interests and approaches to social change, can be derived a number of different, *pure* types of strategy, or 'strategic orientation', in working class politics (see Table 1).

Table 1. Types of working class strategy

Approaches to social change

		Amelioration	Structural change
Roots	Sectional	Sectional-Corporatist	Syndicalist
of	Class	Class-Corporatist	Hegemonic
interest	Community	Integrative	Transformative

I introduce this typology partly because differing political orientations within social-democratic parties invariably legitimate themselves by the use of the same symbols: all claim socialist, democratic, reformist and liberative credentials. Unless it is decided in advance what exactly the perfect Labour strategy should be so that the party's performance can be measured by that criterion, admittedly a popular method,[34] it is helpful to have an independent set of categories to delineate Labour strategies.

It is particularly useful in breaking down the rather limited dichotomies, like left and right, revolution and reform, nation and class, etc., which, ultimately, do not refer to the social effects of what sections of the party are proposing to do. Briefly, these abstract, or pure, strategic orientations may be defined as follows.

A sectional corporatist strategy is one held by a segment which seeks no qualitative structural change and which sets out to represent and promote the interests of a specific group, independently of other groups in broadly similar situations. Its solidarity is based on a simple interest such as that of a trade union or professional group,[35] and, with respect to the Labour Party, corresponds to what Gramsci called the economic-corporate moment where 'the members of the professional group are conscious of its unity and homogeneity, and the need to organize it, but in the case of the wider social group this is not yet so'.[36] It describes particularly well the nature and aspiration of the trade union interest in the PLP.

A class-corporatist strategy likewise subordinates the question of qualitative structural change to the task of defending the primarily econ-omic interests of the working class as a whole.[37] It represents a response to external forces and usually amounts to the demand that a greater share of the rewards of productive enterprise should be distributed to the class of employees.

Integration describes a process, identified in liberal, marxist and sociol-ogical discourse, of gradual incorporation of excluded categories of people into a dominant culture.[38] An integrative strategy is one held by a seg-ment which proposes to act in the interests of all sections of the com-munity, not merely in the economic field, hoping to improve the situation of the underprivileged without transforming the structure of society. The dominant segments in the post-war Labour Party have tended to have this type of strategic orientation: Wilson's technocratic project and Gaitskell's social reformism were both types of integrative strategy.

A syndicalist strategy, though of limited significance in British ex-perience, is one which predicates structural transformation on granting autonomy to producer groups, subject to only loose, central coordination.

A hegemonic strategy is more difficult to define. Gramsci said heg-emony was the moment 'in which one becomes aware that one's own corporate interests, in their present and future development, transcend the corporate limits of the purely economic class, and can and must become the interests of other subordinate groups too'.[39] Qualitative, structural transformation is implied, in cultural and political as well as economic spheres, [40] and it represents the interests of all subordinate groups against dominant social interests. Whether the conditions for the success of such a strategy exist is open to doubt, but there have been few, if any, representatives of such a strategy in the post-war Labour Party.

A transformative strategy is conceived as being in the interests of all sections of the community but assumes that a precondition of a civilized society is qualitative, structural social change. It asserts that integrative strategies are not feasible given the existing parameters of the social order. The Attlee government, I argue, pursued such a strategy.[41]

This typology is a construction of pure types of strategic orientation, defined by the anticipated consequences for a social structure of implementing a concrete programme. In reality, strategies developed in political conflict will, at best, only approximate to a pure orientation. However, the typology is an abstraction from the historical experience of socialist and labour movements in Western Europe. It is not a universal tool, for it does not delineate all possible forms of socialist strategy, a very different formulation being necessary to understand, say, the Bolshevik Revolution. It pre-supposes both a developed civil society, well entrenched and in some degree autonomous of the state, and the existence of established institutions of liberal democracy. No necessary historical hierarchy among types is implied: it is not the case that one automatically or progressively gives way to another, rather all co-exist, though the significance of each for Labour practice varies over time. There is, indeed, a series of plausible, if rough, generalizations about the preconditions for each becoming an active force.

Syndicalism and guild socialist strategies become a force when economic conditions are unpropitious for effective trade union bargaining and when the Parliamentary Party is unprepared or unable to implement reforms which will offset currently felt disprivileges of the working-class, e.g. 1911—14, 1920—26 and 1970 forward. Defensive class-corporatism tends to flourish in similar conditions, though it is a more constant phenomenon given a lack of support for socialist programmes. Strategies of integration are most acceptable either in situations of relative prosperity when sectional bargaining is efficacious and social reforms are sufficient to complement adequately such material gains, e.g. 1950—67, or in times of relative weakness of the industrial working class movement, e.g. 1927—37. However, they remain present constantly in one form or another. Transformative orientations tend to be of moment only in unusual conditions; in Britain they seem to flourish primarily in the aftermath of war in conditions of peculiar social solidarity, e.g. 1917—20 and 1945—8. To outline the preconditions of emergence, however, says nothing of their relative success. Clearly some of these strategies are mutually incompatible and as such provide the basis for intra-party dispute. The primary aim of a segment is to get its strategy adopted and it is the conflict resulting from this, the struggle for segmental dominance, that principally determines the internal dynamic of the Labour Party.

In general the institutional arrangements surrounding the Labour Party tend to increase its cohesiveness. The governmental, electoral and administrative roles of the party, *pace* Rose, all tend to produce cohesion. The historical experience of disengagement by a segment, for example the ILP in 1932, tends to reinforce adherence to a two-party system. Awareness of the consequences of causing a split in the electoral party, the almost certain victory for the Conservative Party, further tends to combat fragmentation. The existence of several segments makes compromise and combination a rational choice. The main contrary pressures lie in disagreement over party strategy, and it is in this sphere that the dynamics of the development of the Labour Party must be sought.

The practical, concrete strategies of segments involved in this struggle usually embody ambiguities and inconsistencies. This is due partly to the constraints towards cohesion within the Party and the need for ways of negotiating compromises between segments, for in general one segment will be unable to mobilize sufficient support to achieve dominance on its own. One aspect of this is that for electoral purposes, party unity is typically obtained by presenting a highly ambiguous programme which means different things to different segments. It is also due, in part, to the diversity of group interests in society. Broadly speaking two types of inconsistency can be distinguished. Some segments appear *internally* inconsistent, either because they try to hold together more than one of these 'pure' types of strategic orientation and hence propose contradictory objectives, or because the justifications for some of their policies undermine others. Other segments adopt an internally consistent strategy but find that in real historical situations the strategy is inapplicable; they suffer from what may be termed *external* inconsistencies or contradictions. In order to understand these it is essential to place the party in its societal context.

Methodologically, I shall identify real strategies, and their inconsistencies, through the study of characteristically distinct ideologies and programmes presented by sections of the Party. By examining the interests expressed, the types of change envisaged, and the specific policies proposed, the strategies encapsulated in them can be exposed. Strategies are then assessed in terms of the structure of possibilities for practice in particular social circumstances. The assumption is that the structure of possibilites is dynamic, generated by social trends and developments, and that segmental strategies interpose in order to control and exploit those possibilities. The result is less a history of ideas and more a contraposition of 'ideologies-in-practice', distinguished in terms of their consequences for social change. The important point is that strategies have a practical reference which ideas as such do not have. The method is a device for connecting explicitly political ideology with social change.

The strategic orientations distinguished refer to social processes, anticipating the directions in which political actions may alter a given social structure or balance of social forces. This has several benefits in clarifying the nature of intra-party division. Firstly it becomes possible to recognize that different ideologies may suggest the same kind of practice. Though two ideologies may have different intellectual origins they may still imply the same kind of political programme. This has, for example, been the case with the dominant segments in the Labour Party since 1950. The strategies espoused by Gaitskell and Wilson were both integrative in orientation, but their respective ideological bases differed considerably. Secondly the same ideology may have a different social significance in different historical configurations. *Laissez-faire* liberalism was once a revolutionary ideology but, adopted by the petit bourgeoisie in the mid twentieth century, it is no longer. Similarly the isonomic aspirations of elements in the labour movement at the beginning of the twentieth century had a transformative potential which they have no longer. The sociological significance of any projection depends upon the nature of the social formation in which it is situated at any particular point in history. Thirdly, ideologies do not necessarily have unambiguous implications for practice. It is often the case that an ideology contains more than one, mutually incompatible, strategic orientation. For example, 'Bevanite' strategy pursued in different degrees, defensive class-corporatist, transformative and integrative orientations all at once, which gives some insight into its predicament and lack of effectiveness.

The possibility of alliance between segments depends upon the nature of their strategies. Some segments with different ideologies may combine relatively easily. Segments with a commitment to community interests, for example, may be able to negotiate an acceptable alliance. The strategies of the Gaitskellites and Wilson were reconciled in practice in the dominant alliance of the period 1965–75. Community interest was defined differently, but they shared a basic assumption that British society fundamentally is, and ought to be, a harmonious community and that the Labour Party must satisfy the demands of all sections of that community. Co-operation on this basis is impossible for a segment which maintains that the purpose of the Labour Party is to promote the interests of the working class in a class-divided society. Such a position, represented at present by the Tribune Group, is not capable of aggregation or reconciliation. On the other hand the pursuit of sectional-corporatist interests of trade unions may be compatible with either an integrative or a defensive class-corporatist strategy, depending essentially on the social and economic conditions pertaining at any particular time. In the 1960s, so long as there existed an economic climate favourable to growth and the Labour leadership refrained from interfering with free collective bargaining, it was perfectly rational for the sectional-corporatist segment to support leadership policy. However once these preconditions dissolved the tendency was for the bearers of that interest to ally themselves with one of *Tribune*'s positions.[42] The sectional-corporatists' concern was never the quality of the total social formation; they calculated in terms of immediate interest in making associations, their overall strategy remaining constant.

My contention is that intra-party conflict can best be understood in terms of competing strategies, where strategy is more than ideology and where segments, as bearers of strategy, are not reducible simply to organized groups with boundaries identifiable through the conscious appropriation of a group identity. To understand the cleavages and the trajectory of the Party its members must be seen as collective bearers of social interests within a complex social system which is a severe constraint on both consciousness and action.

2 The Labour Party and the post-war settlement

The Labour governments 1945–51

The Labour governments of 1945–51 marked the end of one epoch and the beginning of another for the Labour Party. The societal effects of the Attlee administration have been interpreted in two ways. The first, over-charitable, view captured the spirit of the times: widely believed within the Labour Party, and the basis for ensuing ideological debate, it contended that the Attlee governments had laid the foundation of a new, potentially socialist, order.[1] The opposing view was that the Labour government had reconstructed capitalism in a more viable form; that, even in terms of pre-war Labour aspirations,[2] Attlee's administration was a grave disappointment in that it had provided none of the seeds of social transformation, but had integrated Labour into the dominant social order and demonstrated the incompatability of parliamentary politics and socialism.[3]

The argument for the first case rests on the achievements of the governments. Many of the measures promised in the 1918 programme, and subsequently re-iterated, were implemented. As Crossman put it,

> the Government had fulfilled its historic mission. The nationalisation of half a dozen major industries, the construction of an all-in system of social security and a free health service, and the tentative application of planning to the national economy — the achievement of these reforms seemed to have exhausted the content of British socialism.[4]

Crossman, and others, saw these achievements as partly indicating the poverty of British socialism, but nevertheless they were real advances and they did encompass the main demands of the Labour Party of the inter-war period. The Attlee governments created a mixed economy with a substantial public sector and a considerable degree of state intervention; they provided greater opportunities for individual advancement;[5] they developed a superior system of social security which, according to one commentator, was based on profoundly anti-capitalist values;[6] and they benefitted the working class through establishing full employment and improving material standards of living. These were measures which in all probability the Conservative Party would not have undertaken, for, although schisms within the Conservative Party muted opposition at first,[7] hostility was aroused among powerful elements of the ruling classes. Labour, in creating the framework of the mixed economy Welfare State, inaugurated a qualitatively different social order in Britain.

The developments at the time seemed novel and exciting even to the hard-headed,[8] and through the early 1950s they could still be plausibly construed as instalments in the phase of transition towards a Socialist Commonwealth. Any assessment of the Attlee governments failing to take into account the reactions of the Party to the experience of 1945–51 is likely to misuse the privilege of hindsight. At the time the reflections of even the most radical elements of the Party were almost entirely favourable. Crossman's sentiments, that 'we are still unaware of the astonishing achievements of the last five years',[9] were frequently echoed. *Full Speed Ahead*, a Tribune pamphlet, avowed that 'Few would have thought that so much could have been done so soon'. Others thought that a 'revolution' had occurred: Bevan, for example, said: 'having got full employment, having seen to it that all our resources are fully engaged, it has never come home to some people that when that situation has been arrived at a revolution has taken place in human society'.[10] Strachey maintained that the 'nationalisation measures ... have been foundation stones for building a new type of economy' and that 'the real cause of the re-animation of the British economy lies in the shift of economic power and influence between social groups which has taken place in Britain'.[11] For both Strachey and Bevan the changes vindicated a parliamentary strategy; thus Strachey:

> British capitalism *has* been compelled, by the sheer pressure of the British people, acting through our effective democratic political institutions, to do what we used to say it would never, by definition, do; it has been forced to devote its productive resources to raising the standard of life of the population as a whole.[12]

In the field of welfare, satisfaction was even greater: Kingsley Martin believed Labour to have written a 'new list of Rights of Man' and pondered on the question of whether the welfare state was 'a *possible* alternative to socialism'; and Crossman pointed out that the reality of the National Health Service would have been thought 'utopian' in 1935.[13] Both Crossman and Bevan argued that it was in the realm of moral values that Labour had advanced:[14] Bevan thought progress 'is measured by the extent to which the goods and services made available pass into the distributive rather than the commodity sector of the population, and the more and more things that we are able to enjoy without their having to pass through the price system'.[15] In this respect, too, Labour had made progress.

At the same time Labour politicians were puzzled as to what to do next. The problem was put most clearly by Crossman when he argued that 'the Labour Government finished its job sometime in 1948 or 1949; finished the job which the Fabians laid down for it in the previous thirty years. All the obvious things have been done which were fought for and argued about.'[16] Yet he recognized that the 'pattern of values' in society had not altered sufficiently, and that a classless society had not been achieved. Despite very significant changes, which required a 'revolution' in socialist thinking, there was clearly much still to be done.

The second, contrary, interpretation detected that the foundations of capitalism had not been undermined by 1951. On the contrary, Labour's economic policies provided the means for capitalism to flourish. There had been no real attack on property as such. The industries which had been nationalized were infrastructural, basic public utilities which, with the exception of iron and steel, were unaccustomed to making a profit yet whose products were indispensable. Compensation had been paid to the expropriated, which tended to blunt the socialist case against private capital. The organization of the newly nationalized industries was indistinguishable from others in private ownership: there was no form of workers' control, and managerial roles were filled by exactly those who had commanded private industry.[17] Further, given that the great majority of industrial concerns were still in private hands, there was little change in the rationale of economic production: the pursuit of profit still predominated. Even in the area of social policy it was argued that Labour had achieved little. Its system of social provision was considered simply an extension of the existing tradition, not especially favourable to the working class. Also the distribution of wealth did not alter much, although the extent of poverty in the Welfare State was not immediately recognized.[18] On top of all this, Labour pursued a wholly traditional foreign policy.[19]

Neither of these interpretations is adequate on its own to an understanding of the Attlee administrations. The second describes accurately many of the structural features of post-war society, but it would be historically fallacious not to consider the Attlee governments in their own context and in terms of their own intentions. They had not transferred power to the working class nor had they seriously eroded the power of capital and private industry, but they had effected a rearrangement of the balance of forces in society. Recent commentators have failed to appreciate the extent to which the Attlee governments laid new foundations for the post-war social formation. Clearly the outcome was not a recognizable transformation within the terms of socialist theory, as even moderate elements in the Party recognized in the long run.[20] But, most importantly, it was *not* inevitable that the British social formation would become immutably frozen in the mould cast by the Attlee governments. Far more depended upon subsequent developments than is now credited.

Oddly, left commentators exaggerate the efficacy of the formal political system in producing social change. It tends to be assumed that because the Attlee governments did not legislate for a comprehensive socialist transformation the extent of social change must have been extremely limited. Yet this seems to over-emphasize the role of political decisions in the *direct* implementation of social change. Governments, and even new regimes in post-revolutionary conditions, do little more than re-construct the *framework* of everyday life. In Western societies the development of social trends outside the ambit of political control is often more important than political processes. Understanding this, and recognizing the problems it entails, are pre-conditions for accurate analysis.

The Attlee governments made significant structural innovations.[21] While the Conservative Party was still debating the proper economic role of the state, intervention in the economy in peace-time was irreversibly established[22] and the basis for revitalized *laissez-faire* policies was completely removed. The nationalization of the iron and steel industries set a precedent for public ownership of profitable private industry, which could have been copied profusely by later Labour governments.[23] The government also modified the principal mechanisms for the distribution of material benefits in society. It became involved in the process of bargaining between capital and labour. Temporarily it struck the 'remarkable bargain between government, labour and capital' of 1948—50,[24] the first application of national incomes policy, which was later to become a central mode for the regulation of class conflict. The incipient tendency of the TUC to seek extended channels of communication and co-operation, begun before the war, was consolidated by accepting a governmental role in the regulation of industrial bargaining. The full potential of this, as a way of incorporating labour, was not realized until the 1970s, but it provided a subsidiary strategy for the unions throughout the post-war settlement. The distribution of reward was further transformed by the introduction of a comprehensive and potentially coherent system of social provision. Welfare reforms, though based on disparate principles of equal opportunity, minimum security and universal provision,[25] removed some of the insecurities engendered by a market economy, and improved the life chances of the subordinate classes in Britain. The cumulative effect of these innovations, from the point of view of labour politics, was that class conflict became highly institutionalized, mediated by a number of flexible but powerfully constraining institutional nexi which, at least in a period of prosperity, encouraged the social incorporation of the working classes.

In its own temporal context the Labour government embraced a transformative orientation. The Party was united in its intention to transform the social conditions of the inter-war period, and though there was some criticism of the speed of the government's domestic policies, only foreign policy caused internal dissent.[26] Despite the restraints of parliamentary politics and the conventional attitudes of the Labour leadership regarding parliament, and despite even greater economic constraints, the Party used the opportunities presented by the peculiar conditions of post-war reconstruction to pursue a progressive strategy. The upheaval of war and the general public determination that the miseries of the 1930s should be abolished for ever, together with the vast parliamentary majority, created many possibilities for structural change. The basis of the strategy was not the pursuit of working-class interests — community interests predominated — but the necessity to challenge dominant institutional forms was acknowledged. The socialism of Attlee may have been parliamentary, founded primarily on humanitarian concepts of justice and co-operation,[27] but its achievement required qualitative structural change.

That the effects would be disappointing in the long run was difficult to anticipate. Failure cannot be put down to reneging on pledges, for the government was extremely faithful to the promises of the 1945 manifesto which had embraced most of the persistent radical demands of the inter-war Labour Party. An explanation must look to other factors: to the lack of an appropriate theoretical understanding of the likely consequences of their actions, a theoretical and technical ignorance attributable to the lack of a precedent and to the ambiguities of the Labour programmes developed in the 1930s; to a certain timidity and moderation fostered by participation in the war coalition; and to the immense problems of post-war reconstruction. The tendencies to hesitate and retreat in the later stages of the government were compounded of other factors: a resurgence of Conservative opposition; increasing hostility from business; a desire to placate the USA; a fear of being tainted by the label socialist in the climate of the Cold War; an appreciation of the limits of the changes resulting simply from nationalization; and a feeling of exhaustion, combined with complacency, self-satisfaction, and lack of imagination about future measures. None the less, the Attlee governments bequeathed the possibility of further transformative activity. The period 1945—51 witnessed molecular transformation. Labour implemented a series of inter-related, concurrent, progressive reforms, in the circumstances almost the maximum that could be expected from a social-democratic party.

The potential for the further development of government reforms in association with other social forces should not be underestimated. It was far from inevitable that subsequent Conservative governments would accept the new institutions and social principles, the smooth assimilation of which much surprised Labour. The 'post-war settlement',[28] the age of consensus politics, was as much a product of the adaptations of capital as the weaknesses of Labour. Gramsci referred to this kind of process as 'transformism', an aspect of a 'passive revolution' whereby transformation and restoration were two sides of the same process.[29] Transformism denoted the gradual incorporation of antagonistic groups and their political representatives through a pacific, but genuine, change in the structure of power. The character of post-war Labour politics and the post-war social formation should be seen in this light. The antinomies of the condition of the mid twentieth century Labour Party revolve around this paradoxical process of transformism: a transformative strategy revitalized capitalism in the form of the Welfare State; the political representation of working-class opposition entailed the affirmation of advanced capitalism; and a significant change in the balance of social forces re-established the dominance of the interests of capital. The story of the epoch is largely one of unanticipated consequences.

The post-war formation: the Welfare State

Recognizing the novel character of the post-war social formation depends upon viewing society as a totality. Taken separately, its distinguishing attributes — the construction of the mixed economy, advances in welfare provision, the consolidation of the dominant ideology, and the integration of the labour movement — may appear as outcomes of earlier tendencies. But their simultaneous development transfigured British society. The essence of the new configuration can be condensed into a concept of the Welfare State; in Hegelian notation, the concept realized itself in concrete institutions and activities which cohered effectively for two decades but which, from the late 1960s, began to disintegrate as its internal contradictions became manifest.

Often the term 'Welfare State' is used imprecisely. Whilst a common concept of ideological debate, it remains but a casual, descriptive label in social-scientific discourse. The post-war Welfare State has usually been understood as the latest stage in a cumulative process of social reform which began in the nineteenth century.[30] In this view there has been a continual evolution in social provision since the mid nineteenth century wherein the steady, quantitative accretion of social reforms, fed by progressive enlightenment and generosity, had the welcome result of instituting comprehensive social guarantees against individual misfortune. The Welfare State is thus the pragmatic achievement of 150 years of humane liberalism, propelled at times by the legitimate demands of the British working-class movement. But neither continuity nor the influence of British liberalism need be denied while still maintaining that in post-war society a new relationship between social provision and other economic and political processes altered the social-structural significance of welfare services.

Welfare provision, always more than a response to individual hardship and need, has served various functions: since the Elizabethan Poor Law it has been a mode of social control, a way of 'regulating the poor' and maintaining public order;[31] from the time the male working class was enfranchized it has been important in electioneering; by stigmatizing non-observance it has played a key role in inculcating values of work, thrift, and self-help; and it has been a prominent tool for manipulating the structure of the labour force, by maintaining a pool of unemployed and controlling the sexual division of labour. These functions were retained after the war, but with essential additions and modifications. The new functions of public welfare led to its playing an integral role in the re-production of society as a whole, one sufficiently pervasive to designate Britain a 'welfare state'.

The determining characteristic of the British Welfare State was the interdependence of social provision, economic regulation and political control, which generated a particular mode of regulating class conflict. Its central feature was the institutionalization of class conflict, a way of negotiating and containing conflict between capital and labour within established institutionalized channels. Most importantly, these channels were not subject to the direct and formal control of the state. Certainly extended state intervention was a necessary element in the new formation; a public sector in the economy and state-controlled welfare provision were vital. But, nevertheless, many of the determinants of life-chances remained in the domain of civil society; competitive party politics, free and dispersed collective bargaining, market-complementing economic planning, and a meritocratic educational system, left many of the mechanisms of privilege outside of the ambit of state control. The extended, *indirect* mediation by the state in the processes of civil society distinguished the Welfare State from inter-war society; and, in the same vein, it has been the extended *direct* mediation of class conflict by the state which has distinguished the social order of the 1970s from that of the Welfare State.

The accumulation of capital in the Welfare State

Post-war economic reconstruction, presided over by the Attlee governments, provided the basis for the British experience of what has been
called 'the long boom'.[32] Despite occasional fluctuations, the western
economies passed through a period of unprecedented expansion and
stability. The 'age of austerity' gave way to what seemed to be an infinite
'age of affluence'. Economic growth and a rising standard of living in the
1950s and 1960s fostered the illusion that the defects of capitalist economies, so blatant in the pre-war epoch, had finally been cured. But short-
term success obscured certain long-term trends which entailed the economic crises of the late 1960s and 1970s. By then, however, the world
capitalist economy, and the British role in it, had been fundamentally
restructured.

In retrospect it is clear that the workings of the world market after
1945 altered to the detriment of Britain. The decline of the Empire, the
resurgence of the European and Japanese economies, the growing assert-
iveness of non-Western states, and long-term changes in the balance of
trade, removed key supports for the historic dominance of Britain in
the world economy. Furthermore, Britain's burden of fighting a six-year
total war had provided the opportunity for the USA to usurp the roles of
leader, guarantor, co-ordinator and principal beneficiary of the world
capitalist economy.[33] After 1945 the British economy was always dependent on the USA. Despite attempting to maintain sterling as a major
international currency, Britain no longer possessed the economic base
for preserving its dominant position in the world market. The much
stronger economy of the USA, and the subsequent recoveries of other
capitalist economies, rapidly reduced the competitiveness of British
industries. This was partly the result of Britain's initial technical backwardness in manufacturing, a condition which was self-perpetuating.
The outcome was the re-structuring of British domestic capital: a steady
decline in the traditional industrial base was not adequately compensated
for by the growth of new, technologically advanced, industries so that,
gradually, investment in British industry subsided and finance capital
consolidated its leading role within the domestic economy. At the same
time multi-national corporations became increasingly dominant within
Britain, a development which signified a reduction of domestic control
over the economy. The long-term decline of the British economy now
seems to have been inevitable, but so far as the politics of the post-war
period is concerned, a different picture was presented during the 'long-
boom'.

The distinguishing features of economic organization in the Welfare
State were the growth of political control over the economy and the

expansion of public expenditure. The combined effects of an emergent public sector, planning techniques, Keynesian fiscal policy, and public expenditures, restructured the processes of, and inter-relationship between, economic production and social cohesion.

One of the most obvious novel features of the post-war social formation was the increasing role that the state played in economic life. Public ownership and planning in the mixed economy neither undermined the capitalist rationale of economic relations nor fundamentally affected the distribution of power in Britain:[34] in providing both a public, infra-structural base for private industry and a range of economic services the state probably aided the accumulation of private capital. But at the same time it extended public control over the economy. The investment programmes of the nationalized industries were manipulated in a way consistent with the exigencies of overall planning,[35] and the resultant increase in the numbers of public employees permitted governments partially to control the level of wages.[36] The existence of the public sector was one foundation for the institutionalization of economic planning.

The expansion of the role of the state in capitalist economic planning was envisaged by such diverse people as Keynes, Mosley and Macmillan in the 1930s. The relatively successful management of the war-economy was instrumental in making planning reputable, yet still the bipartisan acceptance of planning after the war was significant. It rapidly became obligatory for governments to assume responsibility for overall manage-ment of the economy. In particular, the maintenance of full employ-ment was considered to be politically essential. Various types of plan-ning were implemented after the abandonment of the physical controls of wartime; demand management, wage and price control, market-supportive measures, and indicative planning, were all tried, with dif-ferent degrees of success, in the period through to 1970.[37] Most were related to the interventionist economic theory of Keynes, though some were clearly vulgar applications. Two effects can be noticed. First, the traditional functions of the state — providing the legal basis for private property, balancing the budget and stabilizing the currency — were deemed insufficient: now both the electorate and capital held legitimized expectations that the state would ensure national economic well-being. Secondly, the market was no longer the uncontested regulator of the economic process: planning implied that the free operation of market forces could no longer be relied upon to maintain economic equilibrium or social justice. The modification of market forces was not simply the results of political decision, though, for the accelerating concentration of capital in the monopoly sector and the increasing density of trade union membership, of their own accord, rendered market logic anachronistic.[38]

The role of the state was extended also through the growth of public expenditure, from some 30 per cent of GNP in 1933 to around 60 per cent in 1968, expanding steadily except for a small fall in the 1950s under the Conservative governments.[39] Once again this development can be traced back into the early part of the twentieth century, but simply to consider the long-term trend would be to lose its significance in post-war society.

There have been a number of attempts to classify the functions of public expenditure in the Welfare State, though none are entirely satisfactory.[40] O'Connor's was, perhaps, the most useful sociologically, though marred by the overlap between his categories and the difficulty involved in adapting official statistics to give weight to his analysis. O'Connor distinguished between 'social capital' which, while provided out of public revenue, comprised 'expenditure required for profitable private accumulation', and 'social expenses', consisting of 'projects and services which are required to maintain social harmony — to fulfil the state's "legitimization" function'.[41] (The latter category, 'social expenses', will be considered in the next section of this chapter.) 'Social capital' was of two types, 'social investments' and 'social consumption'. Social investments comprise services which 'increase the productivity of a given amount of labor power': government-sponsored research, the transport network, and the education system in its role as creator of a qualified labour force, fall into this category. The costs of these necessary services are increasingly socialized, provided publicly rather than being a drain on private capital. 'Social consumption' consists of services which 'lower the reproduction costs of labor', including health and social insurance, family allowances, and, again, education. In the British case it is necessary to consider, in addition, direct transfers of money from public funds: subsidies, grants, regional development premiums, and tax relief schemes to private industry and agriculture, all contribute directly to the accumulation of capital. Investment in publicly owned industries also benefits private enterprise in providing a necessary infrastructure which is subsidized by the Exchequer and which, through favourable pricing policies, provides proportionately cheap input factors in private company accounts. The total money-value of such social capital and direct subsidy is probably incalculable, but there can be little doubt that the state provides these supports and that they are pre-conditions for the successful accumulation of private capital in the post-war Britain.

According to Barratt-Brown's calculations publicly provided economic and social services absorbed 37.4 per cent of GNP in 1968 as compared with 18.3 per cent in 1933.[42] The doubling of such expenditure, by increasing political intervention in the economy, had considerable structural effects. Expenditures which were directly economic clearly increased the capacity of the state for control, while those which were indirect often had the same effect. Public expenditure was used to lubricate the economy on many occasions; expansion of public expenditure could be used to increase demand through consumption and, via the 'multiplier' effect, investment.[43] Thus, for example, alterations in public housing policy proved an effective short-term regulator. Though attempts at using such instruments were not especially successful, even when failing they extended the capacity for political control of the economy.

Social services gained a disproportionate share in the new public expenditure. In 1933 social services accounted for only 12.5 per cent of GNP and just over 40 per cent of all public expenditure; in 1948 it constituted 18.6 per cent of GNP and just less than half of public expenditure; by 1968 the figures were 26 per cent of GNP and over half of public spending.[44] Such a concentration of public expenditure is one reason for thinking of the post-war period in terms of the concept of the welfare state. However it would be mistaken to assume, as some radical commentators have, that all such expenditure is directly functional to capital. There is some truth in the notion that the function of welfare is to produce, reproduce and maintain an efficient work-force. All things being equal, a healthy labour-force should be more productive, a secure one more compliant, and an educated one more adaptable. However, despite evidence that enlightened capitalists have reasoned in this way,[45] and despite the fact that most capitalist countries have introduced similar kinds of provision regardless of the character of their political regimes, this argument is inadequate. Firstly, it fails to grasp the intricacies of divisions of interest within capital: as O'Connor argues, the monopoly sector benefits more from this growth of social provision than does the small business sector which remains dependent on market logic.[46] Secondly, it assumes an omniscience on behalf of the state; not only is it assumed that the state is a monolithic agent of capital, but also that it makes correct decisions on all occasions. Thirdly, and most importantly, it ignores the role of the labour movement in the creation of the Welfare State.

Legitimation

Besides providing the preconditions for the effective accumulation of capital, the modern state also sustains the legitimacy of the social order. The manufacturing of consent is a complex process, one which is constantly over-simplified by social scientists. Empirical evidence concerning social values and attitudes does not support the idea that there is a dominant ideology which is transplanted into the minds of all citizens by way of socialization; studies show too great a degree of dissensus on key values to maintain such a position.[47] It seems more likely that the veneer of consent, or, rather, the absence of overt dissent, conceals levels of inconsistency and disagreement on values and norms, social order being maintained by a combination of threats of sanctions, routine behaviour and material compensations. In this view the state's role in legitimation is less one of the direct sponsoring of a dominant ideology, through for example the education process, and more one of fostering consent through institutionalized practices. It is in this context that O'Connor's concept of 'social expenses' is relevant: *social expenses consist of projects and services which are required to maintain social harmony — to fulfill the state's "legitimization" function. They are not even indirectly productive. The best example is the welfare system which is designed chiefly to keep social peace among unemployed workers'.[48] This is to grasp one function of welfare expenditure; social control can be managed, without overt repression, through material compensations channelled through the state.[49] But this by no means constitutes an exhaustive explanation of the role of welfare in maintaining social harmony.

At the ideological level the notion of a 'Welfare State' had a very significant part to play in the legitimation of post-war society. In political discourse it was the encapsulation of the acceptable face of capitalism, and the central element of the politics of consensus. Many members of the Labour Party abandoned their pre-war commitments to socialism precisely because the emergence of a humane, caring, and in some ways egalitarian, welfare system appeared to guarantee mutual protection against hardship within a non-totalitarian regime. For Conservatives too it was not just an acceptable price to pay for social peace but was assimilated with traditions of paternalist Tory social reform. To what extent the ethos of the concept permeated common consciousness is a matter for conjecture, for there appears to be a permanent ambiguity between, on the one hand, berating welfare 'scroungers' and, on the other, lauding the passing of means tests and the insecurities of the 1930s. Nevertheless, at the elite level of national politics and administration, a genuine consensus on the merits of the system of welfare provision can be detected, one which survived into the early 1970s but is now dissolving. This consensus was built upon a coherent social philosophy, a hegemonic formula, which was the key to the maintenance of legitimacy from 1950 to 1970.

The tradition of thought from which the Welfare State emanates is New Liberalism, a tradition running from T.H. Green, through Hobhouse, Hobson, T.H. Marshall and Beveridge to the consensus politics of the 1950s. (It is examined in some depth in Chapter 3, below.) In essence it maintained that the foremost achievement of liberal-democratic societies was the development of universal rights of citizenship,[50] which would incorporate all members of the population through the extension of formally equal civil, political and social rights. What the Welfare State did was to guarantee equal social rights, the most recent stage in the integration of previously disprivileged individuals into society. Welfarism represented the highest stage of the development of individual rights, the epitome of non-compulsive egalitarianism, and the zenith of consensual humanitarianism; as such it had obvious potential for the legitimation of the post-war social order and for the justification of integrative strategies. The post-war social formation was to be the embodiment of this liberal, incorporative doctrine which, it was anticipated, would nullify internal conflict, class division and the inequitable distribution of power.

This ideological syndrome certainly had its problems, for, as Marshall pointed out, there was a vital contradiction between the logic of the market as a distributive mechanism and the rationale of equal treatment for all by virtue of common citizenship.[51] But it was of the utmost significance that the automatic effectivity of the market was not a principal tenet of legitimation in the Welfare State. Just as the role of the market in the production process was modified through state intervention, so its use as an ideological justification for the allocation of rewards was reduced. As Habermas has argued, increasing state intervention, particularly in crisis management, severely reduced the plausibility of traditional bourgeois justifications for the unequal distribution of rewards.[52] The curtailment of the market mechanism and its replacement by administrative or political processes undermines the argument for the naturally fair consequence of market distribution. Instead, as the state claims competence in the regulation of production and distribution, it becomes clear that economic rewards are part of political decision-making. For so long as governments appeared capable of controlling the economic process and generating the resources for increasing material compensation, the new legitimation was very effective. Most remarkable was the way in which, for a time, the social control function of welfare was superseded by an ideologically integrative function. As an idea, the welfare state provided the ideological cement for the dominant political formula of the period; and in practice it furnished various institutional means for securing social harmony. Supported by other social tendencies, welfare institutions provided a channel for averting social conflict. Yet, despite this new role for the state, legitimation at this period remained largely the terrain of civil society and, especially, the political parties.

The institutionalization of class conflict

A historical commitment to promoting the interests of the working class is a constant characteristic of labour movements. The strength of this commitment waxes and wanes, but even though certain sections of most Western labour movements would happily abandon the commitment altogether, the basic political alignments of Western societies, and particularly Britain, still revolve around the axis of class differences.[53] But while any analysis of labour in capitalist society would fail to make sense if unrelated to class conflict and its potential escalation, there is nothing universal about its forms and content. One of the oddities of many analyses of the British labour movement, and of the practical strategems of socialists, is that they take little notice of the historical specificity of class conflict, the varying constraints and institutional mediations which operate in a particular social formation. The oppositional role of the working classes in capitalist society cannot even be described without reference to particular class structures, the ways in which class relations are regulated and negotiated in different epochs, and the class alliances typical of particular periods.

The proposition that the working class shares a fundamental and common interest by virtue of being obliged to sell its labour power in exchange for wages is a useful theoretical axiom for understanding the nature of capitalist society, but is not readily applicable in historical analysis. Among the obvious objections to the axiom with respect to modern British society are that it underestimates the extent of the fragmentation of the subordinate classes, and that it obscures the degree to which fundamental differences of interests between capital and labour are disguised and moderated by various social institutions.

It became increasingly difficult in the Welfare State to sustain notions of an identity of interest throughout the working class because of internal fragmentation. British stratification analysis has distinguished between proletarian, deferential and instrumental workers,[54] all of whom are considered characteristically different from white-collar workers, technicians and auxiliary scientific staffs, who, in some formulations, constitute a 'new working class'.[55] Recent work has detected an even greater fragmentation of social perspectives.[56] These studies, furthermore, remain largely oblivious to two other key lines of internal division within the working class: sexual and ethnic differentiation. If one considers the structural location of women or the role of immigrant labour in the advanced economies,[57] one can hardly avoid concluding that intra-class division, despite recent recognition of 'class fractions' and 'class alliances',[58] creates enormous complexities in the formulation of political programmes.

The socio-economic changes which produced greater fragmentation among the working class also undermined some of the cultural foundations of its political activity. Traditional and impulsive political solidarity weakened. Changes in the occupational structure and the social organization of work, particularly the decline in traditional heavy manufacturing industry, weakened one basis of proletarian solidarity; urban re-housing reduced the social solidarity of working-class communities; wider unionization, in a favourable economic climate, produced a degree of affluence for many, but at the same time probably increased differentials in relation to the non-unionized. Increased intra-generational mobility through educational opportunity improved life-chances for some without recourse to political remedies. Perhaps, then, it is unsurprising that working class involvement in party politics declined.[59]

The period also witnessed developments in institutions which were directly involved in mediating political conflict. State apparatuses played a part, particularly in mediating the distribution of rewards, and so too did changes in the societal role of the labour movement itself.

Barratt-Brown argued, against Miliband, that the state had not just two functions, repressive and ideological, but also a third, a 'conformative role'. Institutions with a conformative role 'contain and moderate the conflicts inside capitalist society'.[60] Among such conformative institutions are the various arms of the welfare system. Welfare provision might be seen as acting in the space between (the effects of) the economic system and the modes of repressive and ideological control, a mediation between the distributive effects of the market and the requirements of political order. Before the war welfare payments and services operated relatively autonomously, a sphere of state activity unrelated to economic management or to attempts to change the structure of inequality in the realization of social justice.[61] Unemployment insurance in the pre-war period, for example, while partly financed through progressive taxation, was primarily a system of self-insurance: it was actuarially independent, and was certainly not considered as a way of balancing the national budget, stimulating consumption, or satisfying social obligations to the unemployed citizen. Welfare was, rather, a contingent palliative. After 1945, however, it was made integral to economic and political practice. Welfare provision became a way of re-distributing wealth, a positive tool in economic planning, and a social right rather than a political expedient: it became a mode of regulating class conflict.

At the same time the institutions of the labour movement came to play a more active, conformative role in post-war society. The 'social democratic consensus' persisted because the institutional agents of the subordinate classes, the party and the unions, were no longer excluded, protesting, peripheral institutions. Although the results of this incorporation of the institutions of labour into the political and state apparatus were mixed, the recognition and the power accorded to them changed the modes of regulating discontent.

One milepost in the progressive integration of the Labour Party was its assumption of governmental office in 1923.[62] It was no accident that the changes in the social composition of the PLP dated from this period, when professionals began to encroach on its uniformly working-class composition.[63] But the constraints of minority government were considerable; there was no sense in which the Labour Party of the inter-war years was responsible for re-constructing the social order. The 1945—51 governments, on the other hand, contributed significantly to the creation of a new framework of society. A situation arose where entirely to repudiate the emergent society would be an admission of failure on behalf of the Labour Party. There were never any signs of this: Labour was undoubtedly proud of its achievements and, having created the post-war formation, it retained a considerable stake in its perpetuation. The Party was responsible for creating consensus politics and was, from one angle, compromised in the process.

'Consensus politics' was not mythical; it signified a real, if temporary, political equilibrium between classes. Britain was politically becalmed. Structural social conflict was minimal. All elements of the social order, including the Labour Party, accepted the rules of the social game: the very different theses of *One-Dimensional Man* and *The End of Ideology* came to the same empirical conclusion, that continued political quietism was to be expected.[64] The Labour Party adopted two, contradictory, roles: it became both a party of management and a party of opposition, involved simultaneously in both the expression and the regulation of class conflict.

The trade union movement also contributed significantly to the social cohesion of the Welfare State. Trade union activity exhibited two distinct tendencies after 1945. The predominant tendency was to operate with a traditional economistic rationale, directed towards improving the rewards and working conditions of their members, by means of autonomous collective bargaining. Claiming apolitical status, and rejecting centralized or state direction, the unions guarded their autonomy jealously and acted subject only to the constraints of the market-capacity of firms and their own organizational strength. Their determination to struggle separately over the distribution of rewards through wage negotiation was, however, highly controlled, for they tried to ensure that struggle was pursued solely through sanctioned channels. Thus not only was a political oppositional role eschewed, but unofficial, shop-floor action was also severely curtailed. In this manner the unions supported the institution-alization of class conflict. Though centralized collective bargaining was the preferred strategy of the unions during the prosperity of the 1950s and 1960s a second tendency, initiated by Citrine and Bevin during the Depression, of seeking stronger formal links with the state, continued to develop slowly. The acceptance of wage restraint in 1948 and 1965, and the increasing involvement in consultations with capital in planning organizations like the NEDC, indicated that an alternative strategy of collaboration with the state had not been abandoned.

Given recent developments, especially the arrangement of the 'Social Contract', it is necessary to distinguish between the institutionalization of class conflict and class collaboration. The institutionalization of class conflict refers to the routinization of dispersed episodes of capital–labour conflict via general procedural agreements which, typically, are only very indirectly mediated by the state. Class collaboration, on the other hand, refers to the containment of class conflict through substantive, universally obligatory agreement between the representatives of class organizations which, typically, are sustained by direct state intervention. The post-war settlement was based primarily on the institutionalization of class conflict; it was assumed that, normally, the negotiation of levels of financial reward among the employed would be the province of free collective bargaining between employers and unions, the role of the state thereby being limited to complementary social reform. While the 'long boom' lasted, and the demands of labour were not detrimental to the continued accumulation of capital, this assumption was generally re-affirmed. Even when incomes policies were introduced they remained temporary expedients. It was the experiences of the late 1960s and the 1970s which led to the conclusion that such institutional forms were unsatisfactory, and attempts were then made to substitute direct negotiations between labour, capital and the state. The tripartism of the Social Contract, based on extra-parliamentary agreements, signified a transition to class collaboration, where the institutional representatives of the labour movement became directly involved in the statutory regulation of class dispute over the distribution of reward.

The post-war settlement

The post-war settlement constituted a distinctive social formation. Integrated institutional arrangements simultaneously secured the accumulation of capital, the resolution of conflict over distribution of rewards, and adequate societal legitimation. Overt class antagonism was largely eliminated: the combination of a regulated mixed economy, free collective bargaining and complementary social reform provided the institutional basis for social harmony and political consensus. This was the structural setting within which the Labour Party was located. Pre-war concerns with market capitalism, private ownership, class conflict, state curtailment of union activity, and social insecurity were all partially deflected. Instead, a dominant strategy emerged, endorsing the new

structural arrangements in a political formula which provided both legitimation and a practical programme for consolidating the welfare state.
That formula was made possible, but not necessary, by the practice of
the Attlee government. Attlee's legacy was ambiguous. Contrary to
Addison, who has argued recently that the post-war consensus was fully
formed during the period of the second world war, the political formula
of the Welfare State was the product of Labour's development after the
implementation of the inter-war programme.[65] The options open were
either to accept the structure of the Welfare State and improve it, or to
develop a new programme which would build on the examples of steel
nationalization and the NHS. The second alternative was elaborated,
rather weakly, in *Keep Left* and *Keeping Left*, pamphlets of the 'Fundamentalist' left, which embodied the transformative impulses of 1945–8.
It was, however, eclipsed by the former, ameliorative tendency, which
was borne forward by the 'Revisionists'. It was they who developed the
post-war settlement. Adopting a different rationale from the practice of
the Attlee governments, and accepting the structures of the 'new society',
they superseded Fabianism and bound Labour's fortunes to the promises
of the Welfare State and its political formula.

3 Social Reformism: the architecture of the consensus

Richard Crossman observed that by 1950;

> the Government had fulfilled its historic mission. The nationalisation of half a dozen industries, the construction of an all-in system of social security and a free health service, and the tentative application of planning to the national economy — the achievement of these reforms seemed to have exhausted the content of British socialism.[1]

The most coherent response to the apparent exhaustion of British socialism came from a group, sceptically christened 'the New Thinkers' by opponents and subsequently referred to as the 'Gaitskellites' or the 'Revisionists', who, instead of reviving socialism, substituted a quite distinct tradition of political thought — New Liberalism. The habit of associating the Labour Party with socialism has largely obscured its connections with liberalism. Without doubting the group's sincerity in claiming socialist authenticity, its ideology was more a development of radical liberalism than a revision of socialism. The segment consisted of advocates of Social Reform, after the style of the Liberal governments of 1906—14. It was these liberal elements which permitted Social Reformism, nutured within the Labour Party, to serve as the central legitimating ideology of the Welfare State.

Early interpretations of Social Reformism deemed it a form of pragmatism, indicative of the irrelevance of ideology in post-war politics.[2] Such a view was later corrected as it became clear that Social Reformism had an ideological coherence of its own.[3] The character and effects of that ideology remained, however, misunderstood. Most commentators, whether sympathetic or not, saw it as part of a unilinear and irreversible trend towards the modernization of the Labour Party. Haseler, in *The Gaitskellites*, contrasted the accurate social analysis and realistic political programme of Revisionism with those of a dogmatic and anachronistic left. He believed the Morrisonian 'shopping list' approach to national-ization extinct, and the left's socialism obsolete. Mistaking the tradition from which Revisionist philosophy derived, and ignoring the fact that it was but one tendency in a segmental Party, he worked remorselessly towards his concluding prediction, its continued supremacy. Bogdanor tended to concur.[4] Those who detested Social Reformism also proclaimed its success inevitable. Coates considered the Gaitskellites to exemplify the ineliminable defects of Labour as a radical party; Burns thought them wholly misguided and beyond hope of correction.[5] Coates, Burns, and others, found Revisionism entirely consistent with Labour's traditions and final proof of the Party's inappropriateness as a vehicle of socialism. Such critiques also mistook their object.

'Moderation', like socialism, appears in many guises. The specific nature of Social Reformism can only be grasped through close exam-ination of the relationship between intellectual conviction and the social context. Characteristic of Social Reformism was its combination of the vision of New Liberalism — social integration through the extension of civic equality — with the acceptance of the existing social structure. Possible only after the reforms of the Attlee governments, such positive affirmation of the basic structural features of the *status quo* was unique in Labour's history. That is not to deny the longevity in Labour ideology of appeals to the national interest and concerns with social harmony; but even the acknowledged pre-war intellectual precursors of Social Reform-ism, Dalton, Jay and Durbin,[6] considered a transformation of social structure to be a pre-requisite of a socialist society. To dispense com-pletely with such a requirement was unprecedented. So long as the social stability induced by the post-war settlement lasted, Social Reformism flourished. But that was neither inevitable nor permanent.

The elements of Social Reformist ideology

Social Reformism crystallized with the publication in 1952 of *New Fabian Essays* and Socialist Union's *A New Statement of Principles*. A spate of literature followed, reaching its zenith in 1956 with works by Crosland, Gaitskell, Socialist Union, and Strachey.[7] Welcoming 'statist' or 'post-capitalist' society, the grouping sought for the Labour Party a new political strategy to turn statism into socialism. But it was to be a new kind of socialism, a socialism which required less a change of social structure than a change of attitude: the socialist project was so re-defined that Crosland could explicitly exclude, as policies of socialist advance, free social services, nationalization, more economic control, and heavier direct taxation.[8]

The ideological positions of the various Social Reformists were by no means identical, but a number of elements were held in common which, when juxtaposed, constituted a particular ideological configuration. The central elements were: the rejection of traditional socialism; a re-vamping of the concepts of class, ownership, individual, and market; a model of the political process centring on a specific view of politics, democracy, and parliamentary representation; and a redefinition of socialism. Embodied in these concepts was both a world-view and a strategy of action for the Labour Party.

Socialism and the 'new society'

The usual starting-point for 're-thinking' was to identify an oppositional doctrine, traditional socialism, and establish its inadequacies *vis-a-vis* the reconstituted post-war society. Rather surprisingly the target for criticism was not the position of contemporaries on the left, but a ghostly marxian economism. Although there had been some revival of marxist thought in the 1930s, which were the formative intellectual years of the early Gaitskellites,[9] it had had little influence since 1940.[10] Durbin in 1940, like Jay before him, had spent a considerable proportion of his time refuting Marx; but there seemed less reason for Crosland to do the same in 1956.[11]

The two defining features of marxism were taken to be the immiseration thesis and the postulate of a capitalist ruling class. According to Crosland such an analysis failed to capture post-war reality.The working class had not become impoverished, and democratic institutions, along with a new stratum of industrial managers, had undermined the power of capitalists. Therefore, marxian socialism (which, it was implied, constituted the content of traditional British socialism) had to be discarded.[12]

A reformulation of socialism was required, and while the manner of doing this was varied (Crosland compared all forms of socialism and made a rather arbitrary selection of themes by elimination and recomposition, while Socialist Union looked back into the British heritage[13]), a common conclusion was reached, that socialism was an ethical ideal concerning social relationships. Socialism denoted the *realization of certain values*: predominantly, for Crosland, the abolition of poverty, social welfare, equal rights, co-operation and economic efficiency.[14]

The idea of the 'new society', current in the 1950s, was central to Social Reformist argument. As Crosland put it, 'traditional capitalism has been reformed and modified almost out of existence, and it is with a quite different form of society that socialists must now concern themselves.'[15] The new society identified by the Social Reformists was essentially a mixed-economy Welfare State. A creature of the Attlee governments, the new society had overcome many of the problems of pre-war capitalism: for example, insecurity, a key motif of Jay's *The Socialist*

Case, had more or less been removed; and the capitalist trade cycle was thought to have been abolished, which led to a general lack of interest in fundamental economic structures. The task was to develop the potential of the Welfare State so that its residual defects were gradually removed. This could be done, the Social Reformists thought, within the context of a genuine social consensus, for affluence seemed to guarantee social harmony.

Crosland implied that Britain was already on the way to socialism, a conclusion which suggested that future actions should be guided by the principles of the imminent socialist society rather than those of the old capitalist order. Socialist Union asked, typically, 'Have we to wait until the last vestiges of class privilege are wiped out before workers will become responsible in their work and take the ideal of fellowship seriously?'[16] In some ways pre-empting the end-of-ideology thesis with their optimistic view that harmonious tendencies inherent in the new order permitted the development of an organic, social cohesion, they advocated policies which pre-supposed 'common interest and equal status'.[17] The immediate consequences of the boom of the early 1950s persuaded them that social consensus had superseded class conflict.

Ownership and control

The notion, explicit in the Party constitution of 1918, that class inequality was a function of property, and public ownership its appropriate remedy, was thoroughly embedded in the consciousness of the inter-war Labour Party. With certain sectors of the economy taken into public ownership Social Reformism concluded that the extant level of nationalization was sufficient.[18] The major turn in the argument was that nationalization was a *means* to an end, not a good in itself, and that common ownership of the means of production was no longer a necessary precondition of socialism.

The Social Reformists re-assessed the goal of public ownership long before it became an issue related to the electoral success of the Labour Party. In an influential, but not entirely consistent, article Albu claimed that while public control of industry had a useful planning function, general arguments for public ownership were redundant: 'The truth is that the most urgent of these (traditional) objects of public ownership have been achieved by other means'.[19] Given full employment, nationalization was only justified as an anti-monopoly device. By and large, the extant level of public ownership was sufficient.

The case against public ownership professed that power had been redistributed in the new society: power no longer resided with a capitalist ruling class but was progressively being devolved onto bureaucratic organizations. Crosland maintained that 'economic power... which rather naturally obsessed pre-war socialists when they were analysing capitalism, now poses fewer problems than other forms of power which have nothing to do with ownership or private industry as such'.[20] 'The enlarged and bureaucratic state', 'a small hierarchy of Court, Church and influential newspapers', and 'those who control the bureaucratic mass organization' were more significant loci of power.[21] The Social Reformists' aversion to bureaucracy derived from a concern with individual liberty in the intellectual climate of the Cold War. Not only was antagonism towards the Soviet Union a principal theme of their position on international relations, but they also sought to dissociate themselves from any taint of communism at home. Their attitudes towards personal freedom, democracy and the market in many ways derived from their critique of social conditions in the USSR: the centralization of power in state bureaucracies was held responsible for the denial of personal freedoms, of speech, movement and combination, for the absence of Western democratic political institutions, and for the absurdities of distributive policies in Eastern Europe.

The other major argument about the devolution of power rested upon a distinction between ownership and control in industrial enterprises. Capitalists as a group of individuals still, nominally, owned the vast majority of industry, but they no longer had effective control as a class. It was asserted that the numbers of people owning shares had significantly increased; that control, or rather oversight, was vested in the people through a parliament endowed with Keynesian techniques; and that direction of industry had fallen to the stratum of managers whose motivations were different from their capitalist-owner predecessors. Hence property ownership was no longer a major evil and the expropriation of owners was not a necessary step toward socialism.

Albu said of managers, who almost became heroes,

> Today the leaders of industry defend their institutions with talk of service to the community; and profit, in place of being an end in itself, has become an expedient. It is now time to take them at their word, to destroy the ambivalence of their position, and to bring the open legal form of our economic institutions into line with the true functions which they perform.[22]

This presaged both *Industry and Society*[23] and Gaitskell's later claim that large private industry was serving the nation well. Albu's position depended upon the claim, which became a central premise of Social Reformism, that managerial power was distinct from capitalist power. Once ownership and control in industry were radically differentiated, antagonism to the capitalist ruling class was misplaced. The advent of the professional manager signified the demise of the profit motive, a contention shared by Harold Macmillan and the 'etatiste corporatists' of the inter-war Tory radicals, so that government planning became compatible with the pursuits of socially responsible managers.[24] Managers appeared as benevolent despots. Without vested financial interest in the enterprise, independent of the shareholders, and not standing to gain substantially from maximizing profits, they operated with entirely different motivations from exploitative, nineteenth century, capitalist factory-owners. The managers' search for status and self-respect, it was argued, stood not on the criterion of profit but on being thought a considerate and humane employer.[25]

The diagnosis of the decomposition of the ruling class had direct implications for Social Reformist understandings of industrial relations, trade unionism and the composition of the subordinate classes in Britain. Adopting a 'human relations' approach to industrial relations, Crosland argued that though there were, and probably always would be, conflicts between managers and workers in industry, these were in no way fundamental structural antagonisms and could be contained by careful, prescient management.[26]

At the same time it was an unquestioned principle of Social Reformism in the 1950s that 'the workers' side must have an untrammelled Trade Union Movement to defend its claims'.[27] Government interference in wage determination, manpower planning, etc., was firmly rejected on the grounds that it was unnecessary and improperly restrictive,[28] a position which proved very useful in raising support for Social Reformism within the trade unions. For example, Williamson of the NUM said that he had been impressed by Gaitskell's 'common sense approach to industrial matters which we in the trade unions regarded as important'.[29] That 'common sense approach' amounted to letting the trade unions get on with what they were doing. This was only plausible on the assumption that there were not fundamental cleavages between the two sides of industry. In conditions of prosperity, given a modified market and the appropriate encouragement of industry towards growth, union practices did not seem to require restriction. Social Reformism condoned the sectional-corporatism of the unions.

Preoccupation with the new managers reinforced the Social Reformist inclination to preserve the traditional functions of the unions. There was internal debate about the propriety of workers' participation in industry (Albu thought the failure of the nationalized industries to change authority relations in industry a major defect, while Crosland expressed 'a certain irritation' at the 'almost obsessive' exposure given to the word 'participation'[30]), but managerial prerogatives tended to be given priority. This was probably because the Social Reformists saw themselves as political managers, professionals, aiming, like their industrial counterparts, at a balance between humanity and effectiveness. Hattersley, reflecting on the changing social composition of the PLP, captured the ethos of the Social Reformists:

> Despite its historical bias the Labour Party has always included a number of men who were middle class in origin, who joined the Party for reasons of intellect rather than of class solidarity. The new men were neither like these nor like the working class socialist who had been the backbone of the Party between the wars. Usually of working class parentage, often with university education and working at middle class jobs, they expected the Labour Party to live up to the high professional standards which they set for themselves. They expected discipline, application, realism and responsibility... Their classless professionalism rejected both the old style class war socialism and sterile disputation about long dead theories and principles.[31]

Professionalism was somehow antithetical to prejudice and interest. It was hypothesized that the function of government was national management, that in politics, just as in an industrial concern, it was possible to take decisions which were in the interests of all the participants in the enterprise. If the managers were good then employees, or citizens, could have only limited cause for dissatisfaction, and structural bases of conflict would dissolve.

Class

Social Reformist analysis presented a radical re-assessment of the nature of class in post-war Britain. The traditional link between class and private ownership, and its corollary that the labouring classes suffer because of their role in the system of production, were both denied. Inequality was recognized, indeed equality was the central critical concept of Social Reformism, but its relationship to class was redefined.

Crosland's analysis claimed that class continued to permeate British society, but through its manifestation as *status inequality*.[32] Class was declared to be not an economic concept, but a 'sociological' one. Britain, Crosland said, 'now presents an unusual paradox to the world: of a society characterised by an exceptionally mature political democracy, growing economic prosperity, and a social order which apparently metes out social justice in a reasonable degree: yet still with an unreconstructed class system, productive of deep collective resentments'.[33] He did not deny the reality of class, for it was a major source of grievance, but he argued that, 'This stratification derives from, and is reflected in, socially recognised relationships of superiority and inferiority.'[34] It was social feelings, differentials in prestige and dignity, rather than inequalities of wealth and power, which underlay the 'class system': among many factors causing stratification, education, style of life and occupational status were particularly important.[35] Income, while significant, was indeterminate, for, as Crosland pointed out, often it was better-paid workers who were most militant, and often there was little difference of income between white-collar and manual workers. The idea of class conflict was abandoned: 'nobody now believes in a theory of irreconcilable conflict', rather, it was the 'failure of social assimilation which creates antagonism'.[36]

The analysis of inequality echoed elements of the British liberal-radical tradition. The case against inequality hung on the ontological equality of individuals which ought to be embodied in equal, formal rights accruing to all citizens. Jay, for example, maintained that the 'ultimate aim' of socialism was 'certain equal rights for all' not the actual equality of individuals. The 'basic economic aim for Socialists' should be 'not literally "equality", but *the minimum of inequality that is workable if human beings are actively to use their talents: not equal shares, but fair shares; not equality but social justice*'.[37] For Social Reformism, income differentials were not important, partly because they were thought to be diminishing, and partly because they were considered functional. Crosland believed that differential rewards were a necessary concomitant of an advanced division of labour and that reward was a function of the importance of a person's contribution to society. As in the Fabian notion of 'rent of ability', ability must be rewarded. Assuaging the collective resentments emanating from class, therefore, depended on manipulating the means by which status inequality manifested itself and ensuring equality of access to privileged positions.

Fairness, justice and equal access were often reduced to equality of opportunity. The socialist project was partially redefined in terms of *meritocratic* principles, as was witnessed in Social Reformist concern with equal educational opportunity through comprehensive schooling. There the focus for change was not the social system itself but the mode of access to privileges within the system. There remained some ambiguity, however, for both Crosland and Jenkins argued explicitly that equal opportunity alone was insufficient:[38] equal access to the race for privilege was inadequate in that it might simply replace a hereditary elite by a meritocratic elite. This ambiguity was irresolvable. It was unclear how equal status among citizens could ever be reconciled with differential reward. And it was fundamentally inconsistent to anticipate the erosion of status differentials when the principal motivation of the managerial stratum was for status and prestige. The ambiguity derived from the initial decision to analyse inequality in terms of status without consideration of the fact that status, in a non-caste society, is predominantly a consequence of the market mechanism itself.[39] The refusal to tamper with market processes of distribution precluded the abolition of status inequality. Nevertheless, the Social Reformist reformulation was quite persuasive, and in fact became an accredited part of sociological orthodoxy.[40] In an era of prosperity, with relatively pacific industrial relations and little awareness of the existence of poverty, the concept of class conflict seemed dispensable; and the alternative provided a basis for an ethical and ameliorative conception of socialism.

The Social Reformist analysis of stratification was connected to a defence of the market mechanism. Competition was made something of a virtue. Gaitskell said, 'we have to weigh up the gains from elim- inating the waste of competition against the disadvantages of destroying the competitive spirit'.[41] He believed that

> it is much easier to get the right atmosphere, and therefore greater efficiency, in large-scale undertakings, if the element of competition is somehow retained. This is especially true of the staff and management grades. It may be regrettable but it seems to be a fact, that most people's enthusiasm about any group to which they belong is enhanced by competition.[42]

Interestingly, differentials in wealth were acceptable while inequitable ownership of landed property was not. Attacks on the iniquities of un- earned income were primarily directed at those deriving from inherited property in land. The inheritance of land was unjust because it was impos- sible to earn property; there was not enough of it to go round, it was already distributed, and individual ownership restricted the use of land by the community. Private capital, on the other hand, though it might be heavily taxed,[43] was not unjust in the same way because all have the opportunity to accumulate. Social Reformists shared Jenkins' view that a surplus from industrial production was vital to re-investment, and thus that profit was not only justifiable but essential. They ignored the distinction between profit and surplus, believing that profit was ac- ceptable because growth, not in the 1950s an obsession but implicit in the argument, required high investment. This was coupled with the con- tention that equality cannot be achieved by further redistribution of wealth, by which they meant that if existing wealth, which the rich hold in excess of the average, were divided up among the poor, the latter would be little better off because of their greater numbers. Almost all the trad- itional socialist arguments about the generation of inequality through the means and relations of production were abandoned. Profit-making, in- cluding financial speculation it would seem, became earned income and, therefore, unobjectionable, providing that all large incomes from profit were heavily taxed, since society had some legitimate interest in its social use.

The Market Economy

To accept profit-making, and to attribute positive value to the market as a system of reward distribution, entailed a revised evaluation of the economic system for Labour. Social Reformist arguments legitimated the existing economic structures, the balance between the public and the private sectors, and the now accepted mode of planning. Crosland urged that since the Attlee governments the majority of the Conservative Party

> would probably concede the right, indeed the duty, of the State to hold itself responsible for (1) the level of employment, (2) the protection of the foreign balance by methods other than deflation, (3) the level of investment and the rate of growth, (4) the maintenance of a welfare minimum, and (5) the conditions under which monopolies should be allowed to operate.[44]

He argued that in some cases the government would wish 'to intervene to override the market allocation of resources within the total allotted to a particular sector',[45] but mostly the mechanism of the market could be left alone.

Jenkins argued vehemently against centralized control over the economy as it would 'restrict liberty' and promote bureaucratization. He proposed, as an alternative, 'a framework of necessary strategic control, and within this to allow consumer preferences to express themselves as forcibly as possible through the operation of a free price mechanism'.[46] He maintained that the old socialist objections to the market — that it failed to maintain full employment or maximum utilization of national resources, and that it inherently tended to unequal rewards — no longer applied. From this was derived a peculiar notion of 'democratic planning' which was presented by Socialist Union:

> Socialist planning has its own definite and distinctive purpose. Its object is to maintain a framework of opportunities — opportunities as secure as possible, as equal as possible and as large as possible — in which each individual can shape his life. Put more concretely, socialist planning aims at achieving economic security, fair shares and an expanding economy. As soon as government intervenes beyond the provision of this framework of opportunities and begins to decide how they are to be used, it invades personal freedom and violates values on which socialism rests.[47]

This,

> Means that a socialist economy is not just a planned economy but a planned market economy. It is through the markets that individuals exercise their freedom of choice.[48]

The Social Reformists suggested that the market of the new society, with its strategic planning, constituted a new and desirable type of economy.

Many elements of liberal doctrine were apparent. The function of the state and economic planning was to provide a framework of positive opportunities within which individuals must be left to determine their

own fate. The state should make only a preliminary and limited intervention and then allow market forces to operate. Production might be
planned or directed to some extent, but consumption should be left to
the market. Social Reformism recognized little, if any, interdependence
between the two spheres even though it seems unlikely that such a separation is possible, freedom to consume implying freedom to produce.
This position was, however, consistent with the Social Reformist concern to escape the taint of bureaucracy — the planned market made it
possible, according to Jenkins, to 'end the belief in a permanent marriage
between socialism and bureaucracy'[49] — and to establish the proper
relationship between the individual and the state.

The relation between the individual and the state is fundamental to
any liberal or libertarian ideology. Social Reformist analysis always
started from, and ended with, the individual, which tended to reduce
their analytic categories to two, the individual, and the nation or people,
to the virtual exclusion of class. The most extreme statement was Durbin's
The Politics of Democratic Socialism which was virtually psychologistic
in assuming unchanging attributes of human nature and seeking lessons
from psychology and anthropology concerning the eternal nature of
conflict and co-operation in society. Although such a naturalistic, atom-
istic ontology was usually replaced in later Social Reformist writing by
the advocacy of equality of rights for all individuals, the individualism
remained.

Democracy

The unquestioning attachment of Social Reformism to parliamentary
democracy was consistent with the affirmation of formally equal rights
for each citizen. Crosland eulogized British democracy:

> We already enjoy in Britain a form of political democracy which is strikingly
> stable, which in no way partakes of mob rule or mass violence, and which, based
> as it is on a long liberal tradition, is exceptionally tolerant of dissent. Even if we
> attained a greater degree of equality, we should still retain our Parliamentary
> institutions, our liberal tradition, and a national character strongly attached to
> personal freedom.[50]

The 'new society' itself had emerged from the throes of a struggle between
democracy and old-style capitalism, a struggle which was steadily being
resolved in favour of the former. The changes in the industrial hierarchy
and, in particular, the success of the reforms of the 1945—51 administration, were proof of the success of parliamentary democracy. The
doubts of the 1930s, as to whether a majority Labour government would
be permitted by the vested interests of capital to pass socialist legislation,
no longer had any basis. Strachey, in *New Fabian Essays* attributed his

renunciation of communism to the achievements made by Labour through the parliamentary system: that the Labour governments 'did in fact appreciably modify the nature of British capitalism' indicated that 'everything turns on the effectiveness of democracy — in the sense of the existence of representative governments which can be made genuinely responsive to the wants of the population'.[51] Strachey, whose optimism was qualified in his *Contemporary Capitalism*, was in fact the only person who bothered even to address such a question. The others uncritically affirmed that the existence of legitimate opposition within Parliament fulfilled absolutely the requirements of a democratic political system. This had a number of corollaries in the Social Reformist conception of the nature of residual political conflict in the new society.

Politics and interests

Panitch argued that the Labour Party, referring to Revisionism in the modern period, could be understood, consistently with its own ideological self-image, in terms of a model of brokerage politics.[52] There existed a whole tradition of Labour which put community before class, which adhered to dominant social values and saw society as an organic whole rather than cleft by class. Adherents to this tradition saw themselves in government as brokers of interests, as adjudicators between the competing claims of pressure groups. However, while the Social Reformists' practice might be analysed using this model, there is little evidence to suggest that they conceived government in such terms. By and large they did not recognize the existence of interests or pressure groups: or rather, while they may exist (and the argument of 1959 that the Labour Party should not represent sectional, i.e. working-class, interest suggested, negatively, that they did), they should be ignored as illegitimate intrusions into governmental practice.

To some extent being the government was an end in itself; it was better to be a government with no purpose than to be in opposition. Crossman's suggestion, that a radical party should only be in power once in twenty years, was met with scorn.[53] But the Social Reformists were not cynical pragmatists. They believed that government should be informed by purpose, but that such purpose was internally generated independent of social interest. They adopted what W. J. M. MacKenzie called the 'exoteric model' of politics, the oldest myth of the parliamentary process, which comprised 'a form of constitution known as responsible parliamentary government, which combines decision by the will of the people in the long run with active administrative leadership in the short run'.[54] Two answers to the question of how governments could know and encapsulate the 'will of the people' emerged from Social Reformist literature.

In some situations ultimate sovereignty was conferred upon the majority of the electorate. Especially after the 1959 election defeat, the Social Reformists argued that only policies which pleased a majority of the electorate should be adopted. At other times this position was rejected; for example Crosland, a decade later, appraising the 1964–70 Labour government, commended its libertarian reforms despite the fact that they reflected minority opinion.[55]

The more fundamental Social Reformist view was to see the purpose of government in terms of the general will. This position bore some similarities with Rousseau's, that interests are base and divisive, and where they exist they should not be allowed to interfere with law-making. Law-making should be the province of impartial law-givers who could divine the nature of the general will as opposed to the 'will of all'.[56] The Social Reformists suggested that in the new society it had become possible to govern without reference to social interests. Governments were entrusted with the honest divination of the collective will: the political citizenry chose its governors on election day and thereafter those governors conducted national business according to their conception of the common good. This is, in fact, the basis of any ethical political theory, one quite consistent with the individualistic and consensual assumptions of Social Reformism. For there to be a general will there must be a predominant area of common interest. The Social Reformists, in the absence of apparent social or political conflict, believed that there was such an area of common interest embodied in the social consensus. In so far as that consensus was imperfect, due to inequalities and injustices, their task was to improve and consolidate it through appropriate legislation.

This attitude to politics distinguished Social Reformists, with the notable exception of Strachey whose doctrinal position was actually at odds with his personal allegiance to the Gaitskellite group,[57] from the Technocratic-Collectivism of the Wilson era, because the latter accepted the existence of divisive interests and the need to manage a compromise between them. Politics, for Social Reformism, was about ethics rather than power or interests.

Ethical socialism

Politics was a *wertrational* activity for the Social Reformists, about decisions made in the common interest of all citizens, where interest and prejudice were peripheral phenomena. Reforming legislation was in the interests of the whole community and hence must warrant tacit consent, independently of the rational-legal legitimacy of political decisions. This was the fundamental basis of Social Reformist thought, nowhere illustrated more clearly than in the publications of Socialist Union, a grouping around the monthly journal *Socialist Commentary*.[58]

Socialist Union's major tract, *20th Century Socialism: the Economy of Tomorrow*, took the ethical nature of the socialist endeavour as its main theme. It was defined as 'a study in applied ethics', sharing 'Keir Hardie's view that socialism is "at bottom a question of ethics or morals. It has mainly to do with the relationships which should exist between a man and his fellows." '[59] The ends to which socialism should be oriented were the ethical values of liberty, equality and fellowship. Interestingly they applauded 'early socialists' because 'what moved them to action was the avoidable suffering and misery which it (capitalism) caused, its sacrifice of men to money'. Today, Socialist Union declared, socialists ignore this, and concentrate instead on efficiency, on national aims; 'high productivity, national solvency, a rising standard of living have become the popular terms of reference'.[60] This has led people to forget that socialist and capitalist philosophies do not mix. Such people put technique above ethics, trying to prove socialism more efficient than capitalism; as Jenkins had argued before, it was an error for Labour to have debated the validity of nationalization on their adversary's grounds of economic efficiency.[61] This disavowal of technical efficiency, though it crept back in when discussing the means necessary to the establishment of the socialist community,[62] underscored both their ethical concerns and their belief that a consensual, community-oriented strategy was on the political agenda.

Their developing conceptions of equality and liberty stressed equal opportunity, 'fair shares', and the freedom of the consumer. The discussion of fellowship was, perhaps, the most revealing part of the document. Workers, Socialist Union asserted, already have a stake in society, and 'as the balance within society is redressed, obligations become more equally spread':

> Obligations are accepted when people feel identified with the community, not rebels against it; when they care about its welfare and know that their contribution counts. This community feeling cannot be achieved by changing the state: society must be changed as well. Society is a network of loyalties which bind people together and make each feel responsible for something more than his own advantage. These are the loyalties which have to be strengthened, if the fabric of a socialist society is to be woven.[63]

It was presupposed that the necessary basis for mutual social obligation already existed. Applied to the sphere of work, people were urged to fulfil their contracts; 'the main voluntary obligations fall on man as a producer, and the first of these is the obvious one of doing a good job of work.'[64] The implication of this, in 1956, was that Socialist Union had a conscious strategy of civic incorporation, though they did not call it that: with society already on the way to socialism, and probably even if it were not, employees ought to feel obliged to fulfil their contractual and social obligations to all others within the community or *polis*.

Socialist Union's work was permeated by a very genuine concern for the plight of the underdogs. There was a clear awareness of the need for social reforms. But the practical projections associated were non-transformative. There was no indication of how remaining evils in structures of economic wealth, political power or industrial authority might be transformed. Only two practical suggestions emerged in the end: that greater state intervention was needed in the realm of co-ordinating planning, which was not antagonistic to existing structures; and that a change in attitude, indeed, a change of heart, was necessary, which would remove status inequality by *fiat*.

Foreign policy

Ethical concern did not, however, penetrate the Social Reformist position on the other major area of policy, foreign affairs. Foreign policy was the only area in which the parameters of intra-party debate were not defined by the Social Refomists themselves. In such polemics they found themselves on the defensive, adopting orthodox, bipartisan positions, and trying to minimize their significance. Endorsing the foreign policy of the Attlee governments and rejecting any notion of a socialist or neutralist foreign policy, they called for 'realism' in foreign affairs, which amounted to support for NATO and the American alliance.

Socialist Union's *Socialism and Foreign Policy* professed to integrate realism and idealism: 'somehow the realism demanded of nations determined to endure must be combined with the idealism which continues to believe in the universal fellowship of man'.[65] But, despite concerns with the rule of law in international relations and an ultimate hope for world government, far more emphasis was put on realism. If the 'long-term aim' was an 'effective world authority',

> in the meantime we live in an anarchic world, where nations pursue their own self-interest, where aggressions are frequent and cruel, and where every country is compelled to do the best it can to preserve security. We cannot pursue our ideals in the ways that are open to us in our own society, where the rule of law is taken for granted. We are forced to look to our defences, and to enter the power struggle in association with like-minded nations. No government can ignore these calls and hope to survive.[66]

It was a constant theme of Social Reformism that Labour must recognize the balance of power in international affairs and since the USSR was the major threat, that British security was best guaranteed by alliance with the USA.[67]

Healey's contribution to *New Fabian Essays* set the tone of Social Reformist foreign policy. Despite a 'determination to apply moral principles to social life' there was little that could be done towards this end in international affairs while the basis for moral agreement did not exist: 'nation states are political entities, not moral entities; with interests and desires, not rights and duties'.[68] With the decline of British power in the world, and in the absence of a moral consensus, Healey argued, Britain must revert to conventional diplomacy.

Social Reformism disdained both neutralism and the 'third force' approach to international affairs.[69] Allegiance to NATO was re-affirmed in the absence of success in negotiations for multilateral disarmament. It was argued in an anarchic world based on a balance of armed force Britain could not but participate. Social Reformist pronouncements on foreign policy indicated absorption into the dominant social consensus, rejection of a distinctive socialist alternative, and acceptance of the lines laid down by the Attlee governments.

The apotheosis of Social Reformism

Social Reformist doctrine, thoroughly matured by 1956, was rapidly embodied in Party policy.[70] The acceptance of the ambiguous policy document, *Industry and Society*, at the 1957 Conference was a key step in the process. In its early sections it made out a strong case for public ownership, but only as a justification for past policies. Full employment, economic expansion, and an unprecedented growth of national wealth vindicated the Attlee nationalization programme; but the success thereafter of the existing balance in the mixed economy, along with changes in the structure of industry, rendered public ownership largely obsolete. Though the right was reserved to 'extend public ownership in any industry or part of industry which, after thorough inquiry, is found to be failing the nation', profit-sharing schemes, a capital gains tax, and government shareholding were considered adequate substitutes for ownership. As Miliband observed, the document 'envisaged as permanent an economic system in which the "private sector" was to retain by far the dominant share of economic power'.[71] At least until 1973 the party suspended its habit of presenting a 'shopping-list' of industries to be nationalized.

Subsequent Party policy documents showed clear signs of the adoption of Social Reformist positions. *Plan for Progress: Labour's Policy for Britain's Economic Expansion* (1958) made no reference to public ownership, contrasting instead 'Tory Stagnation' with 'Socialist Expansion': 'Labour's aim is the creation of new wealth in which all can share'. The pedestrian 1959 election manifesto, *Britain Belongs to You*, was constructed around similar themes. It devoted considerable space to social policies and foreign affairs but based its appeal on Labour's greater capacity for employing economic controls: 'only a Labour Government is ready to use the necessary controls to win full co-operation from the unions by such measures as fair-shares Budget policy and the extension of the Welfare State'.[72] The degree to which Social Reformist thought informed *Britain Belongs to You* can be seen by comparing it with Roy Jenkins' *The Labour Case*, written for the election, which showed concern for economic growth, a satisfaction with private industry so long as it was efficient and continued to invest, a strong emphasis on personal freedom, and a pro-NATO foreign policy.

The post mortem on the 1959 election

A variety of responses emerged from the Labour Party when the Conservatives won the election with a substantially increased majority. Crossman was unsurprised because of the Tories' achievements and unworried because of his belief that Labour could only expect to be in office intermittently.[73] Some saw the defeat as the result of policies which were anaemic by socialist criteria; the remedy, as expressed by Barbara Castle, was to 'go out and make socialists'.[74] The Social Reformists, very perturbed by defeat, focused their attention on resolving what Gay called the 'social-democratic dilemma' — of how to win 50 per cent of the vote.[75] Appraisal of the election results isolated the class image of the party, its identification with policies of nationalization, and its divided leadership, as causes of defeat.

Hinden, in 'The Lessons for Labour', her contribution to *Must Labour Lose?*, argued that Labour carried certain handicaps, the first of which was 'the image that Labour bears of its being the party of the working class at a time when a drift away from the old class allegiances has begun'.[76] The 'cloth-cap' image of 'Keir Hardie's day' was no longer appropriate: full employment, stronger unions, increased earnings, improved education and leisure, welfare services, social mobility, and the decline of the old working class ethos of 'solidarity and mutual help', rendered traditional Labour policies obsolete.[77] Jay expressed the opinion that Labour was in danger of representing a class which no longer existed.[78] Less iconoclastic Social Reformists argued that changes in the structure of the working class had generated new political attitudes. Gordon-Walker said 'the simple fact is that the Tories identified themselves with the new working class rather better than we did'.[79] And Hinden argued, similarly, that 'Labour may stand for the "working class" but not for the increasing number who feel, rightly or wrongly, they have outgrown that label'.[80] Social Reformism subscribed wholeheartedly to the *embourgeoisement* thesis.

Crosland, elaborating on the distinction between 'objective class position' and 'subjective' appraisals of class, urged that the 'unique identification' of the Labour Party and the working class was a 'clear political liability'. He claimed, rather disingenuously, that the solution was to change the Party's 'image', a matter of 'style, presentation and propaganda' which had 'nothing to do with fundamental principle and little to do even with policy decisions'.[81] But at the same time he believed it necessary to 'adapt the Party to social change, and give it a broader and more catholic base, so that it accurately represents the new emerging society and not the society of a generation ago'.[82] In effect, the cultivation of a 'broader and more catholic base' required Labour to jettison its class affiliations. This was expedient: 'the movement will not recover its previous high esteem until it can take, and substantially enforce, a clear national view of such problems as the ETU, unofficial strikes, demarcation disputes, etc.'.[83] But it was also principled:

> To be so identified is not only imprudent, it also betrays a fundamental socialist principle: for a classless society will never be achieved through a wholly class-oriented instrument. The object is to create a broadly-based, national, people's party.'[84]

Crosland, therefore, advocated changing the Party's constitution in order to affirm the supremacy of the PLP, as it was better able accurately to represent the nation.

Abrams' poll, reported in *Must Labour Lose?*, showed that 33 per cent of the electorate identified the Labour Party with nationalization, the most clear association in the sample by far. Crosland deduced that 'this close identification is without doubt a liability; for all the polls show that the majority of the electorate... are opposed to further large-scale nationalization'.[85] He concluded that future proposals for nationalization, if properly argued, might be acceptable, but that 'what is really damaging is the appalling uncertainty as to what the Party really wants to nationalise'.[86] Other Social Reformists, however, anticipating great electoral benefits from the dropping of commitments to public ownership, preferred to avoid such qualification. Hinden argued that all-pervading economic crises were 'things of the past. The techniques to master them appear to have been learnt'. Since people witness improvement '*without* further increase in the size of the publicly-owned sector of industry; they are not likely to be convinced to the contrary short of some new crisis flaring up beyond present control'.[87] Instead, the Labour Party should devote its attention to the 'irresponsible power' of industry, an evil characteristic of both public and private sectors and, hence, not to be mitigated by changes in ownership.

The third diagnosed cause of Labour's electoral failure was its own internal divisions. It was said that Labour must show itself to be a responsible, alternative, governing Party. Crosland began his argument in

Can Labour Win? with a distinction of Weber's, between the ethic of ultimate ends and the ethic of responsibility. The Labour Party must adopt the latter and be primarily 'concerned with political power'; its first task should be to win power, and internal differences should be subordinated to this task. But the conditions for agreement did not exist.

Intra-party conflict and developments in Social Reformism 1959—63

The 1959 electoral defeat precipitated intra-party conflict by bringing existing fractures out into the open. The Clause IV issue, emanating from the Social Reformist proposal that the Party abandon its constitutional commitment to public ownership, was a direct consequence of the election result. The unilateralist controversy, though not directly related to the election defeat, became superimposed on the conflict and led to a struggle for the leadership of the Party. The fate of Gaitskell and Social Reformism was at stake between 1959 and 1962.

The course of events surrounding the Clause IV issue are sufficiently well known not to need repetition here.[88] Its main significance was two-fold: it suggested that Gaitskell miscalculated tactically; and it demonstrated the importance of the trade union interest in the trajectory of the Party. Tactically it was unwise to force the issue, because it prevented any *de facto* abandonment of nationalization policies. The Victory for Socialism movement might have been ignored, its demands for further encroachment on private industry brushed aside, had the issue not been opened up at Conference. Gaitskell was insensitive to the structure of the Party. He also overlooked the degree of attachment to the eventual development of a socialist economy which was apparent in, for example, the debate on *Industry and Society* in 1957, when it was clear that key figures who had espoused consolidationism in the late 1940s, Morrison and Shinwell,[89] spoke against a total retreat from public ownership. The dispute over Clause IV also demonstrated the importance of the trade unions as a force for vetoing unacceptable PLP policies: under existing constitutional procedure within the Labour Party the trade union interest had a restrictive power over the PLP.

A second defeat, at the 1960 Conference, over defence policy, led the Social Reformists to question the role of the labour movement in the determination of Party practice. Despite some concessions to unilateralism after 1958, (Social Reformists were trailing far behind critical opinion in the labour movement[90]), and despite their arguments for a power-based foreign and defence policy, unilateralism was endorsed by Conference. Gaitskell's refusal to accept the decision committed Social Reformism to contesting the principle of the sovereignty of Conference. This intensified intra-party conflict, both encouraging Wilson to contest the leadership on the issue and prompting the Social Reformists' Campaign for Democratic Socialism.

The Campaign for Democratic Socialism was a clandestine organization without any formal membership whose immediate purpose was to secure Gaitskell's position in the Party in 1960.[91] Aiming to mobilize CLP moderates, Clause I of its Manifesto said:

> We are long-standing members of the Labour Party who are convinced that our Movement cannot afford another Scarborough. Rank-and-file opinion must now assert itself in support of Hugh Gaitskell and of those Labour MPs — the great majority — who are determined to resist and then reverse the present disastrous trend towards unilateralism and neutralism.

This manifesto was primarily a request for personal allegiance to Gaitskell over the unilateralist issue; but unilateralism was mentioned in only one other of the fourteen clauses. The rest of the document was given over to an exposition, highly abbreviated, but very typical in both language and content, of the Social Reformist credo: humanitarian conscience and reformism were explicitly stressed in the context of 'the Party's ethical, reformist, heritage'; the concern with market politics and community interest congealed in the claim that 'the Labour Party should be a broadly-based national party of all the people'; more stress was put on the importance of governing — 'the object of political activity is to achieve political power'; increased public services were advocated; public ownership was eschewed; and 'obligations under NATO' were endorsed pending the 'ultimate necessity of world government'.

Commentators have hedged somewhat on the effectiveness of CDS as an agency for mobilizing support for Gaitskell, suggesting that the favourable outcome achieved in 1961 would have occurred anyway.[92] For present purposes, however, the manifesto indicated that the overall orientation of Social Reformist political strategy had not changed between 1956 and 1962. But the consequences of the conflicts between 1959 and 1962, and the election defeat itself, were important because they closed off some of the possibilities left open within the Social Reformist position in 1956. Positions hardened on class, nationalization, the function of the Party, and the Party's relationship to the unions. While *The Future of Socialism* was relatively open-ended, Crosland's *Can Labour Win?*, for example, chose one particular option for Labour. This option petrified several vital inconsistencies, on the relation of Labour to 'market politics', on the relationship between the PLP and the Party in the country, and on Labour's relation to class and nation.

Hinden put the Social Reformist dilemma nicely when she argued that the Party could neither just give 'what people want' nor stand by traditional principles.[93] Crosland, subject to the same tension between

what the electorate wanted and what he thought the purpose of the
Party should be, and fortified by his aversion to 'paternalism', inclined
in 1959 towards playing 'market politics'.[94] This constituted something
of a movement in his position: while in 1956 he defined socialism in terms
of ethical purpose, in 1959 he acceded to the 'ethic of responsibility'. The
attainment of power, and therefore electoral calculation, became his predominant concern.[95] The idea that all people of good-will and good-sense
would support a rational, ethical programme was questioned after 1959
when it seemed that Labour might never be given another chance to implement any programme. The pursuit of governmental power led the
Social Reformists to take public opinion as given, to base their electoral
calculations on what the electorate, or rather the floating voter, would
accept. Policy had to be moulded to extant public opinion, and there
was no guarantee that this led in the same directions as Social Reformist
aspiration.

This inconsistency was continuously apparent after 1959. As was later
demonstrated by Gyford and Haseler, though they possibly overstated
the case, the Labour governments of 1964—70 experienced a considerable
tension between what they called liberal-elitism and working-class populism.[96] Concerned essentially with the reasons for Labour's defeat in
1970, they argued that the Labour government was very successful in
promoting liberal reforms in the fields of homosexuality, abortion,
capital punishment, etc., which expressed a refined social conscience
and a strong concern for personal freedom. Such reforms, however,
failing to take account of the populist attitudes of the working-class,
had caused Labour to suffer electorally. While this argument is far from
proven, it does illustrate two things: it points to the concern of leading
elements in the Party for liberal issues of individual freedom; and it
indicates the ambiguities of Social Reformism with respect to market
politics. If the majority of Labour support came from the traditional
working-classes, to ignore their interests and prejudices at the expense
of other strata would hinder Labour's electoral chances, especially as
Labour's biggest problem in 1970 seemed to be 'turning out the vote'.
At the ideological, rather than the electoral, level this inconsistency re-
appeared as a crucial uncertainty about how far Labour should promote
working-class interests.

The Social Reformist position vacillated between asserting and denying
that the Labour Party was the party of the working-class. Crosland, in a
single paragraph written in 1963, claimed to be on both sides of the
working-class—community divide:

a Socialist Party should be and should be seen to be a national party and not
simply a class party... a Labour Party must make a genuinely national and genuinely
classless appeal',

but at the same time,

> Of course it will continue to draw the bulk of its support from the Trade Unions and the organized working class.[97]

This stark ambiguity, the result of both his concern with electoral tactics and the need for internal party compromise, was never resolved. It merely re-emerged in a different form in the early 1970s.[98]

After 1959 the Social Reformists turned to advocating the sovereignty of the electorate with several consequences for their conception of the role of the PLP vis-a-vis the extra-parliamentary Party, the unions and the working class. The original intention, embodied in the 1918 Constitution, was that the PLP should be responsible to the whole Party through Conference. In practice, especially with Labour in government, this has not been an accurate reflection of the realities of power: the PLP, some would say the Cabinet, has been relatively independent.[99] The discrepancy has usually been rationalized in terms of the PLP having responsibility for the day-to-day running of affairs while Conference broadly determines the lines of policy. The Social Reformists explicitly challenged this rather uneasy semantic compromise, asserting that Conference should have no jurisdiction over the PLP. Clause 5 of the CDS Manifesto said: 'the Party must be seen to represent all sections of society, and it must be made absolutely clear that no one has the power to instruct, control or dictate to the Parliamentary Labour Party'. This was an argument especially directed against Conference decisions on unilateralism, but later extended to cover trade union pressure too. It was deemed electorally unwise, and constitutionally improper, for the Labour Party to be seen as advancing the interests of its active supporters vis-a-vis other members of the population.

Rawson pointed out the practical paradox of such a position with respect to the Party's alliance with the trade unions; without trade union support the Labour Party would be in imminent danger of collapse through lack of funds and votes.[100] The Conference defeats led the Social Reformists to review their previously amicable relations with the trade unions. The editorials of *Socialist Commentary* in 1960 and 1961 contained some vicious assaults on the trade unions as well as on 'sectarian doctrinaires'.[101] Fearing the disintegration of the Party, the unions were attacked because 'the assumption has always been that the unions would not use their voting power to dominate the party *as against the leadership*, and impose political policy on it'.[102] It was claimed that the unions had broken the unwritten rules by attacking the *leadership*, that the unions were applying 'undemocratic' pressure, and that they were an electoral embarrassment.[103] The Social Reformists hastened to affirm the status quo of the 1950s by defending the separation of functions between the unions and the Party. The industrial role of trade unions was acceptable, but because unions represented the sectional interests of their members they must not participate directly in national, democratic politics. The Social Reformist reaction implied, firstly, that the impartiality of parliament as a governing instrument was taken as an absolute presupposition, and, secondly, that the Labour Party could not afford to be seen as a vehicle for advancing the interests of its own members except where those interests coincided with the national interest. The Social Reformists at this stage seemed to be ignoring the need to placate those who saw the purpose of the Labour Party in terms of class and sectional interests. It was hardly surprising, then, that intra-party conflict was bitter and divisive at the beginning of the 1960s.

Nevertheless, in 1962 it seemed as if the Social Reformists were in an unassailable position within the Labour Party. Gaitskell was solidly entrenched as leader, having succeeded in healing over the Party's divisions, rather ironically, on the question of Britain's entry into the Common Market. The desirability of Britain joining the EEC was the main source of internal disagreement within the segment itself. Gaitskell was criticized by his own supporters, by *Socialist Commentary*, and by the Campaign for Democratic Socialism, for his opposition to entry. This, however, was not a vital issue at the time and could no doubt have been patched over.

The success of Gaitskell and the Social Reformists in the power struggle was never quite realised due to the premature death of Hugh Gaitskell himself. Harold Wilson's accession to the leadership caused a different ideological framework to be imposed on the Party. Social Reformists, though profoundly affecting the activities of the Wilson government, suffered a set-back in that, while Wilson still directed an integrative strategy, it had a different set of priorities, a different symbolic clothing, and was founded in a different ideological tradition.

The ideology and strategy of Social Reformism

Given that it never became the basis of a Labour government's legislative programme, Social Reformism was remarkably influential. Its major impact, as must be the case with a strategy developed only in opposition, was in the sphere of ideology, where it had the effect of legitimating the Welfare State. Although critical of the detail of Conservative policy and, by the 1960s, aware of concrete deficiencies in the Welfare State, Social Reformism supported and justified all the essential elements of the post-war settlement. Indeed, it was the Social Reformist wing of the Labour Party which formulated 'the consensus' in British politics and spread it through parliament, the civil service and the media. Such a development was indicative of the principal social role of the Labour Party in the period.

The liberal 'Weltanschauung'

That a Labour Party ideology was able to function as the dominant ideology of the 1950s was a result of its liberal origins. In structure and content Social Reformist ideology closely resembled the doctrine of New Liberalism, which had emerged in the writings of T.H. Green, the British idealist, in the later nineteenth century, and had received its most forceful elaboration by L.T. Hobhouse. In the 1870s British liberalism began to fragment. With the growth of a large, partly organized and partly enfranchised, industrial working class, *laissez-faire* philosophy became increasingly difficult to sustain. The most rigorous attempt to rehabilitate *laissez-faire*, Spencer's *Man Versus the State*, though favourably received in the USA, failed in Britain.[104] Arguments against intervention and collectivism were anachronistic in a Britain where state activity in the spheres of public health, education, poverty, etc., was already well developed. One successor to *laissez-faire* was New Liberalism which, founded on a notion of 'positive freedom', acknowledged inequality and poverty as social problems, and sanctioned certain forms of state intervention to deal with them. New Liberalism never completely dispelled the assumptions of *laissez-faire* liberalism, which affected the inter-war Labour Party,[105] and which continue to have influence in conservative thought.[106] But, having developed as a critical idelogy, New Liberalism was successfully translated into a legislative programme by the Liberal governments of 1906–14 and thereafter formed a hegemonic ideology of twentieth century Britain. It survived, in an unusually pure form, to provide the ideological basis for the post-war consensus.

Like any other ideology, New Liberalism was complex and not simply reducible to first principles. However, from Green, through Hobhouse, Hobson and T.H. Marshall to Crosland, a basic conceptual structure survived. This structure comprised a language of social and civil rights, a conception of modern history as the development of citizenship and a common culture, an individualist notion of liberty, and a central critical concept of equality.

In essence, T.H. Green argued that meaningful individual freedom depended on the guarantee of certain social rights which would permit the individual to exercise his liberty.[107] He argued that a framework of law, guaranteeing access to certain privileges, like education, was the *sine qua non* of an individual's human development. It was not sufficient for government simply to protect person and private property, as *laissez-faire* liberalism had advocated, because the weak would have only formal, not substantive, freedom. He suggested that government intervention in civil society might be justified in certain, limited circumstances; the state had a function of 'hindering hindrances to the good life', a positive function in areas like education, factory acts and temperance. Such intervention was justified because it provided conditions for the existence of free individuals, the ultimate goal.

L. T. Hobhouse, several steps further away from *laissez-faire*,[107] maintained that liberalism had become a 'fossilised creed' and set out to show that state intervention and liberal ideals, (themselves not much different from socialist goals), were compatible.[108] Hobhouse's basic theoretical problem was how conflict between the individual and the social whole might be resolved in a way consistent with the freedom of the individual. Like Rousseau, he concluded that only in a community of moral individuals where each was free would it be possible to have a harmonious society. Harmony required moral consensus, for only in such circumstances would it be possible to make decisions in the light of the common good. The common good, Hobhouse said, 'is founded on personality, and postulates free scope for the development of personality in each member of the community. This is the foundation not only of equal rights before the law, but also of what is called equality of opportunity.'[110] Holding a rationalist and teleological notion of human nature, he believed that the purpose of human existence was to realize the individual potential of each member of the community, a development which could only be voluntary. He therefore required that the state should provide the conditions within which all individuals could realistically pursue their own self-development. The framework for this, he thought, had to be provided by guaranteeing equal rights to all citizens and by abolishing many of the existing material inequalities which rendered formal equality useless. He maintained that the state should intervene to abolish poverty, for an individual living in poverty could never realize his, or her, full potential; he recommended the institution of a 'right to work' and a right to a 'living wage', both of which he considered just as important as rights of person or property; and he favoured high taxation and the redistribution of property. Individual freedom, equality, democracy, and social consensus were, for Hobhouse, inseparable.

On the same theoretical basis, T. H. Marshall developed a theory of modern history. The development of citizenship rights, the extension to all citizens *qua* citizens, of certain kinds of legal, political and social rights, was seen as the principal achievement of liberal-democratic societies. This development was by no means steady and harmonious; indeed Marshall observed two contradictory processes at work. The problem was how to reconcile two opposing principles: on the one hand, the universality of citizenship where 'all who possess the status are equal with respect to the rights and duties with which the status is endowed', and on the other, the system of social class which is a 'system of inequality'.[111] The corollary of the extension of political rights in the nineteenth century was, according to Marshall, a demand for the extension of social rights in the twentieth. Around the turn of the century, said Marshall,

> social integration spread from the sphere of sentiment and patriotism into that of material enjoyment. The components of a civilised and cultured life, formerly the monopoly of the few, were brought progressively within the reach of the many, who were encouraged thereby to stretch out their hands towards those that still eluded their grasp.

He continued,

> These aspirations have in part been met by incorporating social rights into the status of citizenship and thus creating a universal right to real income which is not proportionate to the market value of the claimant.[112]

Thus the satisfaction of certain demands in the realm of social welfare created a new opposition of principles between universal social rights and the market. For Marshall, the search for equal rights, which would guarantee a common level of legal protection, political influence and material subsistence, had the continuing effect of eradicating unjustified privilege and integrating all citizens into a common culture. This account of the historical process recognized class inequality, condoned interference with the market mechanism, and urged the extension of citizenship rights as the precondition of individual happiness and social harmony. It remained, however, individualist, immersed in the problem of how to integrate the individual, in particular the underprivileged individual, into society.

Social Reformist doctrine, though ostensibly socialist, contained most of the central tenets of New Liberalism. The citizenship theory of historical dynamics was embraced explicitly, in the language of New Liberalism, by Crosland who, discussing the movement towards comprehensive education, said,

> I believe that this represents a strong and irresistible pressure in British society to extend the rights of citizenship. Over the past three hundred years these rights have been extended first to personal liberty, then to political democracy, and later to social welfare. Now they must be further extended to educational equality. For until recently our schools have been essentially middle class, plus a few from below who aspired to the middle class or looked like desirable recruits to the middle class. The remainder were given cheaper teachers and inferior buildings and were segregated in separate schools. But today the pressure of democracy under either political party, insists on full civil rights and full incorporation in the educational as in other fields.[113]

The celebrated bonds of citizenship were presumed to be the basis of a common culture, of a shared condition in which it made sense to talk of communal interests. Class became a relatively unimportant concept, referring not to a system of political and economic domination but to residual, status-based, inequalities between individuals. Such inequality was to be regretted since, as Socialist Union declared, equal rights and opportunities were required in order to secure the development of individual potentiality:

> The socialist goal is a society so organized as to provide each of its members with an equal opportunity for the development of his personality. This is the right of everyone, and institutions should be shaped accordingly. But the human personality will not find its full expression unless men are able to live in freedom and fellowship, that is in the exercise of responsibility and in the spirit of service.[114]

The preservation of the British liberal tradition within the Labour Party provided the basis for bipartisan politics and greatly extended the affirmative role of Labour. The sphere of agreement between the two major parties in the 1950s and 1960s was made possible by the Social Reformist appropriation of New Liberalism. Progressive Tories, who would have baulked at programmes of socialist derivation, were sympathetic to the philosophy of Social Reform. And since the Welfare State was in many ways its instantiation, the ideology provided relevant, practical guidance in routine state administration and political management. If, indeed, there has been a hegemonic ideology in twentieth century Britain then it was New Liberalism, (and not conservative traditionalism as suggested by some commentators[115]). Since the beginning of the century New Liberalism has always had an ideological and practical presence. It became a basis for political practice in the period before the first world war. It went into partial abeyance with the demise of the Liberal Party, but was maintained in the inter-war period by Keynes, Beveridge, Lloyd George, radical liberals, some Labour and some Conservative politicians. During the second world war it again revived and was the predominant influence behind Coalition-supported programmes for social reconstruction. It then had another lease of life in the Labour Party after 1950.

Twentieth century ruling ideology or not, the Social Reformist incarnation of New Liberalism profoundly affected the social function of the Labour Party. Labour Party versions of democratic socialism were squeezed out onto the margins of political discourse and it became difficult to see the Party as a whole as a political vehicle of social opposition. Rather, the dominant segment of the Party was the bearer of an ideology which legitimated the basic structures of the existing society. Critical appraisal of existing social arrangements now concentrated only on Britain's failure to meet its own self-imposed social obligations or to achieve its self-professed ideals. The idea of there being a basis for social consensus was publicly endorsed by Labour.

The political strategy

Citizenship theory implied a political strategy different from that of a class theory of history. Crosland made that explicit in asserting that there was a necessary distinction between 'Social Politics' and 'Economic Politics':

> Economic Politics are characteristic of any country to which a Marxist analysis might plausibly be applied. Thus they are typical of periods of growing pauperisation, depression and mass unemployment, falling real wages, and a sharp polarisation of classes. It is at such times, when a direct clash of economic interest occurs between clear-cut productive classes against a background of material scarcity, that economic issues are the main determinant of political attitudes.
>
> Social Politics are characteristic of periods of prosperity, rising income, full employment, and inflation, when attention is diverted from economic to social issues not only for the obvious reason that as living standards rise, and the problem of subsistence fades away, people have more time and mental energy for non-economic discontents.[116]

Under conditions where Social Politics were appropriate, as in post-war Britain, political energies could be directed towards the 'social assimilation' of the underprivileged. The Social Reformists, confident that the conflicts which engender Economic Politics had been removed, offered an integrative strategy for Social Politics.

Social Reformism claimed socialist authenticity: socialism was the ultimate goal. But socialism was presented as a matter of degree. In fact, socialism was the degree to which the 'new society' could be perfected. Crosland surveyed a Britain which was no longer 'pure capitalism' but not yet socialism because,

> the traditional socialist ideals could be more fully realized than they are. To put the matter simply, we have won many important advances; but since we could have more social equality, a more classless society, and less avoidable social distress, we cannot be described as a socialist country.[117]

While much remained to be done, there was clearly no need for a social transformation. Rather, social reforms leading to more equal opportunity, a reduction of social 'resentment', and better public services, would be sufficient to realize the ideals of socialism. Social Reformism, like New Liberalism, was progressive and critical, but it was a strategy of amelioration rather than transformation.

The strategy was isonomic. That is to say, it sought to estbalish a formal equality between all citizens, in the social, as well as the political and legal, spheres. It was thought that inequalities would be removed by extending public provision into areas where private interests would not act but where the absence of services would discriminate against the under-privileged. Greater public expenditure to compensate for the failures of the market mechanism, combined with changes in social attitudes, would permit the incorporation of individuals into the status of full citizenship. This *civic incorporation* was to be achieved primarily through institutions of civil society. True to its liberal roots, Social Reformism was suspicious of the state: the state might provide the framework within which citizens might pursue the good life but its role had to remain limited. In particular it was to refrain from interfering in negotiations between capital and labour in the industrial sphere.

The exclusion of the state from industrial relations and wage bargaining was a basic tenet of Social Reformism and a necessary condition of political consensus. Social Reformism shared the dominant, 'voluntarist' trade union view of bargaining which maintained, *inter alia*,[118] that the industrial sphere inhabited by the unions was quite separate from the political sphere, where the Party belonged. Thus, what was always a potentially major issue of Crosland's 'Economic Politics', the distribution of material reward, was deemed apolitical, only to be engaged indirectly by the state through policies of demand management. The luxury of being able to exclude wages from political calculation was a benefit of the long boom, one which accounted for consensus politics replacing class politics, and for the dominance of Social Reform within the Labour Movement.

The principal reason for the success of Social Reformism in intra-party conflict was the support which it obtained from the trade union interest. Previous analyses have explained this in terms of 'loyalism': a large group of 'loyalists' were always prepared to come to the defence of the Party leadership in times of crisis and disunity, as for example in 1961 in the unilateralist dispute.[119] But, while it is true that trade unionism puts a premium on collective solidarity and that there were great fears that the Party was about to disintegrate, this overlooks the solid, material reasons which trade unionists had for supporting Social Reformist strategy. The apparent long-term prosperity of Britain, heralded by the slogan 'you've never had it so good', worked to the advantage of Social Reformism. In a situation of economic expansion the trade union interest could be satisfied so long as collective bargaining remained free: industry was capable of increasing the real wages of the labour force without incursion into its profit margins. Increased taxation, permitting greater public expenditure, was also bearable. So the function of the Party could become one of implementing social reforms sufficient to *complement* the material gains achieved by sectional bargaining. Such a strategy of civic incorporation, while never likely entirely to reconcile class corporatist or transformative elements of the movement (at this time quite hostile to trade union practice[120]), could satisfy the demands of many social groups including the unions.

With regard to style in intra-party disputes, it is interesting that the trade unionist's traditional suspicion of 'middle class intellectuals' in the Party was employed to abuse the left while support was accorded to the equally middle class and intellectual group of Social Reformists.[121] Although the social composition of groups of MPs does not explain much, the professional characteristics of the bulk of supporters of Social Reform in the PLP casts a little light on their strategy. Professionals, like other technical functionaries in complex industrial societies, have considerable bargaining power by way of their specialized technical capacities and their scarcity, (whether or not that be artificially induced by their own organizations). This is equally apparent in communist societies where the possession of technical qualifications is one of the main sources of privilege.[122] Such power affords these occupational groupings a certain indifference to the overall structuring of society since their privileges can be, and normally are, justified as reward for ability. In this sense the Social Reformists' combination of concern for equal opportunity and indifference to substantive inequalities in the distribution of material reward is consistent with professional interests in that they demand greater access to professional privilege rather than its abolition.

More significant was the Social Reformist attitude to the interests of capital. It is incorrect to assume that the refusal of Social Reformism to grant priority to working class interests implied identification with the interests of a ruling class. The Social Reformists had no special sympathy with either big business or the landed interest, though they had a high degree of tolerance for the former. They posed no major threat to the interests of capital for they guaranteed the legal prerogatives of private ownership and legitimated capitalist practice except insofar as unrestrained profit-making was to be subject to social and political regulation. In fact, the attitude to capital was rather like that towards trade unions; the state should allow as much freedom of action as was consistent with civic equality. To accept a mixed economy was to legitimate a role for private capitalist enterprise, but that role was always subject to a view of the interests of all citizens, to the general will.

Under conditions where class conflict was submerged the political demands of the subordinate classes could be handled quite effectively within existing social structures in accordance with the principles of an integrative strategy based on citizenship theory. Social Reformism developed a degree of public appeal beyond the labour movement. Indeed, having constructed the political formula of consensus it had, by definition, to appear as a practical, if not universally desirable, strategy. The Social Reformists managed to introduce a number of very influential political truisms which were supportive of its strategy. *Embourgeoisement* theory was primarily an invention of the Social Reformists.[123] They also

instilled a wisdom about Labour Party election strategies which went un-
challenged: that nationalization was unpopular, that socialist policies
would never be endorsed, that the majority of the electorate was grouped
in the political centre, etc. There was an element of self-fulfilling prophesy
about such suggestions: the more Social Reformists established their own
doctrines — of responsible government, of the need to wage the Cold War,
and of the dangers of interfering with currently effective economic
mechanisms — the more the Fundamentalist alternative of the left seemed
foreign and fanatical.

While the 'new society' conformed to Social Reformist expectations
the strategy flourished. Though doubts about the permanence of affluence
emerged in the late 1950s, marked by a mild recession in the British
economy and a gradually increasing concern for economic growth among
Social Reformists, it was not until the late 1960s that socio-economic
problems exposed the external contradictions of the strategy. Until then
the ideology was confirmed in social practice and common consciousness,
and while it did contain some internal inconsistencies these were hardly
disruptive.

Social Reformism never happily resolved the tension between a universal, ethical socialism and the existence of divisive social interests. On the
one hand governments and socialists ought to make decisions in accord
with the general will; on the other hand the Party was dependent upon the
support of the working class and was part of a labour movement. This
ambiguity was most apparent in the segment's electoral calculations. The
embourgeoisement thesis, espoused after 1959, suggested that class was
obsolete. But at the same time the Party itself belied the claim: on the
next occasion when Labour lost a General Election, in 1970, Social
Reformists concluded that it was because the Party had taken too little
account of working class interests and opinions. Such uncertainty, however, was the outcome of the real contradiction between an electoral
system which operates on plebiscitarian principles and a society which
divides people into functional interest groupings. That is to say parliamentary elections represent the choices of all citizens as individual
voters in geographical constituencies, whereas the most central social
cleavages are between corporate economic groups, organizations and
classes. This contradiction of political representation, between parliamentary system and party system, though problematic for other Labour
strategies too, was most sharp for Social Reformism.

There was also a persistent ambiguity, hidden while Keynesian policies
were being implemented with success, in the Social Reformist desire
for both a planned and a market economy. On the one hand, it was
realized that economic regulation was essential because a free market
cannot of itself secure equality. But, on the other hand, it was feared

that state control, by tending to centralize power and extend bureaucratic domination, would threaten personal liberty. Moreover, extensive control over economic affairs would necessarily imply some involvement with wage control, which was likely to disrupt the Social Reformist alliance with the trade union interest.

Neither of these inconsistencies was harmful while the conditions for 'Social Politics' survived. Social Reformism was a relatively coherent integrative strategy, successful as a practical political formula governing accumulation, conflict resolution and legitimation during the 1950s and early 1960s. The first signs of its inherent limitations appeared, perhaps, with the Conservative government's stop—go economic policies, the wage norm of 1961—2, and the establishment of tripartite consultations under the NEDC in 1962.[124] Yet although modifications were made to the formula in the 1960s they were not the result of obvious inadequacies in Social Reformist strategy. It was, rather, three associated tendencies emerging after 1967 which undermined Social Reformism, an economic and 'fiscal' crisis, the re-emergence of industrial conflict, and the collapse of the consensus. This can be seen in the reflections of the Social Reformists on the 1964—70 governments and their ensuing attempts to re-state their strategy, a matter dealt with in Chapter 7.

4 Fundamentalism: the ossification of the left 1948–63

As Social Reform flourished, socialism wilted. Most commentators have agreed that in recent history the Labour left has been ineffectual.[1] Though the Bevanites, and later the Tribune Group, proved disruptive, their impact on the Party and on society was very limited.

The most common kind of explanation of the ineffectiveness of the left, prevalent in the 1950s and 1960s, simply assumed that it was bound to fail in the circumstances: socialism had become an anachronism, superseded by affluence and consensus in the Welfare State. In this view, traditional socialist axioms were false and the ensuing practice was therefore ineffective; socialism was a historical residue, a backcloth to the process of the modernization and moderation of the Party. This both oversimplified the role of the left and underestimated the capacity of socialism for survival.

In the same period the only challenge to this interpretation came from those who, recognizing socialism to be an endemic oppositional movement in capitalist societies, believed it still to be on the historical agenda but concluded that the Labour Party itself was an inappropriate vehicle of a socialist transformation. This line of analysis, a constant issue of debate among socialists,[2] centred on the proposition that any party integrated into parliamentary politics must necessarily be incapable of implementing socialist policies. Though easily illustrated by reference to the historical experience of Western social-democratic parties the argument, from necessity, has not been entirely convincing. Coates, for example, argued that the left of the Labour Party always had been, and always would be, the subordinate element in the Party.[3] Quite accurately he observed that concentration on party politics directs attention away from the grass-roots of a mass movement so that passivity is engendered among the rank-and-file while parliamentary representatives tend to see the struggle for socialism as a problem of changing the PLP leadership and legislative programme. He also maintained that the electoral and organizational imperative of party unity constantly acts as a restraint on the left. This argument, however, is suspect in that it rests on the assumption that the dominant segment of the PLP must always be 'right-wing', but this is not, as both he and Miliband contend, inherent in the nature of the British *political* system.[4] Given the segmental character of the Labour Party it is not impossible for a segment with a transformative strategy to achieve dominance. Rather it seems to be the structure of British *society,* its hegemonic institutions and beliefs, which militate against the dominance of the left. Admittedly minimal popular support for socialism is partly the result of past Labour Party practice: if political attitudes are, predominantly, precipitated downwards from the parties and established ideological apparatuses, then the Labour Party, given its unpreparedness to challenge the existing hegemony since 1948, must bear considerable responsibility. Furthermore, exaggerated respect for parliament compounds hegemonic domination by legitimating an important institution. But still this interpretation seems to over-estimate the constraints of parliamentary politics and under-estimate the entrenched social institutions and processes which militate against left dominance. Moreover it tends to direct attention away from analysing left Labour strategies in their own context.

Of the few attempts to examine the modern left in context perhaps the best was Harman's study of the politics of *Tribune*.[5] He argued that the basic ambiguity of Bevanism was its propensity to adhere at the same time to a neo-capitalist domestic strategy and a quasi-socialist foreign policy. He maintained that the Bevanite 'admixture of socialist and neo-capitalist demands was the logical continuation of the politics of 1945'.[6] Harman's analysis was correct in seeing a distinctive foreign policy,[7] but wrong to mistake embryonic elements of the technocratic ideology of the 1960s, present in the writing of Wilson in particular, for the group's domestic and economic policy. In the 1950s the left's proposals for planning, controls and ownership did represent a kind of socialist alternative to current economic orthodoxy. It was also somewhat misleading of Harman to claim that Bevanism embodied the 'logical continuation of the policies of 1945'. The Bevanites fostered but one element of the ambiguous heritage of the Attlee governments, the transformative impulse; they insisted that structural change remained a prerequisite for furthering Labour's purposes. There was some distance between the genuinely neo-capitalist strategy of Social Reformism and that of the Fundamentalist left.

The contradiction which Harman identified in Bevanism, between a neo-capitalist domestic strategy and a quasi-socialist foreign policy, was not the most important one. The basic internal inconsistency of the left after 1950, which persisted into the 1970s, was its incapacity to bridge two distinct strategic orientations, one transformative, the other defensive class corporatist. In brief, the left oscillated between, and failed to reconcile, these two pure types of strategy. Both were always present, but in the 1950s and early 1960s the former was predominant, and in the later 1960s and early 1970s the latter prevailed. The conflict between these two strategies can be seen developing in several stages.

Fundamentalism in the period of reconstruction, 1948–56

Beer called the group around Bevan the 'Fundamentalists', a useful label to describe the left in the 1950s and early 1960s.[8] The segment was fundamentalist in the sense that it understood socialism to be a set of universally-valid principles. Those principles, which had been held by part of the Party between the wars, were constantly re-iterated, for in effect Fundamentalist ideology was little more than these principles: hardly any attempt was made at theoretical re-formulation in the light of new social experiences of the working class or the new theory of Social Reformism. Synonymous with Bevanism between 1951 and 1957, the segment both pre-dated and outlasted Bevan's personal involvement, retaining throughout a constant strategic and ideological orientation.

Prospects of socialism

Fundamentalists were fairly satisfied with the achievements of the Attlee governments. A major *Tribune* editorial in January 1948, attempting to define its socialism, commented, 'Whatever mistakes the Government may have made it is certain that we have been too modest in our defence of Labour's achievements'.[9] The same general satisfaction was apparent in *Keeping Left*, published in January 1950, which was prefaced thus:

> We have all reached the end of an epoch of British socialism. All, and more than all, of the programme worked out in the 1930s has been put on the Statute Book. The 'Utopian' slogans of the street corners — Nationalized Coalmines, the Free Health Service, and so on — have become the law of the land. This outstanding achievement — far more than many of our older pioneers ever hoped to see in their lifetime — has one danger. Since 1945 we have moved so far and so fast that the ideas of the rank and file and the actions of the Government are sometimes a long way apart. Very often this is because changed conditions have demanded changes in method and it is the rank and file who are lagging behind; but sometimes these principles have been over-ridden by expedience, and here it is the attitude of the leadership which is rightly questioned. We could not better celebrate the Party Jubilee than by re-thinking our whole policy in terms of the principles of Socialism.[10]

Thus, despite significant dissatisfaction over foreign policy, and occasional mild criticism of the speed of domestic change, the left was generally appreciative of the government's past record. The future, however, required some re-thinking, an imperative which the Fundamentalists recognized at least as early as, and probably earlier than, the Social Reformists.

There were many similarities between Fundamentalism and Social Reformism at the beginning of the 1950s. Re-thinking was to be organized in terms of principles, the 'principles of socialism' which were inherited from 'a long succession of Radicals who fought against tyranny and privilege, and from those Christians who always knew that their faith must include a struggle against social injustice'.[11] The basic principles, according to *Keeping Left*, were derived eclectically from Rainborough, Winstanley and Tawney, and comprised the dignity of man, a source of livelihood for all, and a democratic *social* order. All were expressed as universal values, in much the same way as the Social Reformists underpinned their theory with universal ethics, and all presupposed elements of equality which were absent, or only partially present, under the existing social order. Furthermore, *Keeping Left* distinguished property ownership from economic control, arguing that Russian experience showed that the abolition of private ownership did not abolish the 'arbitrary power of management over the worker and of the State over the citizen'. It also argued that while the Labour government had been correct to take over the industries it had, nationalization should be used more flexibly: while economic power 'must be made the servant of the community', nationalization was but 'one means to that end'.[12] Competitive public enterprise, it was claimed, was a valuable alternative strategy because nationalization was inflexible, aroused maximum political opposition, involved a lengthy legislative process, and raised problems of compensation.[13] These similarities, later to disappear, should not obscure the differences in emphasis and strategy between the two segments.

Despite the Fundamentalists' intimations that more of the same kind of measures introduced by Attlee would be acceptable, they were never convinced that Britain was coasting towards a socialist society. Private ownership, class and the maldistribution of power and wealth remained central to their critical analysis. They believed that a social transformation had yet to be achieved.[14]

Democracy and accountability

If there was an organizing principle in the Fundamentalist critique of society it was the principle of *democracy*. What was demanded, in many different forms, was control, by politically responsible public authority, of the major mechanisms of the distribution of wealth and privilege. The conclusion of *Keeping Left* argued, typically,

We have seen that socialism has two aspects:
(i) to make economic power accountable to public authority, and
(ii) to increase the participation of the people in the decisions which affect them. The second is at least as important as the first.[15]

Fundamentalism was, literally, democratic socialism.

Democratic reasoning lay behind the defence of nationalization as Party policy. *Keeping Left* proclaimed,

> When we transfer great basic industries and monopolies to public ownership, we are doing it not merely to increase efficiency. We do it because we regard irresponsible economic power as morally wrong; and we believe that a political democracy can become a genuinely democratic society only when economic power has been made its servant not its master. It is the greatest single achievement of the Labour Government to have begun the *conversion of economic power* and so have built the foundations of full democracy.[16]

The same theme, of bringing economic power under democratic control reverberated through Bevan's writing and was the central tenet of his *In Place of Fear*. Only through substantial governmental power over the economy was control by the people possible: it was only in a situation where economic effects of the market, like unemployment and minority control, were abolished that 'the ordinary man and woman is called into consultation and is asked to decide what he himself would put first in the national order of things'.[17] Bevan's criterion of a genuine social transformation was one where political decisions became moral choices undistorted by inequalities of power.

Consistently, the demand for the accountability of economic power included a wages policy: 'economic planning in a democratic socialist economy cannot operate successfully if wage-fixing is left either to the arbitrary decision of a wage-stop or to the accidents of unco-ordinated sectional bargaining'.[18] In this respect *Keeping Left* noted the tendency of all concerned to hedge on this issue, commended the TUC for exercising restraint for a period during the Attlee government, but chided it for its sectionalism, inefficiency, petty jealousies, and irrational organization. What was required was a re-construction of the wages system, agreed by TUC and the government: *Keeping Left* sought a close co-operation with the TUC and believed that a special relationship between trade unions and a Labour government did or could exist. This reconstruction would

> take into account all the factors which must govern our wages structure including the protection of the lowest paid workers, the maintenance of those differentials which are really essential to provide candidates for the highest-skilled and the supervisory jobs, the stimulations of productivity, the need for more labour in the undermanned industries, and the maintenance of industrial peace. Those

factors influence wage bargaining already – but they would be given their proper weight only if that bargaining were universal and not sectional.[19]

It was suggested that the government should 'announce each year a global total for this sector of wages' and that it should be divided up in accordance with the above principles. While in theory this may be perfectly reasonable, the experience of the past thirty years bears witness to the practical difficulties involved except in a wholly centralized economy. How one applies this to the competitive sector of the economy where low wages and an 'anarchic' market prevails is almost impossible to imagine.[20] Furthermore without a complete re-orientation of trade union bargaining practice it would also be unworkable. Indeed the Fundamentalists became increasingly disillusioned and antagonistic towards the TUC. Nevertheless, the basic assumption of the argument, that free collective bargaining and economic control are incompatible, seems inherently correct.[21]

Class, capitalism and democracy

Fundamentalism never forgot about class but it was often a subordinate analytic concept. Given his personal experience, the idea of class struggle probably had more meaning for Bevan than for many of his contemporaries in the PLP. This was suggested to some extent by the language he used: for example, when talking of the under-privileged, he demanded 'redress' of their grievances and recompense, whereas Social Reformists thought in terms of pity and moral indignation. But, nevertheless, when it came to the analysis of conflict in Britain it was to three social forces, 'private property, poverty and democracy', rather than class, that Bevan turned.[22] He said that either poverty and democracy would destroy capitalism, or else capitalism would destroy democracy. Democracy mediated between private property and poverty. But, democracy was parliament, and parliament was democracy: Fundamentalists and Bevan were totally convinced parliamentarians. Thus in giving a critical analysis of parliament as an institution, Bevan, while saying that it was a mollifying and seductive institution, drew the weakest of conclusions – predominantly that MPs should be given more space and secretarial aid.[23] All redress came through the PLP. The transition to socialism was dependent upon parliament increasingly absorbing economic power. Bevan in fact argued that parliamentary socialism was the guarantee of democracy. Capitalism may have brought about individual liberty but, Bevan warned,

People have no use for a freedom which cheats them of redress. If confidence in political democracy is to be sustained, political freedom must arm itself with economic power. Private property in the main sources of production and distribution endangers political liberty, for it leaves Parliament with responsibility and property with power.[24]

Fundamentalism defended parliament against capitalism.

Such an equation was distinctly a-historical in so far as parliamentary democracy has managed to co-exist with equanimity alongside capitalism. But, given the Fundamentalist conception of capitalism, it is perhaps comprehensible. According to Bevan, capitalism was unpredictable, un-principled and unscientific. The 'technical achievements' of modern society had, he said, made human control over the social environment possible, but this had not been realized

> within each nation of the *laissez-faire* type, because such a philosophy by its very nature rejects the propriety of an *a priori* principle. There is no way of saying how far such a society has realized the intentions of its architects, because there was no architect and no intention. There is only an emergent. Science works for predict-ability: capitalist society is profoundly unscientific. It proceeds upon no hypotheses, because that would imply an order of values.[25]

Bevan believed that an anarchic economic base produced an anarchic superstructure in capitalist societies, implicitly assuming that a planned economic system would generate an ordered value system. But behind the epistemologically-confused conception of scientific socialism lay the opposition between *laissez-faire* capitalism and planned socialism, which, being more appropriate to Victorian Britain, gave Fundamentalism an anachronistic flavour.[26]

Britain's world role

The Fundamentalist position on foreign affairs had two principal motifs: that Britain had a moral role to play in international diplomacy, and that foreign policy should not be considered in isolation from domestic con-cerns. While there were some internal differences within the segment, Fundamentalism was predominantly neither pacifist nor pro-communist. In the key disputes of the period, over British rearmament in 1951 and over German rearmament in 1954, the leading Fundamentalist spokesmen clung to a position distinctive within the Labour Party. Firstly they re-mained unconvinced that the USSR was as great a threat as was generally believed at the opening of the Cold War. The principal argument was in favour of conciliation, or co-existence, which, in *Keeping Left*, included the endorsement of NATO, but which later gave way to a neutralist, 'third-force' policy. It was believed that a Labour government had an obligation to ensure that ethical considerations rather than naked power should govern world affairs. Britain ought to eschew partisanship in the Cold War and concentrate on building up a neutral bloc among non-aligned nations from which to influence international affairs. Particular concern was expressed for the autonomy of 'underprivileged colonial peoples' who 'have a right to complete their social revolutions',[29] a right which was unlikely to be honoured in the light of the power politics of the Cold War. This was not, however, pro-Soviet in inspiration: one of the reasons for advocating aid to colonial peoples was to avoid 'driving them into the arms of Soviet Russia'; and as *One Way Only*, advancing a line on the Korean War, put it, 'no one, therefore, except a pacifist or partisan of the Kremlin would argue that military strength is not needed to deter the rulers of Soviet Russia from attempting similar adventures elsewhere'. In this context the second principle, of considering the domestic conse-quences of foreign policy, was brought to bear. The resignations of Bevan, Wilson and Freeman from the Cabinet in 1951 were not over the principle of rearmament but over its extent. Wilson argued that the degree of rearmament was totally unrealistic and would dislocate the British economy;[28] while Bevan, in his letter of resignation, argued that the programme was unattainable, would be inflationary, would reduce working class living standards, and would reduce expenditure on welfare services.[29] Bevan, in fact, later claimed that it was the perpetuation of the Cold War which had 'halted the advance towards socialism'.[30] Fundament-alist foreign policy was distinctive, but whether it constituted a viable alternative is debatable. It was a peculiar mixture of residual elements of the inter-war 'socialist foreign policy', which *Keeping Left* had regretfully admitted could no longer be sustained, and a vision of the overwhelming importance of Britain in international diplomacy.

Hardening arteries: 'the old dogmas are as good as ever', 1956—63

Fundamentalist ideology changed very little in the period 1956—63. While emphases between principles altered in response to a changing balance of strength in the Party and changing economic conditions, the principles remained the same. Both the pamphlets of the Victory For Socialism movement and the columns of *Tribune* restated the Fundament-alist case in primitive form.

Victory For Socialism (VFS) was revived in 1958 in response to two developments, the defection of Bevan on unilateralism and the rise to dominance of Social Reformism. It aimed to put the case for socialism in the Labour Party and to mobilize support for Fundamentalism in the CLPs. Fundamentalism in this period became more acutely aware of the limitations of the Attlee reforms. It was argued that Britain still stood in need of a social transformation; as Warbey pointed out, Britain had 'not *had* the revolution'.[31]

Democracy remained a key concept, one now applied especially to the internal processes of the Party: 'The first problem we have to tackle is the internal democracy of the Labour Party. Unless we can clear the channels through which the creative energies and ideas of the active rank-and-file of the Party can find expression and fulfilment then there is not much hope for us.'[32]

The Party was thought to be floundering on the 'rocks of bureaucracy and the block vote', a state of affairs which could only be remedied by unleashing the socialist sentiments of CLP activists. While it was later shown that the CLPs were no more left-wing than any other group in the Labour Party,[33] the illusion was important to Fundamentalist tactics and ideology.

Once again a residual notion of class conflict was apparent in VFS literature, but its resolution still lay in democracy:

> that conflict can only be resolved by the conquest of capitalism by democracy, by democracy itself owning the dominant sectors of production distribution and exchange.[34]

Democracy was hypostatized so that it became the main source of social change and the guarantee of the ultimate triumph of socialism. The logic of democracy was, it seemed, objectively opposed to the principles of a capitalist order. The task was to make it possible to 'work out a system of social priorities', to 'widen moral choices' unavailable under capitalism: 'to make choice possible is the first step — is socialism'.[35] At the same time it was increasingly emphasized that the basis of an alternative socialist order was common ownership of property. Increasing hostility within the party to nationalization led Fundamentalists to ever more stark invocations of public ownership. With the first signs of the economy faltering in 1956 the calls for nationalization became louder. Lay-offs at Standard Motors, shortages of steel, and the slowing down of car production at BMC, all proved the case for nationalization.[36] As Benn Levy reminded *Tribune* readers, 'the essential thing to remember is that Socialism is an economic system. It advocates the complete transformation of the basic economic structure of society'.[37] Endlessly, in critique of Socialist Union's *Twentieth Century Socialism*, in reflection on the debate on *Industry and Society*, and in discussion on planning, Fundamentalists re-iterated the principle of public ownership as the defining characteristic of socialism.[38] Delargy, typically asserted the principles to guide the Labour Party: 'That political power should be used to transfer economic power. That the more economic power is transferred to the nation, the more we approach our ideal. That our aim is thoroughly to change society, not to patch it up or cover over the cracks.'[39]

Nationalization was defended on the grounds that it was necessary for effective planning as well as on principle,[40] but on that other planning issue, wages planning, Fundamentalism grew increasingly ambivalent. No doubt it was difficult to advocate wage-planning at a time when it was anathema to trade unionists. Fred Lee wrote, in *Tribune*, about wage determination in the public sector:

> Our indictment of the Government ought not to be merely that they have inter-
> fered in industrial negotiations, but rather that they are using managements which
> are physically incapable of paying advances as stooges to enforce a wage freeze in
> the non-profit making industries under their control.[41]

Lee, typical of trade union MPs, presupposed that governments should not
interfere with bargaining, but Fundamentalists were never quite sure
whether or not this was reasonable, as their ambiguous response to Hughes
and Alexander's 'A Socialist Wages Plan' showed.[42] By the early 1960s the
tendency was to argue that free collective bargaining was in principle
deficient, but given either a free-for-all system or Conservative Party
planning, free bargaining had to be supported.[43] By 1963 *Tribune* had
taken to quoting Frank Cousins' adage that 'so long as there is a free-for-
all then the trade unions are a part of it'. Their position was that,

> Ending the free-for-all is a Government job. Planning means the replacement of the
> free-for-all by another method of allocating resources and labour (and incomes)
> within the economy. Only the state can do this, and only a Labour Government
> will make the State do it. And anything short of this is just not planning.[44]

Relations with the unions were very poor in the 1950s and early 1960s,
due partly to the Fundamentalist belief that the union block vote was the
principle obstacle to socialism in the Labour Party, partly to the personal
antagonism between Bevan and Deakin, and partly to the scathing attitudes of Fundamentalism towards the unions. The unions were berated
for their lack of political commitment: as *Tribune*'s Industrial Reporter
put it in 1959, 'they have lacked political fight in recent years. There has
been too much detailed "fitting in" with the Conservative Government —
and not enough socialist thought, talk and action'.[45] Mikardo, in the
course of discussing Party organization, went so far as to say that 'the
Trade Union Movement exhibits an ever greater degree of illogicality and
rigidity'.[46] At the same time, however, *Tribune* never failed to support
wage-militancy and workers: it said of itself, accurately,

> Time and again, *Tribune* has spoken out in support of workers on strike. In the
> Liverpool docks, the factories in Coventry, or the copper mines of Rhodesia,
> workers who down tools to defend their rights and improve their conditions will
> always be backed by this paper.[47]

Fundamentalists staunchly supported working class struggles, but it was
never clear how this was consistent with their political strategy.

Throughout the period to 1963 there was very little theoretical re-
formulation regarding domestic affairs. The election defeat of 1959 was
attributed to Labour's failure to adopt socialist policies. The lesson, they

asserted, was to re-affirm principles, to stress Labour's commitment to public ownership and nuclear disarmament,[48] and to educate people so that they realized the necessity of such policies.[49] The Victory For Socialism manifesto summed it up; the election showed the Labour Party's 'failure to base policy on the principles on which it stands, and to make them clearly understood'.[50] Bevan re-asserted the Fundamentalist position:

> It (the Labour Party) seeks not social justice based upon the vitality of the principle of charity, but the planned organization of the nation's economic life with priorities determined not by those in possession of supreme economic power but by the public conscience.[51]

A key aspect of the Fundamentalist attitude was captured by Michael Foot when, celebrating *Tribune's* twenty-first anniversary, he announced, 'but the old dogmas are as good as ever'.[52]

The columns of *Tribune* clung to its 'dogmas' in the early 1960s too. A letter of Tom Swain, MP, 'Back to old style Socialism', urged, 'let us return to the simple leadership of the Cloth Caps'.[53] Barbara Castle, reviewing Crosland's *The Conservative Enemy*, commended the author for his radicalism and his theoretical acumen, but condemned his devotion to 'proving that we can get rid of the evils (of society) without changing what Socialists have always believed to be the source of those evils: the private ownership of the means of production and their deployment in obedience to the profit motive'.[54]

Perpetual re-affirmation of slogans replaced social analysis and theoretical argument. Principles were asserted without being justified or elaborated. The ideology stagnated at a point where its critique of capitalist society was still a critique of laissez-faire capitalism. Unconcerned with new developments in the post-war economy and class structure, Fundamentalism never acquired a theoretical lever which could re-direct its practice into more fruitful channels. Admittedly, even with an adequate theoretical understanding, it would have been difficult to make an impact in this period; without one it was virtually impossible.

The reasoning behind Fundamentalist foreign policy became clearer in the late 1950s, though it remained faithful to the logic of the position established in 1951. Fundamentalists reaffirmed that foreign policy should be governed by moral reasoning rather than considerations of power, and that a third-force policy, in which Britain played the leading role, was viable. Freeman for example, argued for a neutralist policy, saying he was sure that 'Britain, as leader of a Commonwealth in which India, the most influential of its members, is neutral, could choose a similar policy of neutrality without abdication of Great Power responsibility'.[55] And VFS asserted that the 'Labour Party has a mission to lead the world to peace, and that nothing less than leadership with such a sense of mission is worthy of the people of our country'.[56] The debate over the nuclear deterrent, which was so important in intra-party conflict, gave Fundamentalists the opportunity to apply their policy. It was maintained that Britain would be positively hampered in fulfilling its international mission by possessing nuclear weapons:

> Possessing the H-bomb (without, in fact, the reality of nuclear armed power) ties Britain to US strategy, maintains the illusion that we deter aggression, spreads the fallacy that H-bomb power wins friends and influences people, and thus incites other nations to arm themselves for suicide. To be politically independent, to challenge the fear that perpetuates the arms race, and to lead the majority of nations which are non-nuclear powers, we must therefore renounce the bomb completely and prohibit its use from British soil.[57]

The Fundamentalists continued to seek a greater independence from the USA in foreign policy, less reliance on a balance of armed force in determining international disputes, and a reduction of the arms budget. Though claiming to have no illusions about the foreign policy of the USSR, the Fundamentalists constantly maintained that Labour should eschew involvement in the balance of armed strength. The nature of a desirable policy for Labour was summarized:

> Labour's foreign policy ought to be based on the will to substitute Socialism for capitalism, colonial freedom for colonial overlordship, and international co-operation for the Balance of Power. Socialism ought to recognise that the USSR, though as ruthless and unscrupulous as any other great power in protecting its vital interests, nevertheless wants peace as much as Britain or the USA. Socialists ought to approach Communism as a social challenge and not a threat of military aggression, and to acknowledge that it is fear on both sides which keeps the arms race going. Therefore, Labour's foreign policy should be based on the assumption contained in the UN Charter that there exists a common will to peace. Labour's policy must be directed to articulating the desire of millions the world over to end H-bomb politics and lay the foundations of East–West co-existence.[58]

The emergence of the Campaign for Nuclear Disarmament had a number of effects on Fundamentalism. Firstly, it generated increasing hostility towards NATO and, as an alterantive, greater commitment to the use of the United Nations in settling international disputes. As Harold Davies put it in 1960, 'Labour must get back under the world umbrella of the United Nations. Britain must opt out of the prolific Power Pacts'.[59] Secondly, it provided a potential source for mobilizing political support. Fundamentalists always maintained that the only political home for CND was on the left of the Labour Party and, in so far as they were the only group in parliamentary politics who were sympathetic, there was some political gain to be made from mobilizing CND supporters. To the extent that CND was an expression of moral outrage it sustained Fundamentalis pretensions regarding Labour's role as the party of conscience in international relations. Third, it caused the split between Bevan and his erstwhile supporters. Bevan's position was neither inconsistent with his earlier pronouncements, nor, necessarily, with the Fundamentalist line. However, had he wanted to maintain his old alliances on the left then the language of his Conference speech was injudicious,[60] for though it could be construed in terms of a third force policy, in the context of the emergence of anti-nuclear politics it appeared as a rupture in the left.[61] And, finally, unilateralism divided Fundamentalism from the leadership, partially re-inforcing the cleavage on the Clause IV issue and re-opening the question of the sovereignty of Conference within the Party.

The nuclear arms controversy made explicit the character of the moral foreign policy of Fundamentalism: it meant abandoning power politics, allying with and protecting the interests of the 'little nations', increasing the degree of British independence from the USA, and relying much more heavily on the United Nations.

The other major motif of Fundamentalism, the relation between domestic and foreign policies, appeared more clearly in relation to the debate over entry into the EEC. As the unilateralist controversy died down after 1961, the Cuban missile crisis notwithstanding, the question of the Common Market appeared to heal some divisions within the Party. The Fundamentalists were opposed to entry on two main grounds, that it would prejudice British foreign policy, and that it would interfere with national sovereignty.

The first argument was, in essence, that the EEC was a combination of rich Western nations trying to preserve their economic privileges and to resolve their defence problems. Membership would jeopardize British relations with the Commonwealth, the non-aligned and the poorer nations of the world, and would also further hamper European unity by entrenching the separation of East and West. In VFS's view the application to join was a Conservative ploy to 'preserve NATO' and to entrench capitalism in Europe.[62]

The second argument hung on the character of economic relations within the EEC. It was frequently pointed out that the Treaty of Rome was based upon *laissez-faire* principles and that its statutes would 'make impossible Socialist measures of public ownership (as distinct from capital provided by the State for enterprises run on commercial lines), or planning for social purposes'.[63] The objection was summarized in a VFS pamphlet,

The fundamental socialist objection to the monopoly capitalist EEC under reactionary political management is precisely that it is rapidly bringing about a concentration and unification of European industry across frontiers which makes nationalisation of industry by national means, i.e. by the action of individual governments, impossible, and provides no international means for achieving this end.[64]

It was primarily in this context that Fundamentalism invoked the idea of national sovereignty, (though occasionally it was argued that membership would erode Parliamentary authority): 'surrender of national sovereignty in economic affairs means the surrender of the planning powers necessary to take Britain further along the road to Socialism'.[65] Nairn later argued that the concern with national sovereignty indicated chauvinistic attitudes on the Labour left.[66] There was certainly a degree of insularity in Fundamentalist ideology: there was no intimations of a concern with international working class solidarity. But although *Tribune* did make attempts at populist appeals through patriotic postures when the debate re-opened in the 1970s, its priority was to keep open domestic options. Nairn might be right to argue that after 1970 the socialist potential of British Labour was so slight that nothing could be lost by entry, but the Fundamentalists did not believe that to be the case in 1962.

Fundamentalist strategy

Fundamentalism was a deeply ambiguous strategy, not at all well attuned to the politics of the Welfare State. On the one hand it retained a basic commitment to promoting the interests of the working class, and on the other it espoused a universal ethical conception of socialism. The connection between these two strands of the strategy was never adequately made. Effectively the latter predominated.

Fundamentalists frequently referred back in political argument to the interests of the working class. As *Tribune* proclaimed, support was always forthcoming for any working class struggle; any strike aroused sympathy, and in every conflict between unions and employers it was assumed that the union must have a legitimate claim. They were quite clear that capitalist society was characterized by class antagonism and that socialists were the representatives of the interests of the entire working class. They disapproved in principle of sectional-corporatism because it tended to disprivilege the weaker members of the class — though in practice, in a quiescent era, they welcomed every sign of wage militancy. However, only at the most abstract level was it clear in what sense the working class shared interests in common, and that was by negative inference from the fact of the dominace of capital. Their notion of class was a passive one; it described a condition rather than explaining a process or offering a lever to social change. It was instead democracy, the intermediary between poverty and capital, which was the mechanism behind social change. This substitution, while comprehensible in the light of their ethical preoccupations, marginalized the concept of class in the political strategy.

Primarily Fundamentalism was an ethical ideology constructed on the basis of a set of moral principles. Both its domestic and foreign policies presumed that a rational appreciation of the social world would promote harmony and, providing differentials of economic power were eliminated, that moral decisions could be made about political issues. The essence of the Fundamentalist vision was that once the impediments to moral decision-making had been removed all citizens would count for one in the political process. Democracy would then become fully mature and effective.

The Fundamentalists failed to argue the case coherently, but increasingly they condemned the private ownership of the major factors of production as the principal obstacle to a democratic socialist society. In the early 1950s nationalization was sometimes seen as a means to an end, but, as the Social Reformists gained dominance in the Party, Fundamentalists insistently re-affirmed that nationalization was the *sine qua non* of a socialist society. The essence of the transformatory strategy was a belief that only extensive common ownership of property would give individual citizens equal opportunity to control their own destinies through the channels of representative democracy. The abolition of private ownership would make real the formal political equality created by universal enfranchizement through ensuring the rational organization of production and permitting political decisions to be made in the light of moral principles.

This orientation was logically compatible with a defence of parliamentary institutions. Fundamentalists believed that parliament would both provide an effective channel for a social transformation and be quite appropriate to a socialist society. Their attachment to the parliamentary mode was the result partly of personal affection and custom, and partly of favourable recollections of the Attlee governments. But, most importantly, they believed in a politics of consent. It was advance through parliament, through a peaceful and legitimate transition to socialism, that distinguished them from communists. They believed that the absence of majority consent would only tend to foster an authoritarian and bureaucratic society, towards which they had just as strong an antipathy as the Social Reformists. It followed, thus, both from their moral vision and their choice of organizational instrument, that the catalyst for change would be persuasion and mass education. The role of a political party was to persuade the people that its vision of a rational social order was a just one which would operate in the interests of all. However, in actual practice, far more attention was devoted to changing the composition of the PLP than to mass education — which at least partly supports criticisms of the elitism of the left.[67]

This appraisal of parliamentary institutions was typical of the very narrow focus of the Fundamentalist critique of existing institutions. There was a touching faith in the efficacy of public ownership as a remedy for social inequality and injustice: yet state ownership, without concomitant changes in major institutions, in work situations, in the state apparatus, and in the transmission of the dominant ideology, would probably have limited effects on the life situation of subordinate classes. Despite the challenge to the economic basis of capitalist power there was no reason to anticipate either that effective power would be transferred to hitherto subordinate classes or that social stratification would be radically altered.

It was the failure of Fundamentalism to articulate the relationship between its predominant transformative strategy and its subsidiary class corporatist one which leads to doubt about the real transformatory potential of Fundamentalism. Two types of strategy were advanced simultaneously, but there was no means of reconciling or integrating them. The former required protecting the interests of a class, while the latter envisaged political change by common consent. This anomaly was not simply one of purity of purpose; to promote the immediate welfare of the working class requires compromise and collaboration within conformative institutions which are not themselves socialist. The real anomaly was that the Fundamentalists did not see any problems emanating from the different rationales behind the two strategies.

The relationship between class interests and universal interests has posed a perpetual dilemma for socialist theory. Briefly, it has been argued either that working class interests are necessarily universal interests, or that in the process of transition from a class to a classless order class interests must disappear.

The first argument has taken two forms. In the first form it is postulated that working class interests are inherently universal interests. The second is based in a philosophy of history where history is the process of one, rising, class superseding another, dominant, class in progressive succession. Even if the subordinate class does not embody universal interests at any given point in time, by the logic of history it will eventually.

The second mode of argument has depended upon either notions of crisis or of the role of the socialist party. Scientific socialism, in its positivistic mode, maintained that a crisis in capitalist production would inexorably produce a socialist society. Spontaneist theories also postulated crisis; as the extant system disintegrated a new universal order could be constructed voluntaristically out of the remnants of the old. Alternatively, the socialist party has been granted care of proletarian interests: having upset the old order the party would take power and act for a transitional period on behalf of the working class.[68]

No attempt was made by the Fundamentalists to confront the problem of class interests. There were traces of scientific socialism in Bevan's writing, and of economism in Fundamentalist work in general, but these were submerged beneath their appreciation of the ethical virtue of a socialist society. Fundamentalism had no notion of crisis, or of the inevitability of socialism, or of the universality of working class interests, or of a theory of rising classes. Socialism, for the Fundamentalists, was an ideal which people adopted. But the relationship between that ideal and contemporary class antagonisms was unspecified. If there was any link at all between class interests and universal interests it was the Labour Party itself. Somehow a Fundamentalist Labour Party was believed to have the capacity to mediate between, or to combine, discrepant interests. The very telling quotation from *The Red Sixties* indicated this:

> when the PLP is made up of determined socialists then, and then only, will we see the end of a system which has outlived its usefulness, and now only serves to debauch the nobler impulses of mankind.[69]

The connection between the Party, class and nation, was never explored further. It was simply assumed that the Party had some essential or traditional capacity to integrate class and universal interests.

The Fundamentalists lost the struggle for dominance within the party in the early 1950s. The internal inconsistencies of their ideology apart, they failed both to manipulate the internal balance of power in the party and to adapt to the balance of forces in society.

One reason for their lack of support within the Party was personal. It was feared that Bevan was splitting the Party in an attempt to capture the leadership, but, as the Fundamentalists fared no better after the succession to Attlee was settled, and indeed after Bevan's own death, this must be considered a minor factor. More important was the fact that the Fundamentalists were isolated within the Party, opposed to both Social Reformism and the dominant trade union bloc.

The trade union interest was uncompromisingly hostile to the class corporatist element of the Fundamentalist strategy. It was almost unthinkable that the unions would abandon a sectional-corporatist strategy at a time when free collective bargaining was paying unprecedented dividends in the expanding economy. Throughout the 1950s, despite the emergence of Cousins, the unions were firmly wedded to business unionism. The dominant bloc made a fundamental distinction between political and industrial matters and the respective roles of Party and unions. The Perlman—Richter thesis about the political purposes of trade unions was perfectly accurate in this period.[70] The statements of the union leaders, and the practices of the trade union group in parliament, indicated that trade unions existed to fight industrial disputes for the improvement of the conditions of their members rather than for the working class as a whole.

The Fundamentalists also failed to capture the support of the Labour intelligentsia, for some of whom the painstaking analyses of the Social Reformists were attractive. *Socialist Commentary* in 1955, while accusing 'Bevanism' of doctrinaire traditionalism, slogan-mongering and having 'no alternative home policy', was still seeking an antidote to a 'dangerous vacuum' in socialist thinking: no one, it was said, 'has yet defined the new convincing socialist programme to fit the needs of the mid-twentieth century'.[71] 'New thinking' captured the imagination of *Socialist Commentary* partly because it was the only new approach on offer. The Social Reformists themselves, despite some similarities with Fundamentalism in the early 1950s, were implacably hostile, believing an ameliorative strategy quite adequate to the times: the fundamentalists attachment to the working class, their emphasis on public ownership and state control, their 'unrealistic' foreign policy, and their indifference to electoral calculation, were all anathema to Social Reformism. However, other socialist intellectuals, for example those aligning themselves with the New Left in the late 1950s and early 1960s, while far less alienated from the Labour Party than was the case ten years later, were equally unimpressed by Fundamentalist doctrine. This was at least partly because Fundamentalism totally failed to adapt itself to the particular conditions of the 1950s.

Fundamentalism's failure within the party was paralleled by an incapacity to mobilize any section of society other than pre-committed socialists to its cause. The conditions in which the simple re-iteration of socialist principles might make an impact were absent. Precisely those social circumstances which made Social Reformism powerful in the 1950s and early 1960s rendered Fundamentalism unacceptable. If it were true that the Labour governments had achieved anything of significance then it was odd that the Fundamentalists continued to use an un-revised critique of *laissez-faire* capitalism. With the economy working well and distributing considerable benefits, to the general satisfaction of the trade unions, there seemed no obvious reason for the re-orientation of economic practice. And with the brokers of public opinion, the media, the Conservative Party, and the larger part of the labour movement, exuding optimism and confidence, Fundamentalism seemed something of an irrelevance.

It was not accidental that the greatest impact of Fundamentalism came through unilateralism and CND. CND was a moral crusade, the bulk of its 'middle class radical' membership being opposed to nuclear weapons on ethical grounds.[72] In its dominant, universal-ethical moment,

Fundamentalism identified readily with CND: as Widgery observed, CND 'was the last movement of its kind to be dominated by the Labour Left'.[73] But despite aligning itself with an emerging radical force, Fundamentalism was unable to harness the impetus of CND for wider purposes; disarmament remained specifically neither a class nor a socialist issue.[74] The politics of moral principle, on which plane Fundamentalism primarily operated, proved to be of limited appeal to any substantial fraction of the working class.

The transformative strategy of Fundamentalism, based in socialist ethics, made little impact. But in its defensive class-corporatist moment Fundamentalism was even less successful. In this, its minor strategy, it did little more than perpetuate the idea that the interests of the working class and capital were not identical and that a social transformation was still required to abolish capitalism. In no way did Fundamentalism manage to persuade the working class that its interests as a whole over-rode its sectional interests.

Unable to encapsulate trade union or working class aspirations, Fundamentalism remained an isolated, protesting ideology, attracting support and passion mostly as a result of the tenacity of a tradition of socialist thought in Britain. That tradition has always been a subdued and subordinate one, but without it Fundamentalism would be incomprehensible. The segment clung to the principles which had guided Labour ideology in the inter-war period, to the intimations of *For Socialism and Peace*, and to the transformative elements of the Attlee governments. A lack of theoretical innovation, the limited attempts at political education, the ambiguities of its ideology, and a climate inhospitable to the generation of socialist consciousness, caused its impact to be negligible. Affluence reinforced the hegemonic understandings of the consensus from which Fundamentalism was excluded. No effective challenge was ever posed to the political formula. Meanwhile, despite the excitement caused by Bevanism, Social Reformism continued to hold sway in both Party and society, for the moment throwing democratic socialism towards the margins of political life.

5 Technocratic-Collectivism: the re-structuring of the consensus, 1963–71

The thirteen years of Harold Wilson's leadership of the Labour Party witnessed a transition from the politics of consensus, enshrined in Social Reformist doctrine, to the politics of collaboration, embodied in the Social Contract. In the earlier part of this period, from 1963 to 1971, the consensus itself was re-structured as the Party adjusted its programme and its ideology. A new ideological form was developed, epitomized in the 1964 election manifesto *Let's Go with Labour for the New Britain*. It contained, besides a novel rhetoric, a distinctive political rationale which presaged a new kind of relationship between the Labour Party and advanced capitalist society. In the past referred to only as 'Wilsonism' (Wilson was primarily responsible for creating and sponsoring it),[1] I shall denote it as Technocratic-Collectivism. It was quite different from Social Reformism: in some ways it was antithetical, being neither liberal, ethical, egalitarian, nor individualist. Yet implicitly it carried over some basic presumptions of consensus politics; especially, it assumed that social harmony was a permanent feature of British society. Hence little care was taken to foster or refurbish the legitimating formula of the post-war settlement, a cause of considerable problems in the late 1960s when the Party in government was faced with renewed expressions of class conflict. A reassertion of incompatible corporate group interests, previously defined as beyond politics, compelled the government to intervene directly in a broad range of disputes in order to preserve social cohesion.

Any attempt to understand the Labour Party and its internal cleavages in terms of organized groups would find it very difficult to locate the bearers of Technocratic-Collectivism either inside or outside the PLP. Far fewer identifiable individuals were associated with its emergence, compared with Social Reformism or Fundamentalism; Wilson, Shore Benn, and the personnel of the Labour Research Department seem to have been its principal exponents. Hence, when considered to any real degree distinctive, it has been deemed either an opportunistic pragmatism, or a 'centrist' tactic aimed at establishing unity within the Party.[2] It certainly accomplished the latter, furnishing the basis of a working agreement among segments for some time after 1963, but it was more than a temporary compromise. It was an innovative response to prevailing social and economic conditions.

Elements of the ideology

Technocratic-Collectivism never developed the kind of ideological coherence of Social Reformism. It was a hybrid combination of various themes, which bore some relationship to classical Fabianism, but which drew on several traditions of thought within the Labour heritage. Its principal motif was the idea of a scientific and technological revolution, the pre-condition for modernization of the British economy and a new 'socialist' vision. But underlying this slogan there were a number of elements which combined with it: a distinctive concept of nation which expunged residual concerns with class; a technicist notion of pluralist politics which emphasized expert direction at the expense of democratic determination; and an almost anti-egalitarian idea of social justice.

The regeneration of Britain

The main line of attack by Labour in the 1964 election was an assault on the Conservative Party for 'thirteen wasted years' in office. The suggestion that the Conservatives were failing was not just the partisan ploy of an opposition party, for commentators of many different persuasions diagnosed a malaise in British society in the early 1960s. The idea that Britain was a 'stagnant society' was expressed in several forms. Sometimes this condition was explained in terms of atrophy emanating from affluence;[3] sometimes as a general cultural and political degeneration following from the decline of empire; and sometimes as a result of a deterioration of the moral fibre of the British race.[4] This malaise was apparent in economic, international, moral and motivational spheres: the 'stop–go' cycle and the comparatively low rate of economic growth signified intermittent malfunctioning in the British economy; Britain appeared to have little influence in world affairs; the 'permissive society' was seen as incipient immorality and amorality; and a 'consumer society' was thought to engender complacency and apathy. Against this background of common sentiment the dynamic project for a technological revolution appeared to be a progressive solution.

The Manifesto of 1964 was loaded with metaphors of progress and change which were counterposed to Tory sterility and stagnation. Even the style of the document, with its stilted and terse prose, suggested urgency and energy. For example,

'The country needs fresh and virile leadership. Labour is ready. Poised to swing its plans into instant operation. Impatient to apply the New Thinking that will end chaos and sterility'.[5]

In terms of political content, the motor of change was to be a technological revolution, an event which would regenerate and modernize British institutions, in particular the economy.

The idea of a technological and scientific revolution, though embryonically present in *Signposts for the Sixties*, was fostered by Wilson. Science and technology were the principal motifs of a prolific bout of public speaking after his election as leader. His closing speech to the 1963 Scarborough Conference, which was rapturously received, concentrated on the potentialities and the political imperatives of scientific development. The document he was elaborating on, *Labour and the Scientific Revolution*, was concerned with the speed of change in the 20th century. The scientific revolution, which characterized the post-war world,

> makes it physically possible, for the first time in human history, to conquer poverty and disease, to move towards universal literacy, and to achieve for the whole people better living standards than those enjoyed by tiny privileged classes in previous epochs.[6]

Britain made too little use of its scientists and was too little concerned with scientific development. It was therefore suggested that more higher education places be devoted to science, that the State should support research, and that there should be more planning for a necessarily new occupational structure. In conclusion Wilson asserted the need for new attitudes:

> We are re-defining and we are re-stating our Socialism in terms of the scientific revolution. But that revolution cannot become a reality unless we are prepared to make far-reaching changes in economic and social attitudes which permeate our whole system of society.
>   That Britain which is to be forged in the white heat of this revolution will be no place for restrictive practices or outdated methods on either side of industry.[7]

Wilson re-iterated the message of his Scarborough speech on many occasions between 1963 and the 1964 election. A speech at Birmingham in January 1964 brought together many of the themes.[8] He attacked the amateurish 'Edwardian establishment mentality' fostered by the Conservative governments; he pointed to wasted opportunities, talents and abilities; he berated an absence of effective future planning which had caused industrial stagnation; and he claimed that lost potential had perpetuated unnecessary social injustices. The same theme ran through Benn's *The Regeneration of Britain*:

What Britain needs to-day is more than modernization. What is wrong is that so much talent is wasted and so many opportunities are missed because people are not able to develop their full potential. The regeneration of Britain can only be achieved by releasing energy now bottled up by outdated traditions and methods and the maintenance of obsolete privileges.[9]

For Benn, Britain was characterized by traditionalism and amateurism; its institutions needed to be brought up to date. He argued the need for reform: of an 'amateur centralised Civil Service'; of a 'weak ill-equipped House of Commons'; of the 'creaking piecemeal structure of local government'; and of the legal system. Regeneration depended upon casting off obsolete constraints; 'the worship of status and the entrenchment of privilege behind the camouflage of hereditary pageantry will always kill initiative and frustrate new ideas'.[10]

The idea of a technological revolution was a social mood, a practical programme, and the symbolic expression of a particular political strategy. As a social mood it was important electorally. Peter Shore, reflecting on the 1964 election said that the electorate voted against 'Britain as the "sick man" of Europe' and, instead, for 'a New Britain, strong, modern and energetic, determined to set a new course in its dealings with the world'.[11] As a practical programme it suggested measures to apply modern technology and scientific knowledge to social and economic life, it stressed the importance of educational reform and the expansion of opportunities to the talented, and it advanced a variety of schemes for improving the productivity of the British industrial system. But maybe it was most significant as a symbolic expression of a political strategy which altered the character of Labour aspirations. Socialism was re-defined in terms of efficient administration.

It was Wilson himself who most explicitly re-shaped the socialist vision. In one speech he said 'We must shape our policies at home and abroad as part of an administrative unity. This is what Socialism means, a unity of direction for all the decisions a government has to take.'[12]

He went on to define Socialism:

Socialism, as I understand it, means applying a sense of purpose to our national life: economic purpose, social purpose, and moral purpose. Purpose means technical skill — be it the skill of a manager, a designer, a craftsman, an engineer, a miner, an architect ... Pilot or surgeon: it matters not who his father was, or what school he went to, or who his friends are. Yet in Government or business we are still too content to accept social qualifications rather than technical ability as the criterion.[13]

Socialism, then, became purposeful administration directed by a meritocratic elite. 'Harnessing socialism to science' was a key slogan.[14] To be sure it entailed greater social justice:

> The prospect that the scientific revolution opens before us is a working life which is secure and interesting in a society where machines are subordinated to man; a world in which hardship and suffering are progressively eliminated and the whole range of man's culture is available to enrich the lives of all. This is the true socialist vision which, in the past, want and ignorance have held from our grasp.[15]

But it was one of the most minimalist definitions of socialism ever devised.

Planning and the economy

The principal symbolic connection between the project for the technological revolution and the traditions of British socialism lay in the emphasis placed on planning. The 1964 manifesto outlined plans for everything. There was a National Plan, a Plan for Industry, a Plan for the Regions, A Plan for Transport, a Plan for Stable Prices, and a Plan for Tax Reform. The manifesto claimed that 'At the root of the Tories' failure lies an outdated philosophy — their nostalgic belief that it is possible in the second half of the 20th century to hark back to the 19th century free enterprise economy and a 19th century unplanned society.'[16]

This was no more true of the Conservative Party than the idea that the Labour Party was socialist, but Labour sought to create the impression that it was the party of planning. Labour's planning was really only a method of indirect control, though it was called 'socialist planning'. The first proposal was for a National Plan, run by a Ministry of Economic Affairs, which would 'frame the broad strategy for increasing investment, expanding exports and replacing inessential imports'. The powers envisaged for the Ministry were always limited; it was to engage in indicative planning, encouraging and exhorting industry to abide by targets for the whole economy and for individual industries.[17] It was recognized that success was dependent upon modernization, expansion, and the government's capacity to 'encourage the right type of modern industry' and to 'stimulate enterprise'. Without the co-operation of capital, Labour's planning was doomed to failure. In the Plan for Industry little was promised by way of public ownership except steel and water, the latter being of almost no consequence. Instead the way was opened for the government to set up new industries, justified on the grounds that the 'Government provides over half the money spent on industrial research and development', and, by implication, that private industry was not 'injecting (sufficient) modern technology into our industries'. The other principal, promised impetus was in the area of mobility and training: industrial training was inadequate because faster rates of change within industry demanded greater mobility and re-training. The manifesto said also:

> Skill, talent and brain power are our most important national resources. Yet in Britain under the Conservatives much of the natural ability of the nation is being

wasted. In far too many firms, technicians and technologists, designers and production engineers are held back by the social prejudices and anti-scientific bias of
the old boy network.

This was intended to have some electoral appeal, for if floating voters
were significant in electoral calculations then it was to this group that
Labour's programme would appeal. That they were also integral to
planning only made the programme of 1964 more powerful.

The over-riding rationale behind the planning proposals was to expand
the British economy and run it more efficiently. In this the programme
was not inconsistent with one of the traditions of Labour thought on
planning. From the time when the Fabians supported the National
Efficiency Movement there has always been a view, critical of capitalism
for its propensities to inefficient and wasteful production, which advocated planning as a means of co-ordination for national ends. Wilson
personally had long shown great concern for the health of the economy
as a whole; the use made of national wealth was always a subordinate
matter. He justified his resignation in 1951 on primarily technical
grounds, that the size of the proposed arms budget was unrealistic and
unattainable.[18] His occasional writings between 1951 and 1963 dealt
predominantly with measures for managing the economy more effectively.
In Place of Dollars, framing policies for achieving independence from
American aid, recommended the expansion of overseas trade and more
control and planning towards the 'more purposive direction of our
economic life'. *Remedies for Inflation* gave a concise summary of what
became his later government's economic policy, putting emphasis on the
correct balance of trade, the encouragement of investment in the export
sector and restraints on wages, prices and profits. These aims were to be
achieved through a Keynesian use of the budget, monetary controls, more
control over the investment of private firms, voluntary wage restraint, and
the use of selective weapons against inessential spending. 'A Four-Year
Plan for Britain', though more concerned with associated social policies,
contained the same imperative: 'the purpose of the Four-Year Plan is to
raise the level of investment and to maintain an adequate level of planned
demand so that production can rise at a reasonable rate'.[19] Again, control
and co-ordination were the preferred means: it was control over 'the
commanding heights of the economy' that was required, and while public
ownership was one possible means, any 'sweeping programme of expropriation' was disavowed. Interestingly he insisted that improvements in social
security provision had to be written into the Plan: because it was 'for the
people', but also because it was an important part of the capital investment programme. Gradually, as the economy began to flounder in the late
1950s, Wilson became more attached to a political policy based upon
efficient *expansion* of the economy. Most of his book, *The Relevance of*

British Socialism, was devoted to means by which the economy could be rescued from the ineptitude of Conservative management and particularly from the failure to encourage the necessary investment for future expansion. He explained that the economic problem was the first priority because,

> political conflict, now, is not so much over two competing programmes, but over the measures needed to ensure the increase in production which alone can support the social spending programmes without a lurch into inflation.[20]

For Wilson the question of expansion was unrelated to socialist critiques of capitalist economies, it was simply a case of increasing investment and productivity in all industrial enterprises.

Nation and class

Wilson concluded one article with the declaration that 'a Four-Year Plan designed to recreate a sense of national purpose, and to ensure continued economic growth and real social justice, will enable us to regain for Labour and for the nation the dynamic we have lost'.[21] The concept of the 'nation' was a central unifying theme of the strategy whose importance might be gauged through a content analysis of the 1964 manifesto. 'Nation' was used some twenty times; 'class' was not used at all; and 'socialism' appeared only twice, and then spuriously. Furthermore, 'nation' and 'national' were often used redundantly, as for example 'our national highways', where they added nothing to the meaning of a phrase. Labour almost seemed to be taking over traditional Tory symbols of nation and patriotism. The manifesto concluded:

> The Labour Party is offering Britain a new way of life that will stir our hearts, re-kindle an authentic patriotic faith in our future, and enable our country to re-establish itself as a stable force in the world today for progress, peace and justice.
>
> It is within the personal power of every man and woman with a vote to guarantee that the British again become the go-ahead people with a sense of national purpose, thriving in an expanding community, where social justice is seen to prevail.

The ideas of nation, national unity and national purpose had two distinct sets of connotations, one related to a splendid role for Britain in world affairs, the other stressing the functional wholeness of British society.

The principal thrust of the critique of Conservative foreign policy was that it had allowed Britain's role as a major power to disintegrate. On the question of the spread of nuclear arms the manifesto railed thus: 'instead of throwing Britain's full weight into efforts to relax tensions and to halt the spread of nuclear weapons the Tories were content to play a minor and subordinate role leaving the initiative to others'. The Conservative government was criticized in similar fashion for its 'humiliating' application to join the Common Market. The implication was that Britain remained sufficiently powerful to survive with an independent foreign policy in many spheres. This notion of national influence bore some similarity with that of the Fundamentalist third-force policy in so far as it emphasized Britain's moral purpose in international relations but, in its specific proposals, it was almost entirely consistent with the Social Reformist position and in no sense broke with bipartisan policies. The ultimate aim of foreign policy was 'world government', with the United Nations as the medium, but in the meantime Britain had to support NATO: indeed, claiming the 'NATO Alliance as the basis of Europe's military security', the manifesto commended Ernie Bevin, 'who took the lead in facing the realities of the cold war'. The British role in international affairs was a personal concern of Wilson too. The dual message of *The Relevance of Socialism* was summed up in the final chapter: 'the emphasis is on recapturing economic dynamism by a rapid process of industrial modernisation and innovation and with a stronger and more confident Britain, to play a further part in world affairs'.[22] As Nairn has argued, this form of nationalism or chauvinism has always been present in the British Labour tradition, and has at various times been a major source of party unity.[23] Clearly in the early 1960s there was a desire to see Britain restored to its old glories in international diplomacy, but, whilst one face of the ideological prism of Technocratic-Collectivism, it remained subordinate to the second sense of the term 'nation', which stressed the internal functional wholeness of British society.

Nation replaced class entirely. The Social Reformist position, that Labour should not live under the label of a class party, was not only absorbed but surpassed. Social Reformists claimed that class divisions were of reduced importance and that it was electorally expedient to present an image of Labour as a party for all sections of society. But in retaining equality as its central ethical value Social Reformism contained the residues of class analysis. The technocratic-collectivist idea, that a Labour government could unhypocritically govern for everybody, at the expense of nobody, was a distinctly stronger claim. Any tension between class interest and national interest, present in Social Reformism, was completely ignored as the term class was banished from the Labour vocabulary.

The absence of the concept of class could be explained in two ways: either class interests were irrelevant to politics, there being no real sources of conflict; or conflicts of interest had their origins elsewhere. In the early 1960s Wilson tended towards the former position, but later he came to hold the latter view.

Differences of interest, but not fundamental differences of class interest, were recognized. Corporate interests did exist, expressed by pressure groups of various kinds, but common interests, in an efficiently managed economy, outweighed antagonistic interests. In such circumstances the primary task of government was effective administration, the secondary task was to act as arbiter between interests.

To the extent that Wilson personally had a theory of politics it was a brokerage theory:[24] the government's role was to hear the cases of various interest groups in society and find an acceptable balance between them all. To admit that all interests are equally valid is, implicitly, to accept existing society and reduce social justice to the balance between those interests. In this view the social world comprised nation and interest groups, governments attending to the former and spending a minimum amount of time on the latter.

This view of politics developed between 1964 and 1974. It became apparent in the late 1960s that greater account had to be taken of antagonistic interests in political management. At the time when the first national plan was instituted it was assumed that both sides of industry would happily acquiesce in the technical decisions taken by government. This proved unfounded and gradually the Labour leadership came to accept that government would have to play a negotiating role between capital and labour rather than simply a directing, decision-making one. The subsequent making of the Social Contract assumed less that an administrator could choose the most effective technical route to a given goal, than that a government must negotiate an agreement with relevant organizations of corporate interest, granting them concessions in exchange for promises about their future behaviour.

Technical politics

The idea of a technological revolution was not only significant as a strategy for supporting increased economic growth for, in its deeper layers, it denoted a particular attitude to politics and social change. Whereas Social Reformism put its faith in the maintenance of social consensus which informed the actions of democratically elected representatives, technocratic-collectivism was very much a philosophy of expert *dirigisme*.

It was presupposed that the expert knowledge which was to be applied by the scientists to industry was equally applicable to the realm of politics. The technological revolution was instrumental not only in bringing a new social stratum to prominence — the technologists, scientists and managers — but also in changing the basis of political decision-making. The new political managers of a Labour government were, by implication, as vigorous and progressive as their industrial counterparts: indeed the core of the Wilson cabinet was made up of politicians of 'ability', with qualifications rather than connections. Implicit was the idea that politics was an activity which could be regulated with the same impartial precision as industrial production. Politics was seen as an arena of technical decision, the politician being replaced by the technical expert, because the tasks of government were themselves technical rather than political. The efficient management of the economy was the first goal of political parties, and the distribution of benefits from a growing economy a subordinate one. Wilson himself said so much when he argued that 'political conflict, now, is not so much over two competing programmes, but over the measures needed to ensure the increase in production which alone can support the social spending programme without a lurch into inflation'.[25] The attitude to public ownership had the same rationale; where it was economically expedient it was justified.

This attitude to politics has been described by Habermas as the 'scientization of politics',[26] and by Mueller as part of a 'technocratic para-ideology'.[27] When the political sphere becomes dominated by technical reason at the expense of a substantive practical rationality, when politics becomes a debate about means rather than ends, politics escapes from the realm of collective democratic control into a realm of purely technical decision-making. Politics gives way to administration: questions of values and the nature of the good society are defined out of politics. This had at least two consequences for the Labour Party in the 1960s: first, it was difficult to reconcile with the notion of democracy; and second, it accepted the existing structures of the social and economic order, maintaining only that Labour was better equipped to administer that order. Both were seen as problems by some supporters of Technocratic-Collectivism.

Peter Shore, reflecting on the first twelve months of the Labour government, attacked both problems obliquely in trying to explain the shortcomings in the government's early record. At this point he was quite prepared to sacrifice participatory democracy to expert leadership, but he was aware of the problem of vested interests. He observed difficulties in the realm of the 'mobilisation of democratic power — the power of Government and of Parliament — to impose the necessary change upon the great private and corporate interests which largely control the economy'.[28] A National Plan, operated by experts rather than the old bureaucrats, was the appropriate instrument for Labour to wield, but its effectiveness was hampered by lack of control over industry and the City. As he said, 'how to achieve this essential change, how to transfer power from the amateurs of great wealth to the professional top managers of great ability, remains a missing component in Government policy'.[29]

Benn, later, saw the problem of democracy more clearly. His recent concerns with participation and industrial democracy in many ways constitute an auto-critique of his earlier adherence to Technocratic-

Collectivism. He realized that the unequal distribution of rewards was at least partly predicated on an unequal distribution of power in British society and that, without changes in the structure of power, efficient management of the economy was unlikely to generate significant social change.[30] Technical politics had, in practice, the consequences forseen by Habermas, that it maintained the existing socio-economic structure. This was clearly a disappointment to Benn who expected initially that the strategy would be more radical than it proved in practice. In fact the indeterminacy of the radical content of the strategy was one of its attractions. It was not without a sharp critical edge. Not only was *Tribune* complimentary about the 1964 programme, but so was *New Left Review*. In the latter journal Fanti argued that in 1964, unlike in 1959, there was a clear electoral choice provided by the 'alternative philosophy' of Wilson.[31] Revisionism, he thought, had been defeated and the new approach contained elements of a genuinely hegemonic ideology: 'the defeat of Gaitskellite revisionism was ensured by the *natural* alliance established between on the one hand the centre-left and left-wing groups and, on the other, the main body of corporative trade-unionists'.[32] The strategy appeared to Benn, among many others, to be potentially transformatory: he imagined that, possibly, 'we shall find ourselves embarking upon a far-reaching programme of reform that could be, for us, as important as the Chartist demands were for our grandfathers'.[33] It all depended, however, on what other policies were pursued along with the modernization of the economy, but there was no really good reason for believing that they would be progressive.

Social justice

Modernization, efficient administration, and economic expansion, were all aspirations perfectly consistent with the dominant interests of capital in 1964, a fact which did not exclude the possibility that they would also improve the material conditions of the subordinate classes. So far as changing the structural position of the subordinate classes was concerned, however, the critical aspects of the ideology were weak, the sole guiding concept being that of social justice.

Technocratic-Collectivism was not indifferent to social amelioration, though the reasons behind economic growth often went unmentioned.[34] Some supporters put social reform at the very heart of their understanding of the programme.[35] Wilson frequently referred to social justice in relation to problems of poverty, housing and unemployment, though this was ultimately a secondary concern. Brokerage politics did not need to specify its priorities in the allocation of benefits accruing from economic expansion, though it might for electoral purposes. The principal rationale was to find a balance between *a priori* equally valid social interests, which excluded any basis for generalized debate about them. The technocratic project might be made more or less favourable to the working class, but this remained, theoretically, a secondary concern. This represented the dominant pluralist conception of political administration whereby governments, rather than the market, mediated between competing groups with incompatible demands.

Douglas Houghton's pamphlet, *Paying for the Social Services*, was a superb example of technocratic and brokerage thought. Houghton considered that the year 1909 marked 'the beginning of the modern era of social action by the state'. That era culminated in 1948, since when 'political differences have been mostly about finance — contributions and charges — and not about services and benefits'. This state of affairs he saw no reason to change; his only concern was what the state could afford, and his greatest fear was that improved provision would be economically restrictive. He accepted the delay in introducing graduated pensions and excused inaction on the problem of child poverty on the same grounds that he objected to occupational pensions, that 'it might be highly inconvenient from the point of view of production costs'. In fact Houghton made a virtue of the erosion of universal social services:[36] 'The point of interest is whether the government will depart from 'universalism' in the field of family support. If so, it will confirm the trend of government policy towards more *selective* social security.'[37] He advocated more selective benefits, on the grounds that universalism put inequality before humanity. His view was that with limited funds attention should be concentrated on those social categories whose need was greatest. Such a policy position included encouraging people to pay directly for services; for example, he suggested either insurance schemes or cash payments for health services. While he made the most of the valid argument that there was something odd about universal provision, it being the case that the middle classes tend to benefit disproportionately from many services, the reasoning was dismally conventional. Principally by justifying means-tested benefits, but also by being prepared to risk creating two types of patient in medicine, he was prepared to reject the very values which made the Attlee government's welfare provision progressive. The logic of Houghton's argument was clear: the dilemma of the Welfare State was that demand for social services expands steadily but the wherewithal for providing them is only reluctantly made available. As he put it,

> The competing claims of personal consumption, economic development and social welfare in all its varieties, add up to more than the nation's income. *Private investment* — so essential to economic growth — and *public expenditure* — so essential to social advance — are like two hands in one pocket.
> The level of government expenditure is regarded by many at home and overseas as a reliable guide when assessing our capacity for economic growth. This is where

'confidence' comes in. The question being asked by our overseas creditors and the users and holders of sterling is this: 'Can Britain do it?' How much will people here give up to compulsory rates and taxes, contributions, levies and all, for whatever worthy purposes, without loss of incentive to effort and efficiency, and without pressures for higher incomes which will keep the vicious spiral turning?[38]

Such reasoning led to despair not only on the left, but also among the Social Reformists and the government's own social policy advisers.[39] What, on the one hand, may be seen as realism, on the other, seemed to be a total surrender to the imperatives of preserving the status quo. Vision was wholly absent, and innovative schemes to promote social justice were extremely hard to detect. The problems were the problems of the day; ensuring that foreign creditors retained confidence, allocating funds on the basis of the existing distribution of wealth, and assuming an eternal egoistic psychology. Furthermore, private investment and public expend-iture were given equal moral status and legitimacy: both came from the 'national' pocket. All this may have been perfect administrative logic, but it was wholly divorced from any concern to promote social change. In Technocratic-Collectivist strategy the imperative of economic effic-iency always, in the last analysis, overrode the pursuit of social justice.

Technocratic-Collectivism in practice, 1964—70

The attempt to put Technocratic-Collectivism into practice after 1964 won little acclaim.[40] Its practitioners excused their inadequacies on the grounds of external economic constraints,[41] but hardly anyone else was so charitable. Neither as a government pledged to the regeneration of a deteriorating capitalist economy, nor as a party representing the interests of labour, could the Wilson administrations expect to be viewed favour-ably. Professional economists berated the performance as inept, particul-arly in respect of the subordination of all economic objectives to the prob-lems of the balance of payments and the maintenance of sterling. The PLP (Social Reformists and trade union MPs as well as Tribunites) was disturbed by many aspects of economic, social and foreign policy. Trade unionists were outraged both by incomes policies and the proposals for industrial relations legislation. And left intellectuals and socialists were positively repelled by the government's activities. No doubt expectations were unrealistically high — the 1964 election campaign was successful in this sense — but that was no consolation.

The Wilson governments pursued the logic of their avowed strategy, to renovate the economy before engaging in measures to promote social justice. The problem was, of course, that the first stage, the acceleration of economic growth through effective planning, proved unattainable. Both administrations were overwhelmed, unnecessarily according to

Beckerman,[42] by the problems of the parity of sterling and the balance of payments, which were given first priority.[43] In particular it is now felt that the policy for expansion was fundamentally undermined by the refusal to devalue the pound in the early part of the period of government, a measure unlikely given Wilson's avowal in *The Relevance of Socialism* that 'Labour is determined to maintain the value of the pound, and to take such steps, internal or external, monetary or physical, as are needed to achieve this end'.[44] As Lapping maintained, government practice was a series of adaptive responses to economic difficulties:

> The gap in the balance of payments ... became the national obsession during the years 1964—70. And like the wild, hopeful cure-all of 1925, return to the gold standard, the years of debt were taken up by a succession of public infatuations with the latest way to end the troubles'.[45]

The 'cure-alls' were, successively, a leap into growth, selective intervention, incomes policy, National Plan, return to stop—go, entry into the Common Market, devaluation, reduction of overseas defence spending, and restraint on the right to strike.[46] Of these only a few were consistent with the intimations of the 1964 manifesto: principally the leap into growth, selective intervention and the National Plan. Indeed the government was relatively successful during the first year or so, but was incapable of compensating for the structural defects of the economy in the longer term.[47] The leap into growth and the National Plan were quickly sacrificed in response to the abysmal economic position which Labour inherited. Whether the National Plan would have made much difference is debatable. Granted the situation was worse than even the most pessimistic Labour minister might have anticipated, but as the entire drift of policy was towards rectifying the weaknesses of the British economy through planning the situation was a reasonable test of the viability of Technocratic-Collectivism. As recent commentators have pointed out, Labour planning was inherently deficient: it failed to recognize changes in the character of the international economy induced by the growth of multinational companies;[48] it made no allowances for the possibility that industry might be unwilling to act in accordance with the recommendations of indicative macro-planning;[49] and it took no account of other institutional barriers, like the dominance of the Treasury, to making the plan a priority.[50] 'Selective intervention', by which it was understood that 'government had an important part to play in helping industry, making it more efficient, sponsoring both research and the development of new products, encouraging takeovers of the right kind',[51] was the most successful initiative. Through regional policies and industrial re-organization at the level of the firm, the government did, to some extent, promote the re-structuring of capital. The key institution set up was the Industrial Reorganization Corporation, which sponsored mergers between firms with a view to achieving economies of scale and rationalization, a role it did fulfil in the computer industry, electrical engineering and automobile production, among others. However, the remainder of the policies pursued were either absolutely orthodox or they failed. In the period after 1966 stop—go was re-established, compulsory wage restraint introduced, and legislation was proposed to restrict strikes — all policies which had been explicitly rejected in the early 1960s and which were more appropriate to a Conservative than a Labour government.

The justification for this sad record changed markedly over time. Between 1964 and 1966 Wilson laid the blame for Britain's economic ills firstly on thirteen years of Tory misrule, and secondly on the capitalists, managers and, most particularly, financiers. His well-known rejection of Lord Cromer's repeated advice to deflate and cut public spending[52] was characteristic of the early period of optimism when, despite the small majority, the solidarity of the Labour Party was quite considerable. During much of 1966 and 1967, apparently disheartened about economic revival,[53] Wilson turned his attention elsewhere, but, returning to the subject late in 1967 he began to identify the demands of wage-earners as the main hindrance to economic prosperity. He made several injudicious attacks on strikers, the initial one, widely resented within the labour movement, against the seamen in 1966. From a viewpoint of managing the economy it would have been convenient if demands for higher wages could have been silenced, but this was simply not a viable approach for a Labour government. A Labour government must, if it is to retain support from its own party and from Conference, either satisfy corporatist demands or offer some coherent alternative programme of social change. Wilson did neither.

The issue of incomes policy, and its relation to anti-strike legislation, indicated the existence of a major external contradiction in technocratic-collectivism. Incomes planning was essential to the strategy, as Wilson and Brown clearly realized when they had talked of a 'planned growth of incomes'. But the only source of a greater wages-fund was increased productivity; without a larger pool of resources the planning of wages amounted to simple restraint. Under such circumstances trade unionists were always eager to revert to free wage-bargaining. Even if the Labour government had succeeded in producing a planned growth of wages it still might not have had a very comfortable time for, to the extent that it would have maintained differentials within the category of incomes and constant proportions between profit and wages, then the radical unionists would be discontented. Moreover to the extent that the government satisfied demands for an increased standard of living, independently of union negotiators, then the vested interests of the union bureaucracy would be threatened. Nevertheless, in the absence of the anticipated growth, the government's solution seemed to be at the expense of the working class.[54]

In the field of foreign affairs, which received limited attention because of the obsession with the economy, the Wilson government followed a bipartisan policy. CND declined in importance, though there were no significant alterations in nuclear policy. Economic self-interest increased British dependence on NATO and the USA, but this proved embarrassing because acquiescence to American activity in Vietnam was beyond endurance for a significant section of the Party. The much-vaunted dealings with Rhodesia, intended to be a prestigious venture restoring Britain's reputation in international diplomacy, proved abortive. Withdrawal east of Suez was welcomed, but was bound more closely by the economics of defence spending than by commitment to a principled foreign policy. Similarly, the application for entry into the EEC, a key issue during 1967, was primarily an economic and political expedient.

The governments' record on welfare policy was no better than on foreign policy. Given that welfare provision is ineliminable, the questions to be asked primarily concern its generosity and the principles upon which it is given. Educational policies were quite generous but were inspired primarily by a concern with the 'wastage of ability' identified by the Crowther and Newsom Reports. The expansion of universities and polytechnics had clear technocratic motives, as did the creation of educational priority areas. Though a concern with equality of opportunity lay behind Circular 10/65[55] requiring local authorities to submit plans for comprehensivization, there were no instructions to abolish public schools. The delay in raising the school leaving age also caused some consternation, and the resignation of Lord Longford.

In the realm of social security, Labour's action was fraught with contradiction. Prescription charges were first removed, and then reimposed. The minimum-income guarantee, promised in the 1964 manifesto, was never implemented, and the 'wage-stop' was introduced to prevent people in low paid employment getting more in unemployment benefit than they received at work. Family Allowances were raised and the 'clawback' established, whereby the benefits were taxed so that the rich had them effectively removed. This measure, and the raising of pensions, did improve material benefits for some poorer claimants.

The Labour government introduced a number of selective benefits. The argument ran that since there were insufficient funds to provide all the desired services, benefits should be paid only to the most needy. The problem was that this signalled a return to distribution of benefits through a means test,[56] at risk of restoring the stigma against claimants. One attempt to reduce such stigmata was the abolition of the National

Assistance Board and its replacement by a Supplementary Benefits Commission; but that was little more than a re-naming exercise. Labour's pension plans, apart from taking a great deal of time to mature and never being implemented, gave the clearest indication that the principles behind their social legislation were no longer universalist. Though in suggesting a graduated, earnings-related, pension the inadequacies of minimum provision were recognized, the actual *modus operandi* meant that those who were poor while at work remained poor in old age, and that those with larger wages got larger pensions.[57] Few Labour measures were calculated to redistribute income:[58] the search for equality was no longer a principal element in Labour's welfare plans. Among the government's lasting contributions were a number of libertarian, rather than egalitarian, reforms in the law regarding homosexuality, divorce, abortion and family planning: but these were probably more attributable to the personal influence of Roy Jenkins at the Home Office than any systematic commitment, for when he exchanged offices with Callaghan in 1967 the orientation of policy changed quite considerably — witness the immigration laws of 1968.[59]

The Technocratic-Collectivist strategy

The dominant ideology of the period after 1963 I have characterized as Technocratic-Collectivist. To the extent that it was technocratic it was neither democratic nor ethical: and to the extent that it was collectivist it was anti-individualist.

The ideology was technocratic in that it proposed a particular mode of social management. Society was conceived as a machine whose controls were in the hands of expert social engineers. The many plans might be conceived as a manual for servicing a maximally efficient machine; the role of government was to manipulate, instruct and co-ordinate. In principle this mode of political activity might have been structurally transformative. Thus, for example, in a different historical context Saint-Simon's proposals for a consciously organized order in the 1840s promised a definite transformation in society. But in the context of the 1960s, as conceived by Labour, the potential for transformation was minute. The emphasis on planning, which may have distinguished Labour's proposals from the Conservatives,[60] was not inimical to the maintenance of the status quo. Indeed it has been argued that it was essential to this end; as Shonfield showed, indicative economic planning, which was to be the function of the Department of Economic Affairs, was common to several advanced capitalist societies, to Germany and France in particular.[61]

Catley and McFarlane made it clear that the Labour strategy of 1964—70 was not an aberration in terms of social democratic party practice.

Examining the technocratic strategy of Whitlam and the Australian Labour Party, they argued that it was directed towards making the post-war, neo-capitalist, economy work better than ever, and in fact was heavily based on the recommendations of the OECD.[62] Incomes policy was a means of countering inflation, and proposals for social reform part of a 'package deal' in which increased social services and improved wages and payments to the poor were exchanged for wage restraint;[63] plans for regional development and industrial training became part of an overall strategy for increasing economic productivity. The whole bent of the strategy was towards making the existing economic institutions perform better.

The British Labour strategy, similarly, was an affirmative rather than an oppositional one, one which, given its social analysis, its conception of the nation and of the dynamics of political activity, was essentially integrative. In this framework the concept of democracy became a consenting rather than an active concept: government should be chosen for its expert, administrative capacity rather than because it represented particular interests; and the public had no role to play in the formulation of governmental policy. At the same time the idea that politics was about competing values, and in particular the idea that socialism was concerned with the transformation of social values, was abandoned.

Technocratic-Collectivism was not, of course, without values: it was collectivist rather than individualist, and it was not a species of liberalism. It was collectivist in the sense that the term was used in the late nineteenth century, as the antithesis of *laissez-faire* and radical individualism. The politically relevant units are the social whole and the corporate group rather than the individual. The motivation behind educational reform, for example, was not to foster personality and character, but to contribute to national efficiency. Likewise poverty and unemployment were to be regretted because they were wasteful of national resources rather than because they caused individual misery. The touchstone of policy was its potential contribution to societal machinery, a sort of collectivist utilitarianism where the greatest good of the greatest number referred to the interests of an indivisible state. There was, hence, a total absence of Social Reformist antipathy to the state and the centralization of state power. Effective state administration was the key to social progress, by comparison with which politics, conscientious dissent and interest group organization were superfluous.

There were similarities with Fabianism which, though not technocratic as such, had emphasized planning for efficiency and had rendered the nation a hypostatized entity. The Fabians had tended to believe that certain rules could be formulated for the realization of a social blueprint, which implied a rationality and predictability characteristic of bureaucratic mentality. The technocratic strain was rather more concerned that the expert should have the autonomy to make autonomous decisions in the light of technical knowledge:[64] success in the project of creating the New Britain depended on dynamic experts replacing the amateurs who comprised the Establishment under the Tories.[65] However while it might be acceptable to call the Fabians socialist, it is not plausible to characterize the Wilson strategy in such a way.

The Fabians, according to McBriar, discarded the terms 'class-war' and 'class-struggle' but continued to use the term class 'very much in the same way as Marx'.[66] They saw socialism as a significantly altered, classless, social order. The same cannot be said of the dominant ideology of 1964, which had no use for the concept of class, was indifferent to the question of property ownership, and did not foresee a structural transformation. Given the achievements of the Attlee governments and the nature of the Welfare State a Fabian collectivist strategy would have required radical re-formulation in order to produce a social transformation. Technocratic-Collectivism did, however, share with Fabianism a concept of the British nation-state as distinct from other nations. Semmel pointed out that the Fabians in the early twentieth century combined support of imperalism with the hope of forming a party of national efficiency.[67] While Wilson was no imperialist, patriotic fervour resonated in his concerns for economic efficiency: the flourishing of the British nation provided a symbolic goal to guide the practices of corporate groups.

As Searle showed in his study of the nineteenth century Movement for National Efficiency, such a programme need not be indifferent to the condition of the lower strata in society.[68] Labour in the 1960s genuinely intended to favour the lower classes at least partly at the expense of the rich. Ideas of 'fair shares' and 'social justice' though unrelated to class, contained humanitarian and fraternal elements as well as a degree of political calculation. However, there was an almost total indifference to equality. Despite the fact that its social policy advisers, and British social scientists of the period, used equality as the criterion of social justice, egalitarianism was not part of the system of values of Technocratic-Collectivism. Instead, functional interdependence, co-operation between the differentiated estates of a hierarchical, meritocratically regenerated social order was the operative ideal.

The strategy was, in context, powerful. It had a high degree of internal consistency; the core of the programme was an appealing package of mutually reinforcing measures — technical and administrative rationalization, planning, wider personal opportunities, and economic growth. It was also possessed of an unambiguous rationale, the main thrust of which was that with more good things around, shared amongst everyone, but with special concessions for those who started with very little, all might be well pleased. Therein lay the central conception of community interest which informed the strategy. The additional benefits deriving from growth would be distributed in accordance with the demands of social justice, rather than the logic of the market. But, despite specific commitments to the material improvement of the lower echelons in society, no general redistribution of wealth was contemplated. Technocratic-Collectivism paid less respect to the traditional redistributive demands of the labour movement than had Social Reformism. Relative indifference was also shown to concerns about the balance of class privilege and private property ownership, so that the radical gloss of the strategy arose primarily from proposals for extended state intervention and planning. In fact, the ideology as a whole was phrased in terms of reasons of state. Whereas Social Reform had thought in terms of the general will which represented the collective intentions of individual citizens as members of civil society, Technocratic-Collectivism envisaged the formulation of the national interest, by state and quasi-state agencies, with reference to the sectional interests of organized groups. But despite such differences both segments shared an underlying, integrative, strategic orientation. Technocratic-Collectivism, like Social Reformism, sought to maintain and enhance social cohesion through ameliorative social and economic measures and thereby put to rest the remnants of class antagonism.

Technocratic-Collectivism played a vital role in the internal dynamics of the Labour Party by providing a basis for party unity before the elections of 1964 and 1966. Wilson, in contrast to Gaitskell, seemed to have reverted to the normal role of the Labour Party leader, as mediator between factions.[69] Initially he received wholehearted support from *Tribune*, both on account of his earlier Bevanite credentials and because transformative potential was detected in his thinking. The trade union interest was also supportive: the leadership of the TUC in the early 1960s was favourably disposed towards the idea of a planned growth in wages under a Labour government.[70] Though the trade union group of MPs never have been bound by their trade union affiliations, in many ways it is easier for them to condone wage planning than sectional bargaining. This constituted what Fanti referred to as the combination between centre-left MPs and the corporative interests of the trade unions.[71] The Social Reformists were at first more hesitant, though probably for personal reasons. Wilson, besides having Bevanite affiliations, had been the man who challenged Gaitskell for the leadership in 1960 and he was therefore viewed with some suspicion — which would explain why most Gaitskellites preferred Brown as successor to Gaitskell. But while the ideology of Social Reformism was different, the actual policies of Technocratic-Collectivism were not fundamentally unacceptable. In practice, Ministers like Crosland, on comprehensive education, and Jenkins, with libertarian reforms at the Home Office, found space to pursue legislation which was consistent with their own ideological preferences. Indeed, by 1970 many of the Social Reformists were firmly wedded to Wilson, seduced by the charms, which they had come to appreciate during the 1960s, of economic growth.

In 1964 Technocratic-Collectivism also seemed to offer a promising electoral ploy. The conclusions to the debate on the 1959 election had persuaded large sections of the Labour Party that it must make itself attractive to groups other than the traditional working class. The 1964 manifesto, in its eulogies of the scientists and technicians, went far in appealing to a section of the population which might previously not have been expected to vote Labour. Nevertheless, the stress on technology and the technocracy was not simply, or even primarily, a vote-catching tactic, though this aspect must have enhanced its popularity within the PLP. Centrist coup though it was in part, one sense in which the ideology was technocratic was that it identified the technocracy as a major agent of social change.

Technocratic-Collectivism abandoned any notion that the working-class was a progressive or rising class in society and identified a substitute dynamic stratum, the 'technical-functionaries'. Though conceived as impartial and disinterested in all respects, their corporate interests were, in an important sense, promoted. The suggestion that this stratum was the basis of the revitalization of Britain promised status-rewards automatically; but it also seems inconceivable that they could play the role allotted to them without also advancing their material interests and their occupational autonomy. Such a prospect was apposite to the objective social conditions pertaining: Britain was technologically backward and its stratum of putative technical experts had little formal control over their own activities, little social prestige, and, to judge by the concern shown over the 'brain-drain', little incentive even to remain in Britain. In this way Technocratic-Collectivism might be said to have harnessed the 'techno-stratum' to the working class, rather than socialism to science.[72] Though this alliance need not have been an unhappy one it would be naive to ignore the likelihood that certain corporate demands of the techno-stratum would have to be met in the process. If technocratic politics had to be located in the context of social interests it must be this social group which was represented by it.

On the surface, the strategy was delightfully simple; efficient administration would promote the interests of all sections of society and social cohesion would be preserved as a result. In practice, the major impediment to the creation of the 'New Britain' was the persistence of structural constraints largely ignored by Technocratic-Collectivism — class antagonism, the logic of the market, the international economy, and the traditions of the labour movement itself. Nevertheless, the strategy contained certain internal defects, notable among which were that it left its priorities unspecified, that it failed to reconcile expert leadership with democratic legitimacy, and that it neglected to clarify the relationship between national and private interests.

The strategy was formulated in such a way that it avoided deciding in advance its priorities in policy-making. As Paul Foot summarized the matter, there were a number of questions which should have been answered before Labour came to power: to what extent were welfare reforms dependent upon economic expansion? how far should protection of the pound take precedence over industrial policy? to what lengths was Labour prepared to go in the restraint of wages? and what were the limits of co-operation with private enterprise and finance?[73] The absence of principled decisions to such questions was partly due to lack of foresight, but it was also an integral element of technocratic politics. Flexible responses to changing situations were written into the politics of expertise. Hence, the frequent indictment of Wilson, that his pragmatism was mere opportunism, misses the point. Pragmatism was implicit in technical politics and should not be confused with opportunism. Still, Foot's criticism remains pertinent since many of the reasons for the failure of the strategy, and for the extensive discontent within the labour movement, emanated from the government's uncertainty about its priorities.

Benn's political career illustrates the problem of the anti-democratic implications of technical politics. Benn originally subscribed totally to the Wilsonian vision, yet by the mid-1970s he had become the principal folk-devil of the conservative press. This peculiar development was the result of his concern that expertise should not destroy active, participant democracy, a concern which led him to industrial democracy. Radical thought has usually insisted upon the value of active political participation, whether in industrial or social affairs, an aspiration which technocratic politics renders virtually unattainable. Benn's reflections on the 1964—70 governments, in *The New Politics: a socialist reconnaissance*, brought this problem to the fore. It was a practical problem in so far as 'authoritarianism in politics or industry just doesn't work any more', but it had further ramifications:

> It is arguable that what has really happened has amounted to such a breakdown in the social contract, upon which parliamentary democracy by universal suffrage was based, that that contract now needs to be re-negotiated on a basis that shares power much more widely, before it can win general assent again.[74]

Political legitimacy was threatened by the maldistribution of power: 'the new citizen wants and must receive a great deal more power than all existing authority has so far thought it right, necessary or wise to yield to him'.[75] But technocratic politics was debarred from satisfying such demands for it required the reduction, rather than the extension, of popular control. In both theory and practice Technocratic-Collectivism threatened to reduce the role of popular power in the determination of policies, which provoked resistance unsurprising in the light of labour movement traditions, the Labour Party constitution and rank-and-file demands for workers' control.

The final problem concerned the relation between public and private interests. The national interest, in the name of which the strategy was constructed, is a rather spurious concept. Philosophers searching for some definite meaning to the term have identified a certain range of phenomena which could be said to be in the interests of all but which, if assessed in terms of individual costs and benefits, would be in no one person's interest.[76] This however constitutes a fairly small range of policies; most political decisions benefit some sections of the population at the expense of others. Furthermore, to talk of the nation as if it were homogeneous in its interests is to ignore a basic characteristic of class societies, one well documented in the history of Labour Party thinking, that some groups in society have more power than others. Shore recognized one difficulty, that of persuading capital to act in accordance with policies which were considered by the Labour government to be in the interests of all, the problem of 'the mobilisation of democratic power — the power of Government and of Parliament — to impose the necessary change upon the great private and corporate interests which largely control the economy'.[77] This, an entirely traditional Labour reservation about the willingness of private vested interests to acquiesce in unfavourable decisions, was outside the ambit of Technocratic-Collectivist consciousness, because the strategy was conceived to be beneficial to capital and labour alike. However, enormous difficulties arose in practice when, for example, it was discovered that government had insufficient powers to make capital abide by the price, dividend and investment policies of the National Plan. There were also, of course, problems of the interests of labour in general, and the various trade unions in particular. Subsequently the Social Contract was created in an attempt to obviate this particular problem by regulating the private interests of labour and capital through direct, centralized negotiation, but that subject is treated later in Chapter 8.

The government faced one overwhelming external contradiction. The whole strategy was likely to be acceptable only if rapid economic growth was achieved. Once that was confounded the inadequacies of other aspects of the Technocratic-Collectivist analysis became blatantly obvious. Given rapid growth it might well have been possible both to satisfy the material demands of the various corporate groups in society and to implement the wide-ranging welfare policies which were dear to the hearts of many members of the Labour Party. Without it, the balance of social forces rendered technocratic management impotent. In the first place the power of the vested interests of capital was grossly underestimated: the disagreements with Lord Cromer of the Bank of England indicated this. Unless the Labour government was prepared to deflate, to run an incomes policy and to make stringent cuts in public expenditure, the world financial community would not support sterling. Secondly, the trade unions, leaders and rank-and-file, required some guarantee of return for their co-operation. While a planned *growth* of incomes was not contrary to their sectional-corporate interests, a freezing of incomes, or tight wage restraint, was unacceptable. In this respect the assumption that there was a national interest which over-rode corporate and class interests was inappropriate. While government might gain some control over the market in production, the distribution of rewards still worked on a market principle. Although the market determination of life-chances was not a pure mechanism — corporate organization of employers and employees interfering to a large degree — the allocation of rewards was largely outside the control of government. Incomes policies simply froze the existing differentials in the distribution of income, and the restraints on public expenditure reinforced the existing structure of material distribution. In such circumstances both party solidarity and social cohesion became precarious.

General dissatisfaction within the labour movement could reasonably have been anticipated. The working agreement of 1964 was based on the aggregation of the aspirations of various segments. Either the government had to satisfy corporatist aspirations and ethicalist hopes for better public services, or it had to offer a wider policy of social transformation. But it satisfied neither trade union interests, nor ethical social reformists, nor those with transformatory projections. Wilson's handling of the situation was in some way prescient and in others inept. His handling of strikes, the wages freeze, and *In Place of Strife*, showed insensitivity towards the labour movement: restrictions on bargaining were bound to be unacceptable unless part of a more general policy of social change. After the 1966 election, when government policies did not alter, and did not offer any hope of social transformation, the left was obviously going to be dissatisfied: so long as Labour is a coalition of segments this has to be foreseen. When the government failed to secure increases in real wages the trade union interest was bound to become restive: so long as the Labour Party remains in a close association with the trade unions, in fact so long as there are trade unions, this must be expected. And when the government failed to redirect public expenditure into the social services the ethicalists could find no reason for supporting it. The simple form of Technocratic-Collectivism devised in the early 1960s failed to resolve intra-party conflict or to avert social conflict.

Initially it was assumed that economic expansion would improve living standards for the majority of the population and that the satisfaction of such material aspirations would suffice to maintain political loyalty; social cohesion would be an *effect* of economic success. This was some way from the intricacies of the political formula of the post-war settlement. Consensus politics was not abandoned in the 1960s, but the substance of consensus altered dramatically. No longer was political loyalty courted on the basis of an ethical consensus, as had been the case with Social Reformism. Instead, Technocratic-Collectivism offered a working formula for compromise between social interests. The new formula, despite its genuflections to the ideal of social justice, depended almost entirely upon economic success. In this it encouraged, and almost certainly reinforced, instrumentalist motivations among the population at large. At the same time it gave an inflated impression of the capacities of the state for effective economic management. Technocratic-Collectivism created the situation where economic failure was bound to generate problems of social cohesion too serious to be obviated by mere invocation of the rhetoric of 'nation'.

Ultimately, capital and organized labour refused to co-operate with the government when their interests were adversely affected. The technical and administrative wisdom of state planning left the corporate interests cold. It was the gradual realization of this which led to changed notions of political interest aggregation in the late 1960s. Wilson, by temperament, was disposed to disappoint supporters who, nursing notions of party government, expected a Labour government to favour the interests of the working class and the trade unions. The depth of opposition to 'non-partisan' politics from within the labour movement after 1967 forced him to modify his stance. Already, before the government was defeated, he was prefiguring to some degree the Social Contract, abandoning value-consensus for negotiations between functional group interests. Any simple presumption of the inevitability of social cohesion collapsed, but bi-partisan politics still seemed viable. Nevertheless, having rejected the strategy of civic incorporation, which had been the basis of the post-war settlement, Technocratic-Collectivism had no ready means of containing the resurgence of class conflict at the turn of the decade. What, in conception, had been an ingenious solution to both the British malaise and the internal cleavages of the Labour Party, foundered in the absence of growth sufficient to pacify antagonistic social interests.

6 The crisis of the Welfare State: social developments in the 1970s

The era of consensus just failed to survive the Labour government. Erosion of the substructure of the post-war settlement began in the last two years of Wilson's premiership. By 1973, at the latest, it had been destroyed. Though the origins of changes in the anatomy of Britain may be found before 1968, and though they were not fully worked out by 1973, this was a period of economic and political restructuring. The most visible developments, the oil crisis and entry into the EEC, were but two among many in the process of economic reorganization. Severe problems of financial stability in the international economy surrounded the abandonment in 1971 of the Bretton Woods monetary arrangements; the management of inflation in many western economies began to appear impossible as Keynesian techniques failed; and in Britain, industrial concentration and the further growth of multinational corporations conspired to reduce the degree of government control over the national economy. Problems of the containment of discontent also grew. Radical protest movements — students, nationalists, women and Trotskyists — proliferated. More significant still was the growing antipathy of the unions towards government intervention. Proposals, by both Labour and Conservative governments, to resolve problems of economic management by encroaching upon the legal rights of the unions, provoked concerted resistance. Though not amounting to a transformation of social structure, these molecular changes in economic and political life did entail a crisis of political management.

The delicate balance of forces which characterized the post-war settlement was disrupted. The Labour government, though latterly embarked on redefining the consensus, left the political formula largely intact. Restrictions on collective bargaining, which contravened the formula, had been presented as only a temporary expedient. Meanwhile, public expenditure on social services had been maintained, and an assumption of social consensus had continued to prevail. Strains arose because the strategy for the regeneration of the economy, and thus the expansion of capital accumulation, more or less failed. The transfer of resources into complementary social reform gradually slowed down. The government's dependence on incomes policy to regulate the economy generated conflict, though as yet this was actualized only within the Labour movement. And, finally, the Conservative Party effectively gave notice that it had abandoned the Welfare State consensus when it adopted the programme of 'Selsdon man'.

The political formula of the post-war settlement finally disintegrated during the Heath governments. The years 1971–73 were the most politically turbulent since the 1930s. The mode of institutionalizing class conflict broke down:[1] not only was there an escalation of strikes, despite the fact that standards of living were still rising, but there was a significant crisis of political authority. The rejection of the Industrial Relations Act by the trade union movement was the most important aspect of this, but attempts to alter the character of social provision, especially the Housing Finance Act, also produced dissentient political action. By the end of 1973 it. was fairly common for the press to debate whether Britain was becoming 'ungovernable'. At least in terms of the post-war settlement it was ungovernable. The reason for this lay in the contradictions of the Welfare State itself.

The Welfare State contained an inherent contradiction between the mechanisms of economic production and social cohesion: in essence, the necessary basis for the continued accumulation of capital was incompatible with the established modes of political legitimation and conflict resolution. The logic of capital accumulation necessarily entails an unequal distribution of power and wealth, a condition which has constantly generated opposition. The mechanisms for the containment of that opposition have changed over time, but in the Welfare State they were primarily dependent upon the appearance of increasing equality and prosperity. Once the legitimating illusions were dispelled, the tendency to disintegrate accelerated. At a very general level there are two possible ways of countering this tendency. On the one hand, as Mattick suggested,[2] it might be resolved through the extended public appropriation of the means of production which would, ultimately, undermine the viability of private capital by increasing the dependence of the private sector on the public sector. That is to say the basic nature of the capitalist economy would be changed. On the other hand the social and political relations of the Welfare State might be transformed in order to provide the conditions for continued private accumulation. This would require alteration in the forms of legitimation and conflict resolution. It was the second of these, very abstract, parameters of the Welfare State which was transcended in the early 1970s, for reasons which can be quite closely specified.

The historical origins of the crisis of social cohesion in Britain derived from problems of capital accumulation in the 1960s. Despite a variety of corrective, state-interventionist measures, no satisfactory solution was found to the tendency towards stagnation in the British economy. The economic causes of the halting of economic growth by 1974 remain a matter of dispute, but the consequences for the political formula are quite clear: the disappearance of growth destroyed it. Though initially a subsidiary element in the formula, economic expansion became central because it permitted, or seemed capable of allowing, the long-term alleviation of social injustice without tangling with the politically difficult issue of the redistribution of wealth and power.[3] In particular, growth facilitated rising levels of personal and collective consumption among the subordinate classes, within the existing framework of social institutions, and without detriment to capital accumulation. Its absence, on the other hand, generated competing demands upon government to give financial and ideological support to both accelerated accumulation and expanded consumption. The material basis for the simultaneous satisfaction of both sets of demands decayed in the face of economic decline.

James O'Connor exposed much of the fundamental logic behind the instability of the Welfare State.[4] He realized that one characteristic of the 'Welfare/Warfare State' was its need of high public revenues which it subsequently reallocated in various ways. Its central problem was the incremental and contradictory demands made upon it to increase simultaneously its financial contributions to social capital (productive investment) and to social expenses (welfare programmes). O'Connor envisaged that even in the absence of economic recession demand would outstrip available revenue, because some sections of the population would be unable or unwilling to submit to increases in taxation, while others would pose a threat to political order if the state reneged on the commitments of welfarist ideology. This 'fiscal crisis' was potentially more severe in Britain than in America (which was the object of O'Connor's analysis). While the reaction to high taxation in the United Kingdom was more muted than in other western countries — even though all the political parties promised cuts in direct taxation, for electoral purposes, in 1979 — the breadth of demands upon state expenditure was greater in Britain than in the USA. In Britain the state was more heavily implicated in the financing of capitalist production, both directly through subsidies and tax relief, and indirectly through the provision of economic and social infrastructure; the relative economic backwardness of Britain made the collection of sufficient revenue from industrial sources more difficult; and the ideology of egalitarian social reform had been made absolutely central to political legitimation. In Britain the contradictions implicit in the fiscal crisis were inescapable. The dilemmas of the Labour government after 1974 can be related directly to that crisis. Labour chose to place an over-riding priority on supporting the requirements of capital accumulation. Such a choice could not but have critical implications for the Party and society.

The fiscal crisis engendered particularly severe problems of legitimation for a Labour government whose principal modern commitment had been to social amelioration within the structure of the Welfare State. The principal, politically-controlled, mechanisms for the maintenance of social cohesion in the Welfare State were, first, a steady rise in living standards (personal consumption) and, second, the extension of social provision (collective consumption).[5] Both were means of incorporating the sub-ordinate classes, ways of enlarging the loyalty of the disprivileged to the status quo: the Technocratic-Collectivist strategy was particularly depend-ent upon increased personal consumption, the Social Reformist strategy on collective consumption. Neither, however, could be dispensed with easily.

It is commonplace to assert that both party-political and 'consumerist' ideologies fostered instrumentalist motivations in the post-war period. A desire for, and expectation of, increased personal income was injected deeply into the motivational complex of common consciousness. More-over, governments consciously fostered the belief that improved material conditions were benefits within the orbit of political control. As Mueller argued, governments, encouraged by the initial success of state planning and direction in the post-war period, led the electorate to believe that improved social and material conditions were the effect of conscious policy: governments suggested 'that the political system is autonomous and capable of solving all political problems'.[6] In fact, governments came to justify their own activities, and to legitimate the social order, in terms of their success in satisfying popular, instrumentalist, expectations. The situation arising once governments found themselves incapable of meeting such expectations have been analysed in terms of an incipient crisis of legitimation.[7]

The theory of legitimation crisis maintains that in the process of fostering instrumentalist motivations traditional, 'natural' and market justifications for inequality and hardship have been eroded.[8] With the onset of the fiscal crisis, governments, deprived of the capacity to ad-equately satisfy either instrumentalist or welfarist expectations, could no longer ensure compliance with their directives. Popular motivations which were generated in the post-war settlement no longer sufficed as a basis of political obligation. The effect was the erosion of political authority: as Mueller put it, 'once the structural source of deprivation is perceived as the political allocation of resources, an important condition for conflict has emerged'.[9] In sum, governments, having encouraged new needs and expectations, and having claimed a capacity to fulfil these, generate a crisis of political loyalty when they fail to meet them.

It is doubtful whether, in Britain, this condition will have the cataclysmic effects anticipated by the theory of legitimation crisis. Nevertheless, the theory is germane to an explanation of the demise of the political formula of the Welfare State. The concurrent failure to satisfy expectations of increased personal and collective consumption posed great difficulties for the regulation of class conflict in the 1970s. The political solutions to the crisis threaten to obliterate two main pivots of the settlement: free collective bargaining — the main channel through which increased personal consumption flowed — has been constrained by intermittent incomes policies and industrial relations legislation; and complementary social reform, which supported growing collective consumption, is being curtailed for fiscal reasons. Without these the Welfare State consensus cannot be reconstituted.

The politics of the 1970s lend support to the legitimation crisis theorems. Collapsing levels of personal consumption account directly for a considerable portion of the explosion of industrial militancy in this decade. But they also partially account for increased union membership among formerly non-unionized white-collar and semi-professional occupations, for the attractiveness of Celtic nationalism, and for the emerging political appeal of policies to reduce direct taxation. The impact of declining collective consumption is more diffuse. Because a reduction in public expenditure does not in general have an effect on corporately organized groups, direct implications are obscure. The most obvious case of conflict induced by cuts in collective consumption is, in fact, the increased militancy of public sector employees whose personal incomes and job security are threatened by plans to reduce public spending. The unemployed, the sick, the aged and the young, on whom the direct impact of such 'economies' fall, are comparatively inconspicuous. Nevertheless, individual demonstrations of dissatisfaction, pressure group campaigns and trade union expressions of dissent have emerged in response to the decay of public services and the reduction of the 'social wage'. This almost certainly contributes to sceptical attitudes towards the political system for, as Mueller argued, 'the non-fulfilment of demands stemming from newly established rights (employment, education, adequate housing, medical care, etc.) which, therefore, are legitimate demands gives rise to the sentiment that the structure of government is at fault'.[10] Furthermore, though it remains a hypothesis rather than an established fact, one consequence of of this may be the current volatility among the electorate and, in the longer term, it is also highly likely to refuel the political motivations which generated a Labour Party committed to opposing inequality and injustice.

The crisis tendencies of the 1970s created considerable problems for the Labour Party. In some ways the disintegration of the political formula of the post-war settlement had its greatest impact on the Labour Party, for while it did pose significant problems for capital, labour and the Conservative Party too, there is a sense in which it undermined the entire rationale of the Labour Party since 1945. The Labour Party was highly committed to the structure of the post-war social formation. Not only was the Welfare State the creation of the Labour Party, and a symbol of Labour's success, but it provided ideal structural circumstances for containing the characteristic tensions of a social democratic party in a capitalist society. The Welfare State seemed to contain the potential for meeting traditional commitments to the working class through ameliorative, parliamentary reforms. The collapse of the social conditions for the implementation of the political formula necessarily caused a crisis of ideology and practice within the Party.

The effects on the Party were of three sorts: the character of the various segmental ideologies and strategies underwent a metamorphosis; the balance of forces within the Party, particularly the relationship of the different segments to the trade union interest, altered; and the character of the Party's approach to the maintenance of social cohesion and the regulation of class conflict changed. The following chapters explore these effects in detail.

7 The demise of Social Reformism, 1970 – 78

The social tendencies, outlined in the previous chapter, which led to the collapse of the post-war settlement, most severely affected Social Reformism; if support is required for the axiom that the internal balance of power within the Party is mediated by changing social conditions this is the perfect case. The crisis tendencies, accelerating during the early 1970s, caused the Social Reformist strategy to disintegrate. In the period of the Conservative government there was a growing self-consciousness on the part of the segment's leading intellectuals that their strategy would prove extremely difficult to implement if Labour were returned to government. By the time Labour was re-elected in 1974 the strategy was in a late stage of decay, the preconditions for its success having been swept away.

The pages of *Socialist Commentary* came to be spattered with references to the current crisis; the idea of a 'natural' consensus collapsed into a search for some future basis of national unity; class conflict reared its head; and the problem of providing the revenues for complementary social reform without economic growth began to seem completely intractable. The Party's solution to these problems was the negotiation of the Social Contract. This, though not entirely unacceptable to Social Reformism, was constructed on a very different rationale, one inconsistent with the tenets of the New Liberal *Weltanschauung*. The principal difficulty for Social Reformist strategy lay in the logic of the 'fiscal crisis': barring radical changes in the economic structure the requirements of capital accumulation prevented the government raising sufficient revenue to promote egalitarian social reform, thereby undermining the essential basis of the strategy of civic incorporation through the extension of social rights. What had once been an appropriate and effective strategy became redundant with changes in social conditions. The corollary of this, the demise of Social Reformism, was not long in coming. By 1976 *Socialist Commentary* had re-opened the debate of the early 1950s, that of 'whither Labour and "democratic socialism"?'.

Emerging contradictions, 1970–73

The Social Reformists did not feel it necessary to revise their political strategy as a whole in the aftermath of the 1970 election defeat. Though sometimes critical of the governments,[1] they were in many ways quite satisfied. *Socialist Commentary* commended Labour for having 'become an increasingly *responsible* Government',[2] and Jenkins warned that 'we must not expect a full-scale peaceful revolution every time a Labour Government is elected'.[3] Crosland, too, thought the Wilson governments unjustly maligned. He claimed that, given the constraints under which they were forced to operate, 'solid progress was made on a number of fronts': the increase in public expenditure had been impressive; income had been redistributed; educational expenditure had grown substantially; housing policy was 'far from disgraceful'; regional policy and environmental and libertarian reforms were useful; and the outmoded imperial system had been abandoned.[4]

In the light of such successes the Social Reformist strategy of the 1960s was re-affirmed. In an article written in 1971 Crosland re-iterated his earlier position:

> I believe that a left-wing party's priorities are firstly to relieve misery wherever it exists — to help the deprived, the poor and the underdogs; secondly, to promote greater social and economic equality for the mass of the people; thirdly, to apply strict control to the economic system in the interests of the environment, the consumer and the less prosperous regions.
>
> These objectives, which are in Labour's central tradition of conscience and reform, call for the reallocation of resources and a redistribution of wealth. They require high taxation and public expenditure and rigorous government controls. This is a basic divide between Left and Right; a divide which the Tory Government is now joyously revealing.[5]

Egalitarianism, and the expansion of public services based on economic growth, were Crosland's main themes. His views were shared by *Socialist Commentary* which said, in July 1970:

> In the breathing space that is now before us, a campaign should be mounted to re-kindle the faith and understanding of our own supporters. We have moved beyond the objectives of earlier generations when socialism meant primarily the nationalisation of key industries and the establishment of the welfare state. But the new expressions of socialism — the stress on social expenditure (which means more taxation), the need for some kind of incomes and prices policy, the importance of state intervention in industry, new approaches to financing the social services, creating a gracious environment — all this is not fully understood in the movement and is even distrusted by it.[6]

These features were taken to be the consensual assumptions of the modern Labour Party.

In 1971 the Social Reformists still believed that increased social expenditure was the sufficient condition of an effective civic incorporative strategy. *Socialist Commentary* was quite prepared for the Labour Party to announce that its policies required increased taxation: 'is it really true that high taxes are a bad thing? Ask yourself the question — how else is the constant growth in public and social expenditure, on which the whole fabric of our modern society rest, to be financed'.[7] It was maintained that high rates of public expenditure were a sign of a civilized society, and that further expansion was desirable. Yet even while Crosland distinguished Labour from Tory policy through the former's commitment to increasing public expenditure and public services, he began to appreciate certain inherent difficulties. He said,

> Socialism and equality require a relative transfer of resources from private consumption to public expenditure; economic exigencies may demand a further transfer to higher exports or investment. But under conditions of slow growth, efforts to achieve these transfers inevitably provoke inflation. For since they cannot come from the fruits of rapid growth, they must come from higher taxation of existing incomes. But higher indirect taxes put up prices; higher direct taxes provoke compensating claims for higher wages and salaries. In our slow-growth economy the shift of resources exacerbated problems of inflation.[8]

Intimating that inflation was a problem which could only be offset by faster growth, he argued that an agreement must be reached between the Party and the trade unions on the determination of incomes. But that alone would not be enough because,

> for a Labour Government wishing to allocate resources on a considerable scale, slow growth is an additional cause of inflation. We must, in order to finance our collective spending, reduce the *share* of consumption in total income. But this ... can only be done without extra inflation if the *absolute* level of consumption is rising steadily; and that requires a rapid rate of growth.[9]

The point was reiterated: 'many of the desired reforms will require a substantial increase in public spending. How is this to be achieved? Once again, the first essential condition is economic growth; without that, there is no hope of the increase we want.'[10] Revision of the tax system might help, but economic growth was now the first priority. Crosland had little to say on how this was to be achieved. Rejecting the rhetoric of 1964, he advocated greater competition to counteract the effect of mergers and industrial concentration, competitive public enterprise, and greater public saving to obviate heavy borrowing on the private money market.

The self-assurance of the Social Reformists was far from absolute. Roy Jenkins in his 1972 book, *What Matters Now*, indicated considerable doubt about Labour's future. Using the concept of equality as his critical gauge he examined problems of regional depression, poverty, the

developing countries, work, and urban renewal, finding Labour's performance wanting in all these areas.

Jenkins no longer believed that the abolition of inequality was a simple,
straightforward task. He admitted that 'The social forces that bolster inequality are immensely powerful and immensely persistent ... In the
1950s, many of us thought that the inequalities would diminish as society
became more prosperous. It is now clear that this view was at best simpli-
fied, and at worst just wrong.'[11] Jenkins maintained the position that
socialism was a matter of ideals, and that equality was valuable because
it fostered individual development, but he began to suggest more 'traditional' socialist measures.[12] He came to recognize that the various spheres
of inequality were related; 'we have failed to see the connections between
poverty and serious regional and class inequalities in health care, education, housing and employment opportunities'.[13] To deal with this he
rather gingerly advocated the need for an extension of the public sector
of industry[14] and for 'countervailing action by the State' to correct
regional imbalance.[15] He implied that government intervention was necessary precisely because private industry did have sectional interests and
that the government was better able to decide what was in the public
interest:

> Government, acting through the public sector, can adopt a broader perspective than
> that of any board of directors nominally responsible to its share-holders. It can view
> investment in a much longer time scale. It can estimate the benefit of industrial
> development to the community as a whole, in terms of new jobs and better use of
> social capital.[16]

Jenkins challenged the rationale behind the practices of the Labour
governments. All could not be made dependent on economic growth:

> It is too easy a way out to say that we look to economic growth to solve all the
> difficult problems, helping those in need and everything else. What is undoubtedly
> true is that with sustained growth we can level up both more rapidly and more
> acceptably than without it. But I am not prepared to let everything depend upon
> it.[17]

This indicated something of a return to the ethical socialist stance of, for
instance, Socialist Union, with the first priority being 'wider policies for
social equality', though the practical implications were not made clear.

In advocating egalitarian policies Jenkins had motives other than
simple equity or humanitarian sentiment. He was very much afraid of
social disruption, of the dissolution of the basis for social consensus and
consent. He argued,

> In a world in which the traditional bonds of habit, status and deference are rapidly

dissolving, flagrant disparities of income, wealth and power are likely to pose an increasingly ominous threat to social peace... unless the old deferential order is to be replaced by an accelerating social chaos, in which each group fights with increasing intransigence to defend its own ... we must strike a new and acceptable balance between economic reward and social merit.[18]

The theme of incipient social division recurred constantly. Talking of poverty he warned,

> The main danger is that our society will become increasingly divided between the affluent and the less well off. On one side will be the world of youth and opportunities — on the other the poor, with an increasing sense of deprivation and shut-offness from the affluent world about them... that would be the road to a dangerously split, morally unjust and dangerously insecure society.

Discussing the needs of the regions he argued further, 'If the South is allowed to suck away a disproportionate share of our country's prosperity there can be no real national cohesion ... We cannot allow regional disparities to continue. They will poison and embitter our whole national life.'[20] Again reflecting on work, acknowledging that some conflict was inevitable, he observed that 'if strikes are sufficiently widespread and continous as to cause major national dislocation and widespread inconvenience they are an expression of something deeper than this occasional inevitable conflict'.[21]

Jenkins was becoming aware of certain problems in the Social Reformist strategy, though he did not articulate them directly. Because Social Reformist analysis had never identified any basic source or mechanism of social conflict, the degree of such conflict in the period 1966–73 was almost inexplicable. Status inconsistency was not an adequate explanation, and obviously Jenkins did not think that it was attachment to egalitarian ideals that produced conflict. For him the most worrying aspect of the situation was that the basis for social consensus, the *sine qua non* of a civic incorporationist strategy based in the New Liberal *Weltanschauung*, was disintegrating. The social consensus, the united national culture presupposed in the 1950s, no longer existed in its old form. *Socialist Commentary* pointed out a 'road to disaster' which lay 'in the break-up of the social cement which has so long been a valuable element in British society',[22] while Prentice diagnosed 'a crisis of democracy'.[23] The expression of sectional and group interests led to a renewal of open conflict, probably not actually so great as to warrant Jenkin's concern that the social fabric was being rent asunder, but sufficient to require more radical measures by Labour in the field of public ownership and the alleviation of poverty.

Mitigating class conflict, and pacifying the trade unions in the absence of rapid economic growth, were the major problems of maintaining the social consensus. The role assigned to the unions by the Social Reformists up to the mid-1960s, of pursuing the sectional interests of their members through channels of collective bargaining, was no longer appropriate. They now recognized a need for some kind of incomes policy to control inflation, but they continued to believe that the link with the unions was an electoral liability[24] and were unhappy at the prospect of the unions taking political decisions or being involved in negotiating government policies. The editorial of the November 1971 edition of *Socialist Commentary* said,

> It makes no sense to talk naively about a 'social compact' which seems to imply that the unions should take over the basically political function of allocating national income and expenditure.
>   What is needed is a clear agreement about what are the proper and complementary roles of Government and unions in present-day society. The problem here is that the old understandings on which the marriage between Labour politicians and trade union leaders was founded are no longer valid.

Denying the old division of functions it continued, 'A government *must* now act in areas that impinge upon the unions' traditional preserves. But the other side of the same coin is the need to recognise that the unions' industrial interests are now more fundamentally political than ever before.' The Social Reformist position was that some agreement must be reached, but it should not be one which prejudiced a government's or the Labour Party's freedom of action. The kind of collaborative *bargain* that the Social Contract came to represent, where the Labour Party exchanged concessions in political policies for wage restraint, was not an ideal arrangement so far as the Social Reformists were concerned because it carried overtones of the organization of a corporate state.[25] The Social Reformists recognized that the problem of union pressure could not be solved by an imposed solution, but were unclear about how agreement could be reached without compromising a Labour government through granting special consideration to the trade union interest.

The problem posed by the unions also had repercussions on Social Reformist attitudes to electoral tactics. Crosland, while expressing considerable sympathy with Gyford and Haseler's argument that the Party was not taking sufficient account of the aspirations of 'ordinary people',[26] became generally suspicious of the trade unions. Mainly he was concerned with the 'identity' of the Party: 'we lack a clear *identity* as a party. In particular the public does not know whether we are, or are not, the political wing of the trade union movement.' He went on to explicate:

> Labour's special link is, and must be, with the organized working class, and its solid base is in the trade union movement. Both party and unions represent the same aspirations of their members and their families; and the area of common

interest and mutual need is, and always will be, enormous.

But that does not mean a *complete* identity of interest. Labour is not a sectional or one-class party, nor did most of the pioneers see it as such. They saw it rather as the party of the ordinary people against the rich, the privileged and the powerful.[27]

The Labour Party, he concluded,

should not automatically agree with everything that union leaders say, still less be dictated to by them. For all our special links with the unions, we are a national party, responsible to the people as a whole. If we are thought, as we sometimes are, to be the creature of the unions and exclusively identified with them, then Mr. Heath could occupy No. 10 for a long, long time.[28]

In effect close relationships with the unions were much less satisfactory than in the 1950s, when the unions could be left to play the market. Wage control was an unfortunate necessity but was not an issue around which Labour should stress its special links with the unions in case it over-identified the Party with the unions. This concern of Crosland's was yet another, slightly different, variant of the permanently ambiguous position of Social Reformism towards the relationship between the Labour Party and the working class.

The Social Reformists further prejudiced their deteriorating relationship with the trade union interest by opposing Labour's agreed policy on the major political issue of the early 1970s, entry into the Common Market. The Social Reformists were, most unusually, responsible for one of the two major rebellions of back-bench Labour MPs during the 1970 Parliament.[29] Though the segment was partly divided internally, entry into the EEC had been part of the Campaign for Democratic Socialism's platform in the early 1960s and a constant feature of *Socialist Commentary*'s position.[30] The decision to vote with the Conservative government in 1972 was not inconsistent with their position over the years. Indeed *Socialist Commentary* was so convinced that the arguments had not changed with the passing of time that it found it unnecessary to re-iterate the arguments in 1971.[31]

A supplement to *Socialist Commentary* of March 1971, *Britain 1980 – Out or In?*, did, however, argue the case. It maintained that, outside the EEC, economic growth would remain low so that Britain would be unable to compete economically with American industry or to control multi-national corporations. The case was partly economic, but also partly political. It was argued that national sovereignty was irrelevant because neither finance, the economy, nor defence, was any longer independent. The Commonwealth, lacking any desire for political unity, was no adequate alternative. Entry, on the other hand, would foster economic growth by increasing the size of the home market, without damaging the balance of payments. The prospects of political union were welcomed, much faith being placed in the development of European democratic institutions and their capacity to make central economic decisions.[32] A further major reason for joining the Community was a sense of identity with the social-democratic parties on the continent. Brandt's Germany was looked upon with great respect because of its economic prosperity, its highly developed welfare institutions and its success in constraining industrial conflict.[33] To join Europe would not prejudice British aid to the Third World, and would be a move against stagnation, isolation and declining influence in world affairs.[34] The Social Reformists accused their opponents in the Party of being insular, short-sighted, and anti-internationalist.[35] The outcome of the referendum on EEC entry eventually decided the issue in their favour, but was of little help in reviving a languishing strategy.

The withering away of Social Reformism: 1974—8

The Social Reformists entered 1974 consciously concerned lest social order, social harmony, democracy and the mixed economy were simultaneously collapsing.[36] For a while they remained attached to residual elements of their version of a civic incorporative strategy, in particular the conviction that social policies were essential to the maintenance of social harmony. Thus, the January 1974 editorial of *Socialist Commentary*, 'Who is for Socialism?':

> All talk is of the need for national unity: of the need for people to act in an awareness of common national interest, and in that interest to accept constraints and belt-tightening... It is so manifest as not to need arguing that such an appeal can only decently be made (and, indeed, can only hope to succeed) against a background of government policies that encourage social harmony, that recognise common goals, and, above all, which are seen to be *fair*, so that people can be secure in feeling that any sacrifices will fall most heavily on those most able to bear them.

Berating Heath's tactics of 'confrontation and abrasiveness' and his cutting of welfare, it continued,

> Isn't it self-evident that in the situation we face now and in the period ahead, only the social policies of a Labour Government would be relevant to the needs of national unity, providing an environment in which we could hope to solve our industrial relations problems and pull together in coping with whatever consequences would follow if the oil crisis becomes a continuing part of our economic life.

In the course of a year, however, all the progressive elements of the strategy were banished. Themes of fairness, and especially equality, receded, the occasional echoes of the former philosophy appearing only as utopian afterthoughts, desirable in the abstract, but impracticable given the central issues of the day. The motifs of Social Reformism were now 'liberty', protection of the mixed economy, and 'social justice': the emphasis which older Social Reformists like Crosland continued to put on equality was much reduced in the writings of the younger inheritors of the tradition who formed the Manifesto Group of Labour MPs.[37] By 1975 *Socialist Commentary* had espoused a thoroughly defensive strategy the sole aims of which were to reduce inflation and increase industrial investment.[38] The means for accomplishing this were totally at odds with the political formula of the Welfare State and, one by one, the distinctive elements of Social Reformism were discarded.

One of the most remarkable developments was the enthusiastic support accorded to policies designed to increase the profitability of the private sector of the economy. As economic recession took hold, and the reputation of Keynesian remedies waned, Social Reformists turned to the vindication of what they took to be the most precious element of the *status quo* — the mixed economy. The principal element of their solution to Britain's economic problems was seen as the revival of private industry. *Socialist Commentary*, in an editorial 'Profit and Socialism', endorsed Healey's pronouncement that 'no-one now believes that profit is a dirty word' and that 'we want a private sector which is vigorous, alert, imaginative — and profitable'.[39] The position was usually expressed in terms of the regeneration of the mixed economy, but whereas the left insisted that public guarantees and benefits must be secured in exchange for aid to private industry, Social Reformists had no such requirement. The primary imperative was the removal of impediments to the accumulation of private capital. This was defended partly in the language of 'economic realities' (Britain was dependent upon the operation of the world capitalist system and was subject to pressures from international capital) but it was also advocated for its own sake, as a socialist policy. An identity was established, in theory, between the mixed economy and 'democratic socialism' so as to suggest that the institutional framework for democratic socialism already existed.[40] For example, in contesting the view that trade unions could not be expected to surrender their bargaining power in a non-socialist society *Socialist Commentary* asserted 'But in practical terms we have made so much progress towards a mixed economy that the context in which we are asking for a social policy on incomes is not qualitatively different from what can be expected under democratic socialism.[41] As the left of the Party and the TUC gradually united over an 'alternative economic strategy' the Social Reformists increasingly extolled the benign aspects of the market and the virtues of private ownership. The ambiguous concept of a 'planned market economy', entertained in the 1950s, gave way to the idea of a '"pluralist" mixed economy'.[42] Planning was accorded a minor role.

In *What We Must Do: a Democratic Socialist Approach to Britain's Crisis*, a pamphlet of the Manifesto Group, the role of planning became primarily one of 'help(ing) industries react to changes in market conditions'. Affected by a current scepticism about the efficacy of planning, the role of the state was reduced to minimal proportions: to forming 'a view of the trends in world markets' which 'would enable government to construct a more coherent framework of thinking against which to take individual decisions', to encouraging export trade, and to supporting research and development which 'should be much more clearly associated with marketable output'.[43] Advice and incentives to private capital substituted for state planning, which had been a hallmark of all varieties of Labour thought in the past.

Having rejected extensive planning, and being even more vehemently opposed to public ownership than ever, there was a problem of achieving the necessary degree of regulation over the economy. Two possible means, consistent with the general aim of increasing the rate of investment, were considered, incomes policies and tighter control over public expenditure. Interestingly, the former was subordinated to the latter: 'Their (incomes policies') role in attacking inflation is secondary, the primary role being taken... by proper control of public spending'.[44] It was argued that the application of Keynesian policies in the past had been 'careless':

A failure to distinguish between unemployment due to deficient demand (which the Government could put right) and unemployment caused by organized labour using its bargaining power to push wages beyond what the economy could stand, led to the indiscriminate use of Keynesian expansionary policies. To finance the resultant budget deficits, governments resorted too often (the Tories being far more guilty here than Labour) simply to printing money, which led to high unemployment and high inflation.[45]

The remedy was to avoid raising public expenditure. Though they pointed out that such a recommendation was separate from egalitarian arguments about the virtues of public spending — which in principle they continued to accept — the implication of their position was that the limits to public expenditure had been exceeded and that public spending would have to be curtailed. Indeed the government acted in accordance with this advice, making some severe cuts in public spending programmes and attempting to control the growth of the money supply in their battle against inflation. Whatever effect this may have had on the economy it had vital ramifications for Social Reformism.

As was noted before, increased public expenditure on social provision was the fulcrum of Social Reformist strategy for both social amelioration and social integration. Having made the decision that economic growth was hindered by high levels of public spending, a major ideological dilemma arose. The solution, itself a manifestation of fiscal crisis, proved most remarkable: the commitment to extended social provision was abandoned, not just on the grounds of temporary economic exigency but on principle.

Healey's suggestion in November 1975 that workers wanted more money rather than an increased social wage was frequently reiterated.[46] It became commonplace for contributors to *Socialist Commentary* to recommend public expenditure cuts (or the retention of current levels of spending through the imposition of cash-limits which, in a period of inflation, meant a reduction in services) and to state a preference for private consumption over public provision. This was clearly put by the ex-Gaitskellite William Rodgers in a lecture called 'Socialism Without Abundance'.[47] He argued that in the absence of mass abundance strategic choices were needed about the distribution of public revenue. While affirming that public provision was desirable he argued that it should not be given priority because much of it was inefficient, it lost votes, it did not lead to material equality, and in so far as it was materialistic it was unsupportable. Instead, Labour should expand personal consumption, which would have the desirable effects of increasing freedom (of consumer choice), attracting votes and aiding 'personal equality'. His concept of 'personal equality' referred to the fact that people measure equality and 'classlessness' in terms of their comparative possessions. Rodgers was thus arguing primarily that equality should be promoted by increasing personal incomes, and that political interventions should be limited to those areas of *non*-material inequality like race relations. Even though this argument was expressed in terms of the ethical values of Social Reformism — equality, liberty and fellowship — it signified a major ideological *volte-face*. In policy terms it implied reducing direct taxation, for there was no wish to support wage increases, and cutting public expenditure even further. It was thus far from clear how social harmony was to be sustained, and how any kind of social amelioration was to be pursued. The appeal of Social Reformism seemed to be directed towards the values of civil and familial privatism,[48] values explicitly rejected in the 1950s and 1960s and ones which in general cannot be calculated to increase social solidarity.

It is perhaps surprising that cuts in public expenditure should be preferred to a strict incomes policy. Though the Social Reformists became convinced of the need for an incomes policy of some sort — given their reliance on a wage-push theory of inflation, this was more or less inevitable — they argued against government-supervised, centralized determination of wage levels. They maintained that an incomes policy as rigid as that employed by the Labour government could never be more than temporarily effective and was, in any case, inadvisable on economic grounds. Instead they canvassed the idea that the unions should regulate their own wage demands, internally, in accordance with general governmental directives about permissible levels of growth in the 'wages fund':

> What we want ... is an incomes policy which contains the average level of wage rises and yet responds to market forces within those limits. One method would be for government, unions and employers to bargain annually for the next year's average settlement, and then leave it to the unions and employers to negotiate its distribution.[49]

This, it was argued, would increase flexibility and 'preserve differentials which offer people real incentives to acquire skill and work hard'.[50] Such a scheme, which seems inherently unworkable in so far as trade unions would be loath to accept direct responsibility for determining differentials within and between unions, indicated a general distrust of the Social Contract and a growing hostility to the trade unions. The Social Reformists were never more than pragmatically attached to the methods entailed in the Social Contract. After initial expressions of relief that social harmony had been restored with the election of a Labour government, they became quite critical of the Contract. During the first year of the government, when wages rose rapidly, the Contract was attacked for being ineffective.[51] But even when it began to restrain wages severely they remained unhappy with it. The principal objection was to its political implications, especially to the role it accorded to the trade unions. First it was feared that the special relationship with the unions would jeopardize Labour's electoral chances; before both 1974 elections, and on each occasion when the terms of the agreement came for renewal, *Socialist Commentary* railed against the irresponsibility of sectional interest groupings.[52] Frequently, appeals to the unions to support government policies were backed up by very lightly veiled threats. For example, in September 1975 it was argued that 'hard' economic policies could be instituted without trade union consent and that the government might then 'make the unions the principal scapegoat if economic difficulties increased'.[53] Again, when Chancellor Healey threatened to cut public spending and allow unemployment to rise if the unions did not agree to severe wage control, the Social Reformists raised no objections.[54] The Social Reformists were, clearly, partly worried about militant unionists with left-wing sympathies, but their opposition was still more deeply rooted. It was always maintained that the incorporation of the trade unions in political policy making was a fundamental violation of parliamentary democracy, which in a sense it was. However, to the extent that such an arrangement seemed capable of increasing the power of organized labour something other than outright opposition might have been expected. To understand this response it is necessary to examine the balance of power in the Party in the 1970s.

The influence of Social Reformism declined markedly in the mid 1970s: only strength of numbers within the PLP furnished a power-base inside the Labour Party. An attempt was, therefore, made to restore the segment's position by mobilizing support against the left. For the first time since 1962 a conscious campaign was mounted against the left. The old polemics against marxism were resuscitated and various threats to the party were exposed, from Benn, the Tribune Group, union militants, CLP delegates and entrists from the revolutionary left. The substantive issues at stake concerned intra-party organization and democracy. The most distressing fact was left domination of the NEC, in response to which the Social Reformists attempted to defend the autonomy of the PLP. The NEC was berated for having criticized the party leadership, and for being so inconsiderate as to constitute a 'second opposition' to the good work of the government.[55] And Conference was reminded that its function was only to 'advise and warn' as there could be only one authority in the labour movement, the present government.[56] Further, an attempt to combat the Campaign for Labour Party Democracy, which sought to increase the power of the extra-parliamentary party over the PLP, produced some offensive remarks about the role of CLP activists. (Arguments about the autonomy of the PLP flowed freely and there were some plaintive cries for the reduction of intra-party democracy.) One *Socialist Commentary* editorial, 'Party and Politicians', not only expressed disapproval of participation 'filtered through a distorting layer of political enthusiasts', but also described the proper role of CLP members as negligible:

> What matters is what is done at the national level, and above all by the Front Bench team. The only substantial contribution that local work can make, outside a handful of the most marginal seats, is in the maintaining of postal voters' lists.[57]

The gist of the argument was that members of the Party were unrepresentative of the body of Labour electors and that an MP's responsibility was to the latter. More interesting than the merits of the argument about intra-party democracy, which will always recur when different segments of the party derive their support from alternative sources inside the organization, was the virulence of the Social Reformist campaign. What this seemed to indicate was a clear awareness that their power lay in strength of numbers within the PLP and that their fortunes were declining. It was this which led them to set up organizations to mobilize support.

Three different organizations were created in the mid-1970s: the Manifesto Group of Labour MPs, the Social Democratic Alliance and the Campaign for Labour Victory.[58] The Manifesto Group emerged as a counter-balancing faction against the Tribune Group. A collection of backbench MPs who constituted the second generation of Social Reformism — the first generation having dispersed in the early 1970s — the Manifesto Group provided the principal source of ideological opposition to Tribunism. The Social Democratic Alliance proved to be a short-lived, and potentially embarrassing, grouping contesting the right of Constituency Labour Parties to refuse to re-adopt sitting MPs. The SDA Manifesto reflected the ideological barrenness of the right when it advocated almost reactionary policies by Labour standards. Being convinced that the Party was 'in danger of being driven from its historic course by an intolerant dogmatism' it maintained that the British labour movement had almost no connections with socialist thought: 'The British Labour Movement is deeply rooted in national traditions of radicalism, free co-operation, non-conformity and Christian socialism'.[59]

It went on to plead for the absolute sovereignty of parliament, the rule of law, a pluralistic society, a trade union movement which 'refrains from seeking political power by direct action', a profitable economy, and wholehearted commitment to NATO. Despite an initially favourable reception — *Socialist Commentary* greeted it by saying that 'what it stands for is very much in tune with *Socialist Commentary*'s beliefs' —[60] its strident attacks on the 'legitimate left' of the Labour Party rapidly eroded its support. The Campaign for Labour Victory was an extra-parliamentary organization trying, as the Campaign for Democratic Socialism had earlier, to mobilize support in the constituencies, primarily on issues of Labour Party organization and loyalty to the PLP leadership. As Seyd pointed out, however, what was remarkable about these groupings was their uncertainty about positive policies and commitments.[61] They opposed the left, but did little else.

The people attached to the residues of Social Reformism actually acknowledged their own ideological bankruptcy. *Socialist Commentary* on several occasions proclaimed a state of ideological crisis and confusion. An 'ideological recession' was diagnosed in January 1976; and in November of the same year it was announced that the 'realists' had 'not been clear enough about what they themselves were *for*'. 'A more coherent democratic socialist approach' was required, 'a more organized and systematic effort is needed from the sensible majority of the Labour Party to grapple with these problems and construct a realistic ideology for the Party'.[62] But despite occasional attempts, no solution was forthcoming. In practice they supported the government's policies, especially Denis Healey's part within it, and acted as agents of apology. They approved the government's economic strategy; they were pleased with the outcome of the referendum on the Common Market: they supported the government's foreign policy, re-interpreting NATO as an agency which simultaneously provided defence and promoted detente;[63] and, in general, they bestowed an image of consummate wisdom upon the government. The relatively radical conclusions reached by Jenkins and Crosland between 1972 and 1974 were by-passed and, as a consequence, they ended up supporting the 'moderate' line of Callaghan. Callaghan's election as leader was welcomed, even though it was said to imply a dearth of talent for the 1980s, because he promised a 'quiet' and 'solid time' and signified a 'swing to the right'.[64] For similar reasons the pact with the Liberal Party was also readily accepted.[65]

Social Reformism was disintegrating. The problem was not that the left was actually getting its policies implemented, but that no satisfactory alternative to left ideology capable of achieving sufficient support within the movement was generated. Foremost was the difficulty of placating the trade union interest, for while a few union leaders remained sympathetic to the rump of Social Reformism (notably Jackson, Basnett and Weighell) the majority of the TUC were antagonistic to many of their key proposals. The Social Reformists initially courted unpopularity on the issue of the EEC, for most of the unions, and indeed Conference, wanted to reject the terms offered. Thereafter they advocated economic policies fundamentally opposed to those presented in TUC *Economic Reviews*. The TUC was opposed to cuts in public spending, was sceptical of the degree of support offered to capital, was in favour of a substantial redistribution of wealth and income, and was insistent that the economy should be expanded by boosting demand. Nor could the TUC be pleased with the attitude of the Social Reformists towards its greater influence in the making of political policy. What the Social Reformists failed to account for was that trade union acquiescence over a voluntary incomes policy — which was the main factor in making Labour governmental strategy possible at all — was not to be had without political cost. If free collective bargaining was inappropriate, and rigid and statutory control impossible, then how could an incomes policy be made to stick? *What We Must Do* simply wished that there could be some consensus, that the unions would agree to act as if there were no antagonistic interests involved. But consensus had disappeared in the 1970s; and it was precisely the achievement of the Social Contract to have put some negotiated *modus vivendi* in its place.

The Social Reformists were unable to engineer a coherent response to the collapse of the political formula from within their own ideological framework. Despite remaining influential within the Party, due to their occupancy of key positions within the PLP and the government, they were prevented from making any substantial contribution towards determining the future trajectory of Labour strategy. External developments undermined their strategy.

In the first place, the civic incorporative strategy was far less applicable in a period of economic recession than in an age of affluence. What had been a very appropriate and successful strategy in the 1950s, one which provided the basis for Social Reformist dominance, was far less adequate in the 1970s. With the re-emergence of virulent conflict over wages and industrial relations, it became very difficult to promote policies which were merely complementary to working class demands made through the channels of collective bargaining. Social reform might complement working class gains in a situation of economic expansion but, in other circumstances, the strategy appeared as one directed to a very difficult task, the containment of working class demands.

Secondly a civic incorporationist strategy requires a belief that there are interests held in common throughout the community, that there is a basis for consensus. The Social Reformist strategy had been particularly dependent upon consensus because without substantial agreement among the whole community the idea of a General Will was nonsensical. The assumption of Social Reformism, that class antagonism had subsided, became untenable. The supposition of a post-war consensus could no longer be sustained because sectional and class interests emerged as a hard reality which demanded political management. Conservative government policy of 'confrontation' in industrial relations merely confirmed that in conditions of economic recession the automatic acquiescence of the trade union interest to governmental economic management could not be relied upon.

Finally, the foundation for complementary social reform dissolved as it became difficult to increase public expenditure. The onset of fiscal crisis in the 1970s reduced the amount of revenue which could be directed towards social services of all kinds. The demands made upon public revenue far exceeded the state's capacity to satisfy them so that a choice was required between either devoting funds to investment in productive industry or allocating them to public welfare. This basic problem of a mixed economy, delineating the limits of the Welfare State, could not be solved within the terms of Social Reformism.

8 Tripartism: a collaborative solution to crisis, 1972–79

The fiscal and legitimation crises, which had rendered inoperable the classic integrative strategy of Social Reform, were confronted by the Party's leaders by re-casting Technocratic-Collectivism. The pursuit of consensus was abandoned between 1968 and 1973, being replaced, as a basis of social cohesion, by the Social Contract, a scheme for class collaboration. The new strategy, 'Tripartism', was an approach intended simultaneously to re-establish internal unity, ruptured in the late 1960s, and to develop a more practicable form of integrative strategy. The ensuing mode of political management was an ingenious solution to the dilemmas of social-democratic party practice, although the arrangement between the Party and the unions, upon which it was based, proved difficult to sustain. In part built on foundations laid by the left, Tripartism was re-appropriated by the leadership in 1973–4 in order to restrain any potentially radical implications.

The general disillusionment with the Labour governments of 1964–70 had little immediate impact on the Party leadership or programmes. Neither of the 1969 policy documents, *Agenda for a Generation* and *Labour's Economic Strategy*, presented new orientations, although they were much more cautious about the ease with which a future Labour government could promote efficiency, equality or democracy. Nor did the 1970 election defeat make much difference: as Nairn pointed out there was a vacuum in Labour Party thought, there was no post-mortem and the Party remained in a state of suspension until it was revived by the debate on the EEC.[1] Technocratic-Collectivism was not renounced, but it was transformed, almost by default of its protagonists.

The Labour leadership scarcely participated in intra-party debate while the Conservatives were in office: for the first time since the war political initiative was displaced from the PLP leadership. It allowed the left to lead Labour's attacks on the Conservatives and avoided most polemical issues, bar that of entry into the Common Market. As in 1962 this was the issue through which the leadership tried to manufacture Party cohesion. Using the argument that the terms negotiated by the Conservatives were unsatisfactory, substantial majorities were obtained in Conference for renegotiation and, eventually, for a referendum on continued membership. This vacuum permitted the left to increase its influence on official Party policy through mobilizing the support of the beleaguered trade union interest. Wilson himself only returned to the stage to contest *Labour's Programme 1973*, the creature of the left-wing NEC, which he feared would jeopardize election prospects.[2] By then much ground had been lost and it took a degree of ingenuity to align his putative policies with those being developed by the Party in Conference. Using the prerogative of the Party leader and the Parliamentary Committee to draft the election manifesto, however, the thrust of the radical programme was parried by producing an ambiguous, unifying election platform. It included many elements of *Labour's Programme 1973*, but provided a means of avoiding their radical implications.

When Labour was returned to office in 1974 the government was committed, on paper, to more radical policies by Conference decisions. The 1974 manifestos contained more *specific* radical proposals than had their predecessors, the language changed quite significantly, and in the new Social Contract Labour carried a potent political weapon. But many of the policies from *Labour's Programme 1973* were omitted, and once again the ambiguities of policy proposals allowed a vast degree of flexibility in interpretation. The January 1974 manifesto, *Let Us Work Together — Labour's Way Out of the Crisis*, for example, showed some signs of the impact of the left in the preceding years in that it contained specific proposals for public ownership and social welfare. It bore some semblance to the kind of economic strategy advocated by Stuart Holland (subsequently published in *The Socialist Challenge*)[3] and supported by the radical NEC of the early 1970s. However, it still concentrated primarily on Labour's capacity to 'rescue the nation' by reversing and compensating for the policies of the incumbent Conservative government. The first task was still to cure Britain's economic ills, though there was no mention of technology and efficiency. In addition, it was claimed that only Labour could resolve the problems of social cohesion which had become apparent in the period of 'confrontation'. The principal concept remained 'the nation', but now Labour was both the ideal manager of the economy and the guarantor of social order. Despite the radical veneer, the rationale behind the strategy was not very different from that of 1964. Like its predecessor it could be construed as a radical strategy: whether or not it was depended upon the way in which it was put into operation.

The immediate task of 1973—74 was to reconcile obeisance to the radical programme with the twin objectives of regenerating British industry and restoring social cohesion, without actually undertaking transformative change. In the event, the leadership assimilated the three major new instruments to which the party was committed in its manifestos, the Social Contract, Planning Agreements and the National Enterprise Board, (NEB). All were, originally, designed to regulate the relations between government, private capital and labour, and were inspired by the need for effective control over the economy. The first was concerned with co-operation between the trade unions and the government, the others with the relationship between government and industry. The government re-directed or avoided each in turn, managing to keep them firmly under control. As employed by the government they signified neither new economic policies nor new social and political priorities, though they did generate a new conception of politics within which unreformed techno-cratic aspirations were pursued. The Social Contract was turned into a formula for securing the collaboration of the trade union interest; and the NEB, the new institution most favoured by the left, was contained within a role consistent with a truncated version of Technocratic-Collectivism.

The National Enterprise Board and Planning Agreements

The radical potential of the NEB was steadily blunted as it passed through the stages of being an opposition Green Paper, a government White Paper and a practical instrument.[4] In conception it was to be part of a general assault on the power of private capital; for parts of the Tribune Group, for example, it implied that the state would take a controlling interest in a considerable number of leading, profitable firms in Britain. But even at this stage it was not conceived as a remedy for capitalist injustice or immorality. Once embodied as government policy, even under Tony Benn at the Department of Industry, it already began to appear as an extension and revitalization of the 1963–4 strategy rather than as a traditional 1930s socialist measure. The Party's October 1974 manifesto, *Britain Will Win With Labour*, promised to set up a NEB with powers to invest in private industry and to take particular industries into public ownership, in accordance with the Department of Industry's White Paper, *The Regeneration of British Industry*, published in August 1974.[5] But it was quite clear from the first paragraph of the White Paper that public ownership was only a means to regenerate the mixed economy:

> We need both efficient publicly owned industries, with a vigorous, alert, responsible and profitable private sector, working together with the Government in a frame-work which brings together the interests of all concerned: those who work in industry, whether in management or on the shop floor, those who own its assets, and those who use its products and depend upon its success.

It continued, in paragraph 4,

> Industry and the Government should also be partners in the pursuit of objectives which spell success for industry and prosperity for this country. This requires a closer, clearer and more positive relationship between Government and industry, and the construction of that better relationship requires the development of new institutions.

The maintenance of a balance between the interests of the various parties to the agreement, conceived as the interest of the nation or the community, was the central objective of Labour's strategy. The goal was the prosperity of all. Talking of Planning Agreements and the NEB the White Paper said:

> The Government believe that this new initiative will contribute to the achievement of greater industrial efficiency, more and better investment, and a higher return on investment. By thus entering into explicit partnership with industry, the Government expects to raise the quantity and the quality of manufacturing industry's contribution to the development and growth of the economy on which the prosperity of us all depends.[6]

Fundamentally there was little in the brief of the NEB inimical to capitalist planning, at least as it was conceived on the Continent.[1] The first concern was to increase productivity, through the rationalization of industrial practice, regardless of to whom profit accrued. The aim was, explicitly, to moderate, regulate, and control market forces. The White Paper described one of the functions of the NEB as 'to secure where necessary large-scale sustained investment to offset the effects of the short term pull of market forces'.[8] Benn made the same point at the Tribune rally in November 1974:

> We know now that the market mechanism has not worked here in Britain, and it does not serve the interests of our people. As Socialists we must now be prepared to take political responsibility for planning Britain's industrial recovery on a national scale, using the instruments we have devised to implement a national plan for British industry.[9]

There were different ways of interpreting the proper function of the NEB and it was Benn's particular activities through the NEB that caused alarm. The NEB need not be construed as progressive *vis-a-vis* the interests of the working class, for in principle the NEB did not fundamentally challenge the basic tenets of economic orthodoxy or capitalist relations. The White Paper said of the NEB 'It will compete with companies in the private sector and be expected to operate in accordance with suitable financial objectives. Its guiding financial objective will be to secure an adequate return on that part of the nation's capital for which it is responsible.'[10]

Much as *Industry and Society* of 1957 would have wished, the State was being encouraged to become a participant in capitalist economic practice through competitive public enterprise. Also, consistent with the dominant Labour conception of the 1960s, the government should be permitted to take over those sectors of the economy which are 'failing the nation'. But such a strategy had a strong sting in its tail in a period of economic recession. At a point in time when capitalist enterprise was floundering, the State appeared to be encroaching rapidly on private property. In a prosperous climate the buying of shares in private enterprise for the purpose of increasing regulative control over industry might be gradual and pass unnoticed. In recession, however, the government was obliged to make massive intervention. The apprehension of capital towards Benn was based on the fact that when the economic cycle began to turn upwards there could have been quite a substantial transfer of economic assets to the State, though in the long term the NEB might have acted in a way consistent with the interests of capital.

In the course of implementing the policy its radical potential was further reduced. Benn was quickly removed from the Department of Industry and the total budget of the NEB was reduced to comparatively minor proportions. The pursuit of community interest once again seemed to result in greater concern for the interests of capital than anything else.

The Social Contract

The major ideological innovation for the 1974 election campaigns was the development of the notion of the Social Contract. It signified a change in Labour's conception of politics by effectively abandoning the assumption that there was a natural identity of interests in the nation as a whole. Though it continued to use the rhetoric of nation it embodied a hard-headed view of the role of corporate interests. Rather than being the broker or arbitrator of group interests, government after 1974 was to become one institution involved in the *direct* negotiation of a bargain or compromise between interests. The lesson learned from the period 1964–70 was both that the representatives of capital and unionized labour have to be placated, and that the unions have to be persuaded, rather than coerced, to accept governmental economic policy. Government in effect becomes less the province of technical, expert decision-making, and more one of aggregating corporate interests and negotiating between the representatives of labour, capital and the state.

The nature of the Social Contract was specified in the document *Economic Policy and the Cost of Living* produced by the TUC–Labour Party Liaison Committee in February 1973. The document discussed the contemporary economic situation under the Tories. It said 'the Government's policies have steadily undermined the possibilities of co-operation

in our economic life ... it seems to have equated what it describes as its
electoral mandate with a freedom to ride roughshod over the interests of
great sections of the community'.[11] It argued that 'the problem of inflation can be properly considered only within the context of a coherent
economic and social strategy — one designed to overcome the nation's
grave economic problems, and to provide the basis for co-operation
between the trade unions and the Government'.[12] Such a strategy was put
forward, based on price control, repeal of the Housing Finance Act,
public ownership of all land required for house building, 'a large-scale
redistribution of income and wealth', and the channelling of resources
into the social services. In discussing how to finance such a programme it
was said that there 'must be agreed policies on investment, employment
and economic growth. And the objective must be to get faster growth'.[13]
The problem of investment was deemed to be fundamental, and part of
the solution was to develop new public enterprise and public supervision
of the investment policies of large private corporations. Control of capital
movement overseas and rejection of the terms of entry into the EEC were
also required. The final section of the document, 'Industrial Democracy
and Economic Democracy' said that,

> In the control of capital and the distribution of wealth there will be more economic
> democracy, and the growing range of functions of the trade union movement will
> bring about a great extension of industrial democracy. The collective bargaining
> process is the essential means whereby the most important factors affecting the
> livelihood of workpeople can be subject to joint regulation.

Rather ambiguously it maintained that there should be both a 'movement
of bargaining in many industries from national to plant level', and, 'equally
there has to be a development of common lines of action at national level
and, indeed at international level'.[14] It went on further to explain that
because of the complexity of the problem,

> Policy in this field can only be based on agreement and not on compulsion, though
> there is great scope for seeking to reach recommendations through tripartite
> machinery along the lines of NEDC. But in the field of collective bargaining, such
> recommendations can only be incorporated in collective agreements voluntarily
> reached by the process of negotaition.[15]

Finally, the document referred to an earlier agreement between the NEC,
the TUC and the PLP on the repeal of the Industrial Relations Act, and
claimed that,

> this statement on Economic Policy and the Cost of Living will further engender the
> strong feeling of mutual confidence which alone will make it possible to reach the
> wide-ranging agreement which is necessary to control inflation and achieve sustained
> growth in the standard of living ... It will be impossible to specify what will be the

precise economic circumstances in which the next Labour Government will take office. Nevertheless it will be the first task of that Labour Government on taking office, and having due regard to the circumstances at that time, to conclude with the TUC, on the basis of the understandings being reached on the Liaison Committee, a wide-ranging agreement on the policies to be pursued in all these aspects of our economic life and to discuss with them the order of priorities of their fulfilment.[16]

The emphasis on co-operation between a Labour government and the trade unions was unprecedented; Labour in fact promised to conclude an agreement on policies and the order in which they should be implemented. The implications were far-reaching. The TUC was granted, in principle, a considerable degree of influence in the determination of government policy; and at the same time its further integration into the state apparatus was accomplished. The outcome was uncertain: either the TUC might strike very hard bargains with the government in the protection of its members interests; or it might simply increase the conformative role of the TUC within the state.

At the same time Labour made an equally grave alteration in its ideology by replacing the concept of social justice with that of co-operation. It seemed that community interest was not only predominant, but that co-operation amounted to no more than peaceful coexistence between social groups under the present social structure. Wilson's Foreword to the October manifesto ran, 'In February the country rejected, as we had urged, policies of confrontation and conflict and 'fighting to a finish' philosophies. We put before the country the policy of the Social Contract.'

The manifesto even went so far as to apply the traditional metaphor of the family to society: it was suggested that there were no fundamental cleavages in British society, the irony of which being that their entire election campaign and subsequent practice were directed towards containing and regulating such cleavages.

Tripartism: a note on the concept

The importance of the Social Contract has been recognized in the growing debate about the emergence of a corporate state. The discussion of corporatism has become increasingly subtle; early predictions that a quasi-fascist, corporate state was developing have given way to quite complex distinctions regarding the types of co-operation and compromise which have been established between state, capital and labour in contemporary European states.[17] Some agreement exists about the novel characteristics of recent policies and the procedures for their formation. A general trend is discerned towards the involvement of the national executive bodies of business and labour organizations in the formation of governmental, especially economic, policies. This significantly affects the nature and practice of plebiscitarian and parliamentary democracy because it changes effective decision-making procedures and constitutes a new way of containing conflict over the distribution of reward – through institutionalizing agreements, mediated by government, at the level of the elites of capital and labour.

This general development has not by-passed Britain, though there are some peculiarities about the British case. It has been observed, particularly since 1974, that the CBI and the TUC have gained increasing influence over government policy,[18] and that this represents a movement towards institutionalizing extra-parliamentary channels for determing policy. The most useful characterisation of the new situation, of 'Tripartism', was presented by Jessop.[19] He argued that the growing involvement of functional interest groups, primarily capital and labour, in the making of state policy through extra-parliamentary negotiations, signified the emergence of a 'hybrid form of state', a cross between parliamentarism and corporatism. He maintained that certain essential elements of parliamentarism, which is a form of state where all citizens participate equally through elections in the determination of policies which are enacted in parliament and executed by a permanent administrative staff, had been superseded 'owing to the participation in corporatist decision-making of representatives of the parliamentary executive (or government) and the participation in parliamentary decision-making and administration of corporations (e.g. unions and employers' associations)'.[20] Tripartism is, in other words, a system of rule where institutions with previously autonomous spheres of jurisdiction become formally interdependent, mutually constrained under the aegis of the state. Whilst at the general level, at which Jessop was working, this comprehends an important tendency of the last three decades, its precise significance for Britain and the Labour Party in the 1970s has not yet been grasped.

Discussions of Tripartism, or 'liberal corporatism' as it is more often called,[21] have frequently assumed that such a system is based upon a 'consensus' between labour and capital. But, certainly in Britain, this is a misleading presupposition.[22] To suggest otherwise is to confuse consensus with accommodation or compromise. The political ambience of the Social Contract was entirely distinct from that of the post-war consensus. The post-war consensus was constituted in a hegemonic ideology which presupposed the dissolution of class difference as the basic political issue. The Social Contract represented an explicit recognition of the antagonistic interests of labour and capital which, despite the rhetoric of co-operation, was little more than a working compromise to regulate class conflict. Tripartite consultation becomes a likely, even a necessary, development once the state adopts an interventionist role in economic affairs, as it has throughout Europe since 1945. Tripartism *as a form of rule*, as a governing formula, is a different phenomenon. Its adoption by the Labour government entailed a revised political practice and the partial supersession of Technocratic-Collectivism.

Tripartism in practice: the Labour governments 1974–9

The period 1974–9 was politically volatile. The grip of the two major parties over the electorate was significantly reduced, with the Labour Party having an overall majority in Parliament for only half the time. Labour failed to achieve a majority in the February 1974 election, so that Wilson's first government was carried on in the clear awareness that another general election was imminent. In the October election Labour won 43 more seats than the Conservative Party, but Nationalist, Ulster Unionist and Liberal Parties took 40 seats. Losses in subsequent by-elections removed Labour's working majority and Callaghan, who became Prime Minister in 1976, deemed it expedient to conclude a pact with the Liberal Party in March 1977.[23] The period saw a significant struggle over the question of Britain's continued membership of the EEC. Besides setting a precedent for referenda, the issue created an open division within the Cabinet and the Party, some members supporting, others, predominantly of the left, rejecting the re-negotiated terms and campaigning for withdrawal from the EEC. The left of the party, fortified by *Labour's Programme 1973* and considerable support in Conference, kept up a moderate rearguard defence of the programme on which Labour was elected, staging several embarrassing rebellions — over incomes policy, public expenditure cuts, defence expenditure and pay beds — but with little consequence for the government. On the other contentious and time-consuming issue, devolution, political alignments were less predictable. However, the principal matters before the government, on which it staked its reputation, were the management of the economy and the maintenance of social harmony.

In the first year of office, despite the economic problems resulting from the 'Barber boom', rising oil prices, international currency instability, and a huge balance of payments deficit, the government went some way towards honouring the promises made to the trade unions under the Social Contract. Pensions were raised immediately, the hated Industrial Relations Act was repealed, a variety of measures relating to conditions of labour were introduced (the Employment Protection Act, Health and Safety at Work Act), and the Housing Finance Act was removed from the Statute Book. Thereafter, few of the radical measures contained in Labour's programme were ever seriously entertained by the government:

the elimination of poverty, the promotion of social and economic equality, the increased accountability of industry, and the fundamental shift in the balance of power and wealth, were not in evidence.[24] Instead the government's principal orientation was towards providing the most favourable conditions for the recovery of British capital. In the sustained attempt to reduce inflation the Labour government concentrated on restraining wages, reducing public expenditure, and providing incentives and security for private capital investment.

One of the most remarkable aspects of government policy 1975—78 was its success in restraining wage increases. By invoking the Social Contract, and with considerable help from Jones and Foot, the government presided over a period outstanding for the low level of wage increases and the small number of days lost through industrial disputes. The various annual targets for wage increases — £6 flat rate increases in 1975—6, 4½ per cent increases in 1976—7, and the 10 per cent ceiling 1977—8 — were, with the support of the TUC, almost achieved. Certainly, prices rose faster than wages and the real standard of living of the working class fell without significant retaliation from labour. The Government espoused a wage-push theory of inflation: from 1975 onwards it consistently implied that economic recovery depended upon union leaderships regulating the wage claims of their members in fulfilment of their obligations under the Social Contract. Whether the government was intellectually convinced of the cogency of such a simple, traditional response to economic recession as cutting wages is perhaps debatable, but it remained throughout the most consistent element of economic policy. The mission to regenerate the economy and restore social harmony was made dependent upon the degree of wage restraint secured by the TUC: the government's political reputation come to depend on the index of wage increases, an unfortunate dependence when, after three years of severe restraint, wage claims increased significantly in the winter of 1978—9.

The government was far less successful in meeting the other goal of its economic policy, the regeneration of the economy.[25] An outstanding feature of the Labour government was its accommodation with capital: from 1975 onwards endless concessions were made to promote profitability in the private sector. Not only did leading members of the government make unprecedentedly candid speeches reassuring private industry that Labour had no predatory intentions, but a whole range of policies were implemented to help private enterprise through the trough of the world recession. The Industry Bill was substantially moderated through the intervention of Wilson, corporate tax rates and taxes on small businesses were reduced, price controls were steadily relaxed, and stock appreciation relief was made permanent. Economically-related social policies, like regional development, were implemented through offering favourable incentives to private profitability. But possibly the most symbolic concession to the private sector was the re-interpretation of economic planning undertaken during the government. Planning has been a motif of the Labour Party since its origins: even segments of the Party opposed to further expansion of the public sector were committed to governmental control over the activities of private industry. Planning had always implied a degree of compulsory direction of private capital by government, the critical edge of the concept being precisely that the un-restrained pursuit of profit could not possibly be in the popular interest. Yet the organization of planning after 1975 dispensed with that assumption. Shanks noted the demise of governmental direction in economic projections embodied in the NEDC document of autumn 1975, 'An Approach to Industrial Strategy', which abandoned the idea of another National Plan in favour of sector planning.[26] Shanks explained,

> The new style of planning was to be less numerical, less comprehensive, more oriented to objectives, issues, constraints and opportunities than previous plans. It was to build from the bottom up, rather than the top down. To this extent it accorded much more closely with the views of industry than had been the case in the past.[27]

In effect the government, instead of trying to impose national guidelines, would ask industry for its investment plans, accept them as the basic data, and then attempt to co-ordinate the various schemes through the NEDC. Such a method of planning hardly produced anguish in private industry.

Shanks summed up the government's economic strategy as, 'in the next upswing of the business cycle priority must be given to exports and to capital investment in the private sector; at the cost of private consumption and public expenditure'.[28] The Industrial Strategy was the name given by the government to this exercise. Under the influence of the Bacon and Eltis thesis, that Britain's problem was the shrinking of the productive sector of the economy, the major aim was to stimulate private invest-ment.[29] This entailed using the National Enterprise Board as primarily a state holding company for various firms which had failed, e.g. Rolls-Royce, Leyland, Ferranti, etc. The NEB, though it had some success in supporting worker cooperatives and fostering small, new companies, became a pale shadow of its initial conception, given insufficient funds or encouragement to take holdings in profitable private corporations. Planning Agreements, the other relic of the 1973 programme, were made voluntary and thus, with the single ill-fated exception of Chrysler, never materialized. That the Industrial Strategy would not succeed might have been anticipated. The underlying principle that capital should not be forced into doing anything it would not wish to do meant that it was unlikely that private investment in industry would rise since there were more lucrative ways of employing capital, abroad and in non-industrial spheres. So, as is often the case in recession, many companies made substantial profits but refrained from re-investing them in ways which would increase the productive sector of British industry. The government had neither the will nor the means to make them do otherwise.

Public expenditure plans began to be cut from 1975 onwards. Though there were occasional fluctuations in the trend, originating from the need to get successive phases of the incomes policy past the TUC, Healey successively pruned public spending; some £4,500 million disappeared in 1975 and 1976 alone. Subsidies on food and to the nationalized industries were phased out; there were cut-backs on housing, education, health and the personal social services, with conspicuous effects on the qualities of the services provided. The number of people employed by the state evened off after having expanded at a steady rate for more than ten years. The real level of public expenditure fell despite increased spending on unemployment relief and on schemes designed to provide temporary employment and industrial training. The government presided over a period of high unemployment, unprecedented since 1945; on official figures unemployment rose from some 3 per cent when Labour came to office to around 6 per cent in 1978. Without employment subsidies, training programmes, job creation schemes, etc., the figures would have been much higher. Such levels of unemployment, which had until recently been considered politically suicidal, along with the reductions of public spending on the social wage, might have been expected to generate considerable protest. That these conditions did nothing else but fuel wage demands in 1978—9 was a quite remarkable triumph for the government's management of social conflict, yet they were sure signs that the modes for containing conflict under the post-war settlement had withered away and that the Labour Party had radically altered its own political trajectory.

Tripartism as a political strategy

The strategy of the government is not easy to analyse in the manner I have adopted in other parts of this book because its ideological foundation was almost completely inexplicit. Uncharacteristically, for the Labour Party traditionally has offered elaborate ideological justifications for its policies, there was almost no attempt to develop a theoretical basis for its strategy. Perhaps this was because it was very difficult to square the policy objectives of the government with any recognisably Labourist tradition of thought. To have made the strategy explicit would have been to alienate further activist support for the Party. An analysis of what the Government did, and how it was presented to the media by Cabinet ministers, does however suggest a degree of coherence in the government's practice.

The strategy pursued by the government after 1974 was a truncated and shadowy form of Technocratic-Collectivism. The progressive elements of Technocratic-Collectivism, as it was formulated in the early 1960s and reformulated between 1972—4, were abandoned. The technological revolution, technicist *dirigisme*, and the pursuit of social justice, disappeared from the agenda. What remained was a strong ideological appeal for national unity and a rather tenuous hope that industrial capital could be persuaded to re-structure itself if the government could manage to contain trade union pressure. The centre-piece of the strategy, the Social Contract, turned out to be an arrangement for securing social cohesion through the compliance of labour whilst waiting for the problems of capital accumulation to be solved.

The Social Contract was a response to the collapse of the post-war settlement and, in particular, its mode of containing class conflict. Once working-class interests could no longer be accommodated satisfactorily through free collective bargaining and complementary social reform, it became necessary to develop an alternative means of conflict regulation. The solution alighted on by the Labour Party was to further incorporate the trade union leadership into the central administrative agencies of the state. Using a mixture of threats, seduction, persuasion and concession the Labour government, at least temporarily, inveigled the trade unions into guaranteeing the conditions for the restoration of social harmony.

The initial appeal of the Social Contract to the trade union interest was the concessions it offered; as negotiated in *Economic Policy and the Cost of Living* the Contract offered a *quid pro quo* to the unions, certain political policies being exchanged for wage restraint. The agreement was facilitated by two enduring traits of the trade union movement. Historically the protection of the legal position of union organizations has always tended to induce political solidarity among them. Thus the traditional antagonism between the unions and the Conservative Party, acutely aggravated by the latter's industrial relations legislation, predisposed the unions to reach an agreement with the Labour Party which entailed repealing the 1971 Act. A second tendency of union behaviour, the steadily increasing involvement of the unions with the state since the 1930s, was also exploited. The unions' sporadic search for direct political influence through cooperation with governments made a political concordat a viable proposition. While, contrary to much common wisdom, the agreement was as much an index of the unions' industrial weakness as of their corporate strength, it provided grounds for a political compromise with a Labour government.

In practice the adherence of the unions to the Contract was of major political significance but of little benefit to the unions themselves.[30] The real standard of living fell between 1975 and 1978, so that the obligations imposed by the Social Contract became embarrassing to the union leaderships. Given that unions are primarily corporate interest groups, the reputation and source of authority of the elite depends primarily upon the benefits which accrue to the membership as a whole. When, therefore, the leadership fails to act in support of rank-and-file industrial grievances, that authority is eroded. One effect of the Social Contract was that the government diverted some of the opprobrium attached to reducing real wages towards union hierarchies, a fact witnessed by the number of unofficial strikes. Nevertheless, the TUC was fairly effective in policing wage restraint and minimizing strikes, especially between 1975 and 1978. The resolution of the trade union hierarchies in this respect requires explanation. No doubt they were partly afraid of the return of a Conservative government and punitive legislation. Furthermore, the general aim of the government to increase industrial investment was in itself attractive to some unions in the manufacturing sector whose strength was being eroded by falling employment and membership. Also, the unions probably internalized some of the government's definition of what was economically possible: there was little dissent to Healey's lightly veiled threats that if wage restraint was not forthcoming the government would have to both cut public expenditure and sanction increased unemployment. Such warnings were accepted, and the idea of co-operation pending the regeneration of the economy was quite widely reiterated by union leaders. So although Trade Union Congresses remained critical of government policy, generally giving support to measures from the left's 'alternative economic strategy' and counselling the government that cutting public expenditure and increasing unemployment would jeopardize their capacity to enforce wage restraint, the unions at the national level were generally acquiescent. Indeed, though union leaderships were unable to guarantee strict control over wages in Phase III, or secure the continued compliance of their members in the winter of 1978–9, they remained committed to the idea of a compact.

Co-operation was also supposed to extend to the relationship between government and capital. Initially capital was sorely afraid of the implications of the Social Contract lest it produce socialism, nationalization, and trade union domination. To the extent that their fears were genuine, rather than inventions of parts of the press, they were soon allayed. As Marsh and Grant observed, the CBI was very hostile to the new Labour government but, after 1975, when government policy began to correspond to CBI advice, its antagonism moderated.[31] The source of the antagonism probably derived from the fact that the Social Contract was initially an agreement with the TUC and in the search for social peace the Labour

Party had first of all cemented the relationship with the unions. Having defeated the left in mid 1975, the government began to make considerable concessions to industrial capital. The role of the NEB as embodied in the Industry Act was considerably reduced; planning agreements were made voluntary and clauses relating to the disclosure of information were modified; the *Approach to Industrial Strategy* abrogated national for sector planning — 'consensus planning' being a strong guarantee of CBI interests; significant tax concessions aided capital; cuts in public spending were at least a form of symbolic appeasement; price controls were covertly relaxed; and the interests of 'small businesses' were consulted assiduously, even to the point of assigning a minister for their protection. Along with the various ministerial apologies for private capital such a combination of measures represented substantial concessions to private industry and a high degree of commitment to the maintenance of a mixed economy and the regeneration of private capital within it. Indeed, it is difficult to see how the Labour government could have done more to accommodate private capital consistent with the latter's long-term interests. When Wilson and Callaghan exulted in Labour having become the 'natural governing party' they were intimating that Labour had consciously become the party most capable of protecting capital by placating labour. That the government's policies had only a marginal effect in the re-structuring of capital indicated, however, that Labour, even when adopting such priorities, had a limited degree of control over capital. The absence of increased levels of investment, which the Labour government's policies were designed to promote, again suggested that voluntary co-operation with capital is ineffective in persuading the latter to do anything that it would not do of its own accord on the criterion of profitability. That is not, however, to deny the significance of Tripartism.

Tripartism, both as a political practice and as an ideological construct, was a response to the collapse of consensus in British society. In the attempt to foster social integration under crisis conditions the concept of the nation was made to play a vital rhetorical role. The key theme was community solidarity, the main appeal was to an ingrained patriotism, and the primary intention was to persuade people that there was a solution, in the interests of all, to the problems of the mid 1970s. The permanent attachment of the Labour Party to a sense of national unity has been eloquently described by Nairn.[32] The Party has often encouraged a social solidarity which puts nation before class, a solidarity which is promoted by appeal to established institutions, to historical traditions deriving from Britain's imperialist past, etc. Yet the Labour government and its ministers, in 1974–79, took the concept much farther than usual. Probably this was because it became almost the only ideological symbol remaining in their armoury to mobilize the labour movement behind their programmes. With the down-grading of the concern with social justice and the abandonment of schemes for directive national planning, which had rendered Technocratic-Collectivism acceptable to the labour movement, all that was left to them was patriotic symbolism. Up to a point such appeals fell on fertile ears among the British working class and elements of the Party and the unions, for the idea of the British nation is a lasting component of British hegemony. Yet patriotism must be a frail support for a Party whose strength derives from working class loyalties, especially when national unity was premised on a conception of politics which identified discrepant interest groupings as the units of political practice.

The Social Contract signified the acceptance that politics dealt with competing interests, especially with the corporate interests of capital and labour. Tripartite representation and administrative arrangements rendered it transparent that the government was concerned with mediating between the interests of employers and unions. The Social Contract was nothing if not a compromise between powerful, opposing interest groupings. These were not represented as class interests as such, rather they appeared as the interests of two umbrella institutions, the CBI and the TUC. Yet the entire vocabulary of politics marked the reality of contesting corporate interests. For purposes of legitimation an attempt was made to mask the conflict by insinuating that these were non-antagonistic interests, and that actually there was a unity of interest between manufacturing capital and productive labour. Originating in the concern with de-industrialization, the suggestion was that Britain's industrial sector was contracting and that economic viability depended upon altering the balance between the sector producing marketable products and the non-productive, service sector.[33] It was argued that growth, rising living standards and reductions in unemployment, could best be obtained by expanding industrial production, whether public or private, and that there was hence a basis of common interest between capital and labour in the productive sector. Given that the objectives of these proposals were endorsed by industrial trade unions faced by redundancies and declining memberships, the idea was fleetingly attractive. This putative identity of interest between industrial capital and its employees has a foundation in the socialist tradition in the writings of Saint-Simon, whose conception of *les industrielles* envisaged that all productive workers, managers and technicians as well as labourers, entertained common interests vis-a-vis the non-productive, parasitic classes.[34] Subterranean intimations of the nation-as-all-producers, which seemed to be the operative assumption of Tripartism, were, however, difficult to develop fully, for they were smothered by trade union common sense about industrial relations and by recognition of their consequences for unions organizing workers in the 'non-market' sector.

Thus, there was no way open for the government to establish any real consensus to underpin its practice. The genuine consensus which had been reflected in the bipartisan politics and political quietism of the post-war settlement was unrecoverable. The post-war settlement had been effective because its integrative capacities inhered in both the social and the political spheres. Though social integration in the 1950s and 1960s was fostered by political agencies, it was also reinforced in common consciousness and everyday experience by the institutions of civil society. That is to say non-political institutions, and particularly non-state agencies, confirmed the claims of the political formula. When it disintegrated, the Labour government was impelled to resort to a substitute form which was evidently politically induced and sustained entirely within state institutions. As Habermas pointed out, establishing an artificial, administratively-generated consensus is practically very difficult:[35] themes of legitimation derive their authority from established traditions and are not instantly re-creatable to administrative requirement when those traditions are broken. The Labour government tried to create an alternative mode of consensus, without the longevity and pervasiveness of the New Liberal tradition, which was founded on new institutional arrangements permitting elite representatives, of capital, labour, and government, to reach a negotiated compromise about the advancement of their respective interests. Tripartism, as a legitimating formula, required people to accept that this arrangement constituted the basis of a new consensus, a way of establishing the content of the national interest. It failed. Instead social consciousness absorbed the idea that politics is about the articulation of corporate interests, and rather naked interests at that.

In practice the Social Contract made little impact as a legitimating formula; it remained instead an administrative mechanism for containing conflict between labour and capital. Its primary function was to contain working-class pressures by creating channels of class collaboration. Class collaboration I defined above as a mode of securing the compliance of labour through the incorporation of union leaderships into the state apparatus thus enabling governments to mediate directly in the struggle over the distribution of material rewards. The effectiveness of the Social Contract as a form of rule depended directly upon the degrees of co-operation afforded by the TUC and the latter's capacity to control individual unions and their memberships. While co-operation was forthcoming, especially between 1975 and 1978, the government managed to contain the conflicts which bedevilled its Conservative predecessor. Once withdrawn, the government's strategy and credibility vanished. That this was the key to the government's success or failure is demonstrated by its declining reputation in 1979: the only thing that really changed after 1978 was the retraction of acquiescence by the TUC under pressure from inside the trade union movement. At that point no combination of favourable economic indicators were sufficient to generate popular support for the Labour Party.

The Social Contract must be considered as a new departure for British politics and the Labour Party. Firstly, the political centre was explicitly moved from the Parliamentary arena. Although the real power of Parliament had for a long time been less than was pretended, the formal acknowledgement that central political decisions emanate from extra-Parliamentary negotiation was significant. In comparative context this was by no means unusual, for quasi-corporatist arrangements are common-place in Europe.[36] But the co-existence of such structures with a two-party political system, where the Labour Party was institutionally closely bound to the unions, fundamentally affected inter-party relationships. Because the same structures are not available to the Conservative Party, they are more unstable than in other countries, which makes the issue of union collaboration politically more important. Second, the Social Contract is a distinctly new stage in the incorporation of the union elite into the British state. The permanent and obligatory nature of the 1973 agreement marked a break in the form of union-state relations. While it is true that incomes policies had existed at various times since 1948, and that they had depended upon trade unions surrendering autonomous bargaining power and policing wage claims, they were always intended to be temporary and did not confer any specific political obligations on the unions. The wages freeze of 1965—67, for example, was an interim measure which did not entail the government making any special concessions to the unions. Other tripartite arrangements, like the setting up of the NEDC under the Conservative government in 1962 and the increasing involvement of unions on Royal Commissions, were entirely consultative and reserved no powers to compel or direct. In contrast the Social Contract, while 'voluntary' by definition, was construed as a new long-term agreement which conferred new powers and obligations on the TUC. If one wishes to think in terms of theories of corporatism then the implementation of the Social Contract was the key development in the British case. Finally, Tripartism was significant as a Labour Party strategy which reformulated the relationship between class and national interests. It was a clever attempt to recast Labour politics by reducing working-class interests to the concrete demands made by the union hierarchies and fusing them with those of industrial capital. The strategy was one of integrating the working class through co-opting its elite representatives into the administrative apparatus of the state.

The contradictions of Tripartism

One contradiction runs right through Tripartism, a contradiction between the structure of class interests and the conditions for social integration in contemporary Britain. This contradiction was inherent in the initial formulation of the Social Contract and generated all its subsequent problems. The Social Contract was called into existence to resolve a crisis of legitimation apparent in the overt antagonism between unionized labour and the Conservative Party *qua* representative of the interests of capital. The Social Contract was a format which postulated that this overt clash of interests did not exist, or at least was given a wholly disproportionate importance in relation to the over-riding mutual interests of capital and labour. It presupposed that through negotiation between the representatives of capital, labour and government, a form of compromise could be reached which negated antagonism. Yet there was no attempt to transform the structures which gave rise to conflict. In practice the government did nothing to remove the pre-conditions of the crisis of legitimacy. Instead it attempted to manage the effects of structural antagonism by providing institutional arrangements which would contain or avert open class war. It dealt with effects rather than causes; it tried to introduce a cohesive political formula on the basis of a recognition of the incohesive character of society. The Social Contract placed a veneer of harmony over a yawning discrepancy between social interests which had resulted from the compound crises of the period. These crises, openly admitted to exist by the Social Reformists, were scarcely confronted: there was just the act of faith that a temporary relief of pressure on capital through wage restraint would provide the opportunity for a return to sustained growth which would, of itself, restore the conditions for harmony characteristic of the 'long boom'.

Tripartism was precarious from the point of view of economic management. The signatories to the tripartite compromise were only prepared to co-operate if it served their interests: the government proved to be somewhat ineffectual in forcing either side to co-operate beyond such a point. The most obvious feature of the government after 1975 was its incapacity or unwillingness to direct private capital. It foreswore the economic instruments which would give it directive power over capital, relying instead, almost entirely, on persuasion and incentives to increase industrial investment. The pattern of capital investment in the period was little influenced by the government. The only period when investment revived was during the few months between recessions: the hope that capital might invest in advance of an up-turn in world trade so that it could take advantage of international recovery was in vain. It was simply capitalist logic that determined the pattern of investment. In consequence the fiscal crisis of the state remained unresolved: more and more resources were poured into supporting investment at the expense of social provision. At the same time unemployment increased, living standards fell, and the British economy continued to flag. Thus the necessary conditions for the continued collaboration of trade union leaderships were eroded: the Social Contract was exposed as a mode for the containment of labour and consequently disintegrated after 1978.

The government was hardly more successful in its attempt to restore social integration and mass political loyalty. It avoided the recurrence of the open hostilities of 1972—73 but, as a long-term project, tripartite agreement was distinctly less satisfactory than the Welfare State consensus. Part of the problem was that social integration was even more directly dependent upon economic performance than before. For there was no alternative source of mass support other than the satisfaction of economistic interests: the stability of the political compromise depended entirely upon its overt results. Having denied itself the aids to integration provided earlier by complementary social reform and Keynesian intervention, and having become directly responsible for income determination, the government had no secondary supports to fall back on to mobilize popular support. This created political problems at the national level and within the labour movement.

As a political formula designed to maintain electoral support, Tripartism was unreliable. Had the government's economic policies worked out satisfactorily then the Social Contract would probably have been a resounding success and a major electoral asset when compared to the failings of the previous Conservative government. Labour could then have claimed that it, and only it, was capable of securing industrial co-operation through its agreement with the unions. But given an unsuccessful economic performance there were few other grounds on which to campaign for re-election. There was an ironic paradox as regards electoral popularity in the government's relationship with the trade unions. The government's entire strategy depended upon the special relationship between the Party and the union movement, which had the effect of indissolubly linking the reputations of both. The government impressed upon the public that its major achievements were to be measured by its capacity to restrain wage increases as a counter-inflation policy. It thereby represented the unions as rapacious, greedy, sectional organizations, the control of which depended upon the special relationship. At the same time the basis of both the relationship and Labour's electoral appeal was that the unions' general consultative and participatory role should be enlarged. The government thus encouraged the public to identify the Labour Party with selfish trade unions, potentially discrediting itself by association. If, say, Phase IV of the government's policy had held, this might not have mattered. But as it happened Labour went into the 1979 election in the worst possible circumstances, identified with the ill-reputed unions and apparently unable to exercise control over them.

Tripartism had contradictory implications as a party strategy too. It was initially widely accepted because it was yet another ambiguous, unifying formula capable of gaining the support of the left, the right and the trade unions. But sustaining that support was bound to be problematic. Union support depended upon the results of the implementation of the Social Contract and when few benefits emerged it necessarily became precarious. Particularly in intra-party affairs union opposition persisted, for even while collaboration was at its height the TUC continued to present alternative economic programmes and to support the left within Conference. So far as a second coming of tripartism is concerned — the Party officially re-endorsed the arrangements in the Liaison Committee document *Into the Eighties: An Agreement*, and in the 1979 election manifesto — the unions are likely to want more substantial guarantees from the Party leadership about the character of its policies than were forthcoming between 1975 and 1979. The implementation of Tripartism was grossly unsatisfactory to the left also, although for reasons explained in Chapter 9 they remained attached to the idea of the Social Contract.

The greatest ideological inadequacy of Tripartism in practice was its resolution of the nation—class dilemma. The Labour government increasingly opted for affirmative, nation-centred legitimations of the most traditional kind. Whether or not this made sense electorally, it was a doubtful ploy in a mass party with the self-image and structural location of Labour. For not only does much of its support, and particularly its activist support, derive from its radical pretensions, but its existence within the British political system depends upon it presenting the appearance of being the oppositional political agency. To actually become the 'natural governing party' would both upset the two-party political order and undermine Labour's capacity to perform an oppositional role.

In conclusion, Tripartism was inherently unstable. Its effectiveness as a strategy of economic management was limited because it gave insufficient power to the state to ensure the re-structuring of capital in a way consistent with the demands of labour. As a mode of social legitimation it was markedly inferior to the Welfare State consensus: it was bereft of the ideological force of the latter because the language of national unity was belied by its obvious foundation in the antagonistic interests of labour and capital. It provided no antidote to the decay of political support from the working class, for it lacked elements of social amelioration relevant to the non-unionized and disprivileged, and, as an administrative arrangement at the level of corporate elites, it was of doubtful popular-democratic legitimacy. Finally it was unfitting for bipartisan application, it not being a formula which the Conservative Party could adopt. As an affirmative strategy designed to restore the mixed-economy and the Welfare State it was rendered inadequate by the logic of economic and fiscal crisis. So though a re-markable temporary innovation, a strategy which will almost certainly be tried again, it is unlikely to be successful a second time round, either for the Party or the 'nation'.

9 The Tribune Group and the crisis of the Welfare State, 1964–79

One normal sign of capitalist crisis is the recovery of left and socialist thought, and the British experience of the 1970s was no exception. Organized loosely as the Tribune Group of the PLP,[1] the left manufactured a major revival in the early 1970s which was a direct, if delayed, result of the failure of dominant Party strategies to deal with the collapse of the post-war settlement.

What distinguished the strategy of the Tribune Group from Fundamentalism was an inversion of priorities: the primary, ethical, transformative orientation of Fundamentalism was subordinated to a class corporatist rationale. Tribunism developed around a constant concern to protect the interests of the working class, as a class, in a period of capitalist crisis. From 1966 to 1973 this objective was expressed in an inchoate, predominantly defensive form which appealed to the economistic motivations and solidaristic traditions of the trade union movement. The Fundamentalist aversion to British trade unionism was overturned, to such an extent that the left in the 1970s proclaimed that the unions were the principal institutional base for socialist advance. This new appreciation of the unions was of the utmost importance for the left for, once cultivated, it furnished a source of support within the movement which enabled the left to capture a locus of power on the NEC. Out of this came a series of proposals, adopted by the Party Conference but rejected by the leadership and majority of the PLP, which formed the basis of what became known as the 'alternative economic strategy'. The origins of that 'alternative' lay in the left's critique of Wilson's attempt to implement Technocratic-Collectivism, and in particular from the apparent preparedness of Labour governments to resolve the problems of capital accumulation at the expense of the labour movement. Primarily the alternative strategy was a programme of economic and industrial change: its objectives were, perhaps, not so very far removed from those of Wilson himself in 1964, but the means for accomplishing them were markedly different.

The reconstruction of the strategy of the left was a lengthy and painful process which fell broadly into four periods. The first was an era of transition from Fundamentalism, 1963–66, characterized by a pervasive, but increasingly cautious, optimism about the potential of Technocratic-Collectivism for securing significant social-structural transformation. This was succeeded by a period of deep despair, 1967–71, during which the PLP leadership was thought to have completely abandoned any commitment to socialism or the interests of the working class. Activist support for the Party declined and the potential socialist constituency of the Labour left departed into other organizations and fields of activity. Meanwhile the Parliamentary left was both bereft of ideas and torn by the problem, which after all had not occurred since 1931, of what to do about a Labour government whose practice they found abhorrent. The only source of comfort in this depressing scenario was the fact that the trade union wing of the movement was equally discontented. It was consolidation of the emerging alignment with the trade union interest which marked the next period, 1971–75. An era of renewed hope emanated from the combined action of the Tribune Group and the TUC to counter the policies of the Heath governments, in particular the Industrial Relations Act of 1971. The PLP leadership effectively lost the initiative in the day-to-day direction of the Party and the left managed to mobilize the larger part of the trade union movement to its cause within the Party. By 1973 the left was actually in a stronger position within the Party than at any time since the war and it succeeded in committing the Party officially to its most radical programme since at least 1934. This programme, which emanated from various policy committees under the auspices of a left-wing NEC, provided a strategic rationale for Tribunites which was both coherent in itself and officially endorsed by the Party. In the first year of government it appeared that the programme was to be followed, in a slightly diluted form, and the Tribunites were relatively well pleased. The end of this period was quite abrupt: in May 1975 the left suffered a double defeat, first in the referendum over the EEC, and second with the removal of Benn from the Department of Industry, after which the government rapidly abandoned the controversial, transformative aspects of *Labour's Programme 1973*. The subsequent years were ones in which the left fought a rearguard action against the government, but, unlike the period 1966–70, they retained some leverage through their continued predominance on the NEC and their, somewhat ambiguous, alignment with the unions. Greater preparedness to use that leverage in intra-party dispute, and renewed theoretical confidence, prevented them from falling back into despondency. Though still not prepared to threaten the government to the point of causing its downfall, the left, equipped with alternative proposals sanctioned by Conference, was able to maintain a critical stance against the government.

An era of transition: Tribune, 1963−6, and the emergence of reactive politics

The Fundamentalist left of the Party maintained its coherence and continuity for so long as the issues on which it was mobilised in the late 1950s, unilateral disarmament and Clause IV, remained alive. As CND petered out, and with Clause IV formally saved, many of the Bevanites and Fundamentalists aligned themselves behind the Technocratic-Collectivist strategy of Wilson. Pragmatic, electoral calculation and personal affiliation to Wilson aside, many shared a genuine belief in the technocratic programme as a way forward to a socialist society.[2] Technocratic-Collectivism provided a real, unifying platform for a short period, one which inspired a good deal of optimism on the left. Relief over Labour's return to office in 1964, coupled with the small parliamentary majority, ensured that criticism would be muted during the first period of the Wilson government; but when the government's policy failed to change, despite the increased majority in the 1966 election, disillusionment set in and soon became chronic.

The return to government saw a significant change in the character of left strategy. Instead of going back to first principles the Tribune Group concentrated on an immanent critique of the technocratic project: the government's performance was measured in terms of its promises. As Wilson weaved his way from disappointment to crisis, *Tribune*'s criticism followed each new step in purely reactive fashion. Though the principles of Fundamentalism were not specifically rejected they were abandoned as a major pillar of argument and replaced by a series of responses to situations. There was, nevertheless, a rationale behind left criticism, the rationale of a defensive, class corporatist strategy.

The Tribune Group took over one strand, the theoretically subordinate strand, of Fundamentalism and elaborated it in relative isolation from the other. When the technocratic strategy failed either to increase standards of living substantially, or to eliminate 'public squalor', the defence of working-class interests became a priority for those who believed that Labour's roots were in the working class. The Tribune Group, operating on such a premise, concentrated overwhelmingly on defending the economistic interests of the working class, an orientation which temporarily detracted from their commitment to socialism and altered the character of left strategy.

Before the 1964 election *Tribune* believed that its aspirations coincided with those of Wilson, whose speeches were extensively quoted in the run-up to the election.[3] It was thought that he would pursue a unilateralist policy and at least almost-socialist domestic policies.[4] Immediately after the election Michael Foot asserted that, 'Harold Wilson shows every sign that he intends to exploit (political initiative) to the maximum and with the fullest sense of urgency'.[5]

The elation of the election victory soon turned to critical apprehension for contributors to *Tribune*: doubts about the government began to be expressed as early as December 1964, when a *Tribune* editorial suggested that the government was being over-reassuring to the City, that the delay in increasing old age pensions was undesirable, and that the confirmation of the contract with South Africa for Buccaneer aircraft was ominous. Pointing to the failure to renounce contracts made by the Conservatives with private oil companies with interests in the North Sea, the editorial also observed that 'the Government seems to be developing an altogether exaggerated respect for business contracts however vicious they may be'.[6] Ian Mikardo, writing in the same issue, was also having his first doubts about the Government's intentions, though he anticipated that at the impending Conference criticism would be tempered by consideration of the inherited economic chaos, the small majority, and the short duration of the Wilson administration.[7] However, the main areas of dispute with the government – foreign and defence policy, and the distribution of rewards – had become apparent by mid 1965.

Tribunites, remaining wedded to many Fundamentalist positions on foreign affairs, trusted Wilson to pursue a principled foreign policy. They were therefore dismayed by his approach to Rhodesia, nuclear weapons, Vietnam and NATO. Over Vietnam, subservience to the aggressive Far Eastern policy of the USA produced demands for a principled 'British initiative'. And over NATO, the initial hope, that a Labour government could exert influence to transform it from 'a purely military alliance' into an 'association of States for agreement on disengagement' and for 'collective security in Europe', soon proved illusory. Membership of NATO was also irritating to the left because it was expensive, causing apprehension, exacerbated by the White Paper of February 1965, lest the failure to implement defence cuts would jeopardize domestic reforms. Thus *Tribune* argued that,

> the temptation is for the government to respond to the economic crisis by delaying the improvement of the social services. If at the same time it clings to a huge programme of military commitments, then it will have no option – slum clearance, schools, hospitals, pensions – all will have to wait while we continue to pour money into Polaris submarines, BAOR, and the whole chain of overseas bases.[8]

Some satisfaction on this issue, in July 1965, was hailed as 'The First

Victory', but, as the numbers of resolutions to Conference on defence and foreign policy suggested, these matters continued to cause much tribulation.

In the domestic sphere Tribunite criticism was concentrated on the failure to re-nationalize steel, on Prices and Incomes policy, and on the government's attempts to manage the economy. The first was condoned once it became clear that without support from the Labour MPs Donnelly and Wyatt, or the Liberals, it could not be passed through parliament with Labour's tiny majority. The other two issues remained problematic.

The left was divided between two distinct positions on incomes policy: one, bearing similarities to that of *Keeping Left*, saw an incomes policy as essential, the other, a sectional-corporatist type, resented any limitation on free collective bargaining. George Brown had relatively little difficulty in contracting the voluntary agreement embodied in the Declaration of Intent in 1964. It was acceptable to the trade union leadership because of the promised 'planned growth of wages' which was to follow from steady and continuous economic growth: and it was welcomed by the major strand in *Tribune* because it was 'to distribute the benefits of faster economic growth in a way that satisfies the claims of social need and justice'.[9] The editorial position of *Tribune* was,

> We have always believed that an incomes policy could be a real instrument of socialist advance, provided that it was always based on a firm commitment to re-duce inequality and secure real improvements in the living standards of working people. An incomes policy will only work within the context of an effectively planned economy.[10]

It was initially assumed that inequality would be reduced and that there would be a planned growth of incomes as part of the process of modern-isation of the economy. However the government's incomes policy soon became a tool of fiscal control in relation to the balance of payments problem which implied a very different rationale. Thereafter defenders of incomes policies became increasingly concerned that wage restraint was accompanied by returns for the working class. It became common to argue for greater government control over prices, and the criterion of an improving standard of living was frequently invoked. The dilemma was simple. On the one hand free collective bargaining was neither planned nor subject to the criterion of social justice. As Henry Collins argued, against Clive Jenkins, 'Collective bargaining is primarily defensive':

> Collective bargaining is an indispensable means of preventing an increased rate of exploitation. As a means of winning for the workers a significantly higher pro-portion of the wealth they create it is a non-starter.[11]

On the other hand there was a fear that in practice wage restraint was not operating in the interests of the working class. As one contribution to the debate argued,

> Controlling inflation is not the business of trade unions but of Governments; what the unions must do is use their power not just negatively to protect their individual positions in the market, but positively to pressure the Government into policies which strengthen the whole position of labour over against that of property.[12]

All the while *Tribune* also carried articles completely rejecting incomes policies. Clive Jenkins's column in particular expressed unremitting hostility to any interference with free collective bargaining. He maintained that incomes policy should be nothing more than a 'short-run *emergency* stop against inflation';[13] that the unions should not be beguiled by the veneer of non-compulsion;[14] that the National Arbitration Court was a step towards a corporate state and a threat to democracy;[15] and that free collective bargaining was 'the one consistent factor in favour of the employed as against the employers'.[16] As time passed this position found increasing favour, but in 1965—6 there was still sufficient optimism, and still a sufficient degree of uncertainty about how the National Plan would work out, for the voluntary incomes policy to retain support.

Despite reservations it was believed that a substantial majority achieved in the 1966 General Election would enable Labour to throw off the constraints of the previous two years: the first *Tribune* headline after the election victory exuded optimism — 'Socialism is right back on the Agenda'.[17]

The process of disenchantment: 'Tribune' 1966—70

Hopes raised by the election victory rapidly gave way to unmitigated gloom. The government's technocratic plans for economic modernization failed. In their place came a stringent incomes policy and proposals for industrial relations legislation, both anathema to the left. Furthermore, in the absence of anticipated levels of growth, increases in public expenditure on social welfare were restricted and benefits allocated on selective principles. Finally, the government's foreign policy in Vietnam, Rhodesia, Greece, and South Africa, and its application to join the Common Market, were abhorred.

Economic management was the main bone of contention. The development of incomes policy — from 'early warning' legislation, to wage freeze, to the Prices and Incomes Bill of 1967 — gradually reduced confidence in wage planning. It was argued that these policies failed to contribute to social justice or to the improvement of working-class living standards, and that they were part of a sustained attack on trade unions rather than on capital. Heffer, for example, in 1967 declared 'The Government has followed anti-Socialist policies and has got away from the feelings of the people. Strong Government has become synonymous with attacks on the workers' conditions instead of the entrenched power and privileges of the City of London and all that they represent.'[18]

While it was still common in 1966–8 for *Tribune* to defend the principle of incomes policy,[19] the case for a return to free collective bargaining gained many adherents. Scanlon observed that 'the most important lesson (of 1967) is that in a mixed economy the trade unions cannot and must not be an instrument of government ... (their) major job is to look after the interests of their members'.[20] The contention that free collective bargaining encouraged growth became popular; and the more cogent argument that most of Labour's planning was directed toward wage restraint rather than control over capital began to be aired.

The discontents led *Tribune* to identify itself with the interests of the unions, a tendency which was cemented when the government proposed to introduce industrial relations legislation along the lines set out in *In Place of Strife*. *Tribune*, by treating *In Place of Strife* as an unnecessary and ineffective response to Tory hysteria,[21] increasingly gained the confidence of the union interest. Panitch pointed out that the influence of the Tribune Group on the PLP Trade Union Group increased substantially in late 1968 when the former's prognosis of the effect of income legislation proved true.[22] The Trade Union Group voted in December 1968 in favour of the voluntary approach to industrial relations suggested in the Donovan Report. Once the government abandoned voluntarism and threatened to introduce sanctions against strikers, the Trade Union Group developed a momentum of its own against the government. *Tribune*, for its part, used the findings of Donovan to upbraid the government's proposals: compulsion would not work, the 'cooling-off period' would be ignored, and pre-strike ballots would increase the number of strikes.[23]

Tribunite disenchantment was also expressed in back-bench revolts, which reached enormous proportions, over public expenditure, immigration, health charges, Vietnam, Nigeria, reform of the House of Lords, the Common Market and social provision. In the field of social policy *Tribune* doggedly defended the principle of universality and decried the cuts in public expenditure on welfare services which led to the re-imposition of prescription charges, the postponement of raising the school leaving age, the reduction of the housing programme, etc. In response to counter-arguments about costs, Tribunites pointed to the size of the defence budget and suggested that it be trimmed first.

Despite a number of documents produced between 1966 and 1969, there was little evidence of a coherent Tribunite alternative: their overriding priority was to manage the economy more efficiently so that a surplus would be available with which to improve the standard of living and social services; the logic of this was similar to that of the government. 'Never Again', a statement signed by some 70 MPs reflecting on the effect of the July 1966 measures, said, 'We have sought to eliminate our balance of payments deficit only by sacrificing economic growth, deliberately creating unemployment and cutting overseas aid. This is no solution ... Only when we can maintain a payments surplus, full employment and economic growth all at the same time will our economic problems be solved.'[24] In the short run it was proposed that capital should be repatriated, further exports of capital restricted, selective import controls imposed, and defence commitments reduced. In the longer term more effective control over the City was advocated, along with a new National Plan which included a 'planned investment policy' and 'major tax changes'.

It is true that the Tribunites began to suggest more radical measures towards the end of the period: the 'Socialist Charter' of June 1968 was a more full-blooded statement than many of its predecessors, demanding 'public ownership as a real weapon for socialism' (a call which had disappeared from their literature over the previous four years), 'redistribution of wealth', 'full public accountability', an end to discrimination, 'an independent foreign policy', and a break with 'the Politics of Consensus'.[25] But this seemed to be primarily symbolic; for in early 1970 a *Tribune* editorial, commenting on the squeeze of the previous two years proclaimed, 'Only when such economic growth is taking place does the argument about what we are to do with it make sense. As socialists we wish to see growth being used to alter the basic structure of our society, particularly by increasing the amount of money which goes into public expenditure in all its forms — for that is one of the most important ways in which equality is made real in our society.'[26] By reacting primarily to the issues thrown up within the consensus they tended to reflect the concerns of the dominant segment in the Party rather than to create any clear alternative.

From 1966 onward there was an on-going debate in *Tribune* on 'What is wrong with the Labour Left?'[27] As early as June 1967 Michael Foot had claimed that 'rank-and-file morale is at an all time low'. Aware of criticism that the Labour Party was an ineffective vehicle of socialism it was felt necessary to justify the parliamentary road. Heffer announced that he regarded 'Parliament as a weapon to transform society on the basis of Socialism', and there was frequent repetition of the old adage that the left's role was to act as 'the conscience of the Party'.[28] The path from conscience to power was a troubled one, however. The tactics of the left were made plain by Foot who, when asked why the government had not pursued more radical policies, blamed the 'determination of the leaders of the Labour Party'. In the circumstances, of 1969, he saw the main glimmer of hope coming from the trade unions: 'The most hopeful phenomenon in the party is the development of greater independence in many of the trade unions, and strengthening of their political activities. I believe they can revive the Labour movement, and will revive it.'[29]

As the election of 1970 drew closer *Tribune* began to moderate its criticism and to make what it could of the occasional achievements of the government. Both Scanlon and Jones wrote pieces explaining why the Labour government should be re-elected. Jack Jones said

> We recognise the fundamental contribution which Labour is making to working people — the way in which comprehensive schooling will help to bring a fair deal at last for the children of ordinary families — the determination of Labour to protect and extend the health service, and to keep the atmosphere of the means test out of social security.[30]

But that aside, almost all the reasons given for re-electing Labour were negative: Labour should be supported because the election was about 'class issues' and it was necessary to keep the 'ugly Tories' out. Only editor Clements sounded a note of relative, and naive, optimism in saying that Labour's achievements, in a 'transitional' society, were acceptable: 'I believe that a large part of the electorate understands this fact well. To them the Labour movement is *on their side* in the struggle to gain better conditions and a better society.'[31] Presumably the majority of the electorate did not understand that, for, contrary to expectation, the Labour Party lost.

The revival of hope: 'Tribune', 1970—74

The return of a Conservative government in 1970 provided ideal conditions for the Tribunite segment to flourish. No longer faced by the embarrassing prospect of criticising a Labour government, the defence of working-class interests became easier and more congenial. The actual policies of the Heath government, the entry into the EEC, the Industrial Relations Act, and the Housing Finance Act, were excellent targets for *Tribune*. Particularly important was the attack on the established rights of the trade unions in the Industrial Relations Act. Whereas the unions had baulked at the possibility of over-throwing a Labour government they were prepared to engage in confrontation with a Conservative government. *Tribune* became increasingly optimistic during this period as the weight of the trade unions appeared to be behind attacks on the Conservatives and attempts to get the Labour Party to adopt more radical policies. The alignment of the trade unions with the Tribunite position promised a new era in Labour politics when the left might have an unprecedented degree of influence on the making of Party policy. The combination with the unions in defence of their interests was the predominant feature of the period 1970—74.

The post-mortem on the 1970 election was unenlightening. Besides a few technical criticisms of the Labour campaign it was unanimously urged that the solution was to 'get the policy of the Labour Party back on the road to socialism'.[32] With Labour back in opposition the way lay open for advancing rather more radical measures. Norman Atkinson captured the mood in stating that it had to be established that socialism was not outdated. He wanted a classless society, and industrial democracy, 'but it is our journey towards an economic democracy which remains paramount and concerns the most fundamental aspect of our overall struggle for democracy — that of the ownership of wealth'.[33]

The issue which monopolised attention in the immediate aftermath of the 1970 election was entry into the EEC. Tribunites were opposed mainly on the grounds that membership would impose enormous restrictions on planning the British economy. The Treaty of Rome was described by *Tribune* as 'a panegeric (*sic*) in favour of the idea of maintaining a modern and efficient capitalist system in Europe'. It was hence opposed on the grounds that 'there must be no surrender of our rights to plan the British economy and to make progress towards the type of socialist society which we want to see established in Britain'.[34] The Party's decision to oppose entry on the terms negotiated by the Conservatives, the outcome of a special Conference held in June 1971, greatly pleased *Tribune* not least because it signified a victory over the Labour Marketeers who, according to Atkinson, were all 'social-democrats',[35] but also because it meant the 'end of a five year bipartisan policy on Europe'.[36] The issue also produced a scapegoat for British economic ills; unemployment and underinvestment were laid at the door of 'the free-enterprise philosophy of the EEC'.[37] Arguments about sovereignty were also freely employed.

The EEC issue fell into abeyance as domestic concerns recaptured attention. *Tribune* gradually contained its obsession with growth and, as the influence of the left grew, began to press for a more radical package of measures. Returning confidence was apparent in Clements' announcement after the 1971 Conference that 'The annual conference... marks the beginning of a new era in British politics. It was a decisive move by the Labour Party away from consensus politics as a whole, and away from those in the party who have tried to convert it into a shallow, reformist grouping.'[38] The left platform had been presented, just prior to the Conference, in a document 'Forward with the Left: a statement of socialist policy issues by the Tribune Group'.[39] In economic policy it argued against the 'stranglehold of the Treasury'; against the power of the Bank of England and the City; for a more redistributive and progressive tax structure; for the nationalization of 'the big insurance companies', the aeronautical, shipbuilding and pharmaceutical industries; for the establishment of new enterprise by the state; and for a national minimum wage, equal pay, and an entitlement to retraining after redundancy. It was said that 'Only a programme as bold as this would make it possible for the next Labour government to pursue those policies of planned expansion which are urgently required if the British people are to be enabled to use to the full their skills and the wealth they have created.'[40]

The rest of the document attended in turn to questions of industrial democracy, social policy, housing and land, and foreign policy. It was suggested that, apart from repealing the Industrial Relations Act, a charter of trade union rights, including provision for trade union participation in management, should be produced. In social policy the Tories were attacked for moving away from the principle of universalism in provision, for 'a general weakening of the firm principles upon which the post-war Labour Government founded Britain's new social services'.[41] Public ownership of parts of the building industry and existing privately rented accommodation, were the main proposals on housing; and in foreign policy the statement sought a 'real spirit of internationalism', cuts in defence expenditure, an increase in overseas aid, and close co-operation with the Third World.

'Forward with the Left' was something of a hybrid combination of radical Technocratic-Collectivist and traditional socialist policies.The demand for economic growth to maintain employment levels and finance more social services was typical of the former; while demands for redistribution of wealth, public ownership of profitable enterprises and industrial democracy, were part of the latter. The same mixture of policies was advocated by Allaun in the conclusions to *No Place Like Home*,[42] a study of housing, in which he suggested that growth, along with a wealth tax, defence cuts, and the nationalisation of land, should be the basis of a Labour housing policy. The aim was to combine growth with socialist reforms but the latter without the former was never considered. This indicated something of the rationale of the general political strategy; the first priority was to protect the living standards of the working class, the second was to introduce socialist measures.

It was this order of priorities which led to criticism of *Tribune* from elements of the Labour left. 'Forward with the Left' was accused of being weak and 'mealy mouthed' within the correspondence columns of *Tribune*.[43] Other organs of the Labour Left, *Militant* and *Voice of the Unions*, were suspicious of the moderation of *Tribune*. A 'Voice' editorial of March 1972 maintained that 'the Parliamentary puppets have shown themselves incapable of moving towards socialism, however slowly. The Unions must now step in and show them how to do the job'.[44] Both in attitude and in language *Tribune* appeared to be outflanked by militant rank-and-file opinion which put far more emphasis on workers control and on punitive measures against capital.[45] In response, Fletcher summarized the Tribunite position: the party was essential to overcome the sectional interests of each union since 'legislation serving the general interests of the working class, as distinct from the particular interests of sections of it (which are better bargained for), thereby becomes possible'.[46]

Tribune expressed increasing affection for the TUC and the trade unions. The almost total opposition between the trade union interest and the Conservative government permitted *Tribune* to bury ambiguities about whether or not to support an incomes policy by concentrating on the issue of a threat to the traditional legal rights of unions. The old antagonisms between the left of the Party and the trade unions now seemed to be resolved. Earlier criticisms of the restrictive nature of the union interest were forgotten as the links between the unions and the Party were eulogized. Heffer, for example, located the Labour Party: 'despite everything, it is the mass party of the British working class precisely because it is based on the unions'.[47] Atkinson expressed his faith in the unions when arguing for common action by the TUC and the Labour Party against the Conservatives: 'it must now be the trade unions who take the leading role in protecting working class interests. They must be backed by bold and effective Parliamentary argument'.[48] And *Tribune*, reflecting on the TUC Conference of 1970, went so far as to say that 'the trade union movement which exists in Britain today bears hardly any resemblance to the movement which existed say 10 years ago'.[49] *Tribune*, throughout the years of the Conservative government, steadfastly supported all trade union action, against the Industrial Relations Act, against the National Industrial Relations Court, and against attempts to administer an incomes policy. Thus the alignment of the left and the unions was reinforced.

At the same time, however, the left was beginning to formulate a more constructive position. Hatfield, in *The House the Left Built*, described the manoeuvring inside the Party which led to Left majorities — in Conference, on the NEC, and thus on various policy committees — producing the radical document, *Labour's Programme 1973*. Pitt of the Research Department, Benn as Chairman of the Party 1971—72, and Holland as an external adviser, all had important parts to play in the formation of an economic and industrial policy which placed overwhelming emphasis on the need for greater state control over economic affairs. This impulse revived emphasis on public ownership, producing very controversial debates about committing a future Labour government to nationalizing twenty-five, or even two hundred, leading private companies.[50] But overall the proposals were directed towards the broader objective of making macro-planning more effective.[51] Out of these deliberations came Planning Agreements, the National Enterprise Board, and a whole range of policies which would, if implemented, have made substantial changes in the character of British society. Not surprisingly, Tribunites were delighted, and Clements, looking forward to an election, was not altogether deluded in claiming that 'For the first time Labour has a comprehensive answer to the ills of our society. It is a direct attack on the failings of the capitalist system as it exists in Britain. It is not popular with the media, but it provides the real basis for changing society.'[52]

But majority support in Conference and the TUC for NEC policy was not a sufficient guarantee of social change. It was not simply a question of the internal ambiguities of the proposals, between incentive structures required for growth in a private economy and promises of redistribution and industrial democracy, but also one of persuading a Labour government to implement those policies. Tribunites shared the Fundamentalist belief that the Labour Party was the repository of socialism and, hence, rejected the dominant view of political representation: the Party, they believed, should be representative of its members, especially of its rank-and-file activists and trade union supporters, rather than of the electorate or the nation. Towards this end a Tribune Group pamphlet, *Labour — Party or Puppet?*, made a series of suggestions about improving party democracy. It argued that the decline in the number of party activists between 1964 and 1970 was due to a lack of internal democracy. As a remedy it proposed that Conference decisions should be made binding, that both ministers and MPs should be made accountable to Conference, that procedures for the selection of parliamentary candidates should be improved, and that the NEC should be elected by Conference. Though fruitless at the time, the proposals provided the basis for an extended campaign when the next Labour government failed to act in accordance with the Party programme.

Tribune's judgment about the politics of power within the Party was fairly realistic. However, when it came to taking a position on the key issue of 1973, the making of the Social Contract, the left, by endorsing it, undermined its own source of renewed influence. *Economic Policy and the Cost of Living* was welcomed as a formalization of the links between the unions and the Party: 'it is an acknowledgement that, organically, the two movements cannot exist in separation'.[53] The agreement was thought to signify a new relationship between the two wings of the labour movement and to be a radical document resulting from rank-and-file pressure. Reinforced by the apparent shift to the left among key union leaders,[54] the Tribunites believed that the next Labour government would be compelled to adopt policies far more radical than those pursued between 1964 and 1970.

Tribunites and the Labour government, 1974—9

The crisis tendencies, and the demise of Social Reformism, opened up considerable opportunities for the Tribunites. Between February 1974 and May 1975, despite some reservations about the government's foreign policy and defence estimates, Tribunites were optimistic about the prospects of social change. The government was committed to a radical programme,even though the two manifestos of 1974 were diluted forms of *Labour's Programme 1973*. Benn at the Department of Industry was preparing to mount a strong NEB, to enforce Planning Agreements and to sponsor industrial democracy and co-operative enterprises. It was believed that these new instruments would extend state control over the economy and revive British industry in a mode consistent with democratic socialist convictions: thus the White Paper, *The Regeneration of British Industry*, and the Industry Bill of February 1975 were well acclaimed in *Tribune*.[55] Also, in the early days of the administration, the trade unions seemed sympathetic to left policy. This was the principal source of optimism during the first fifteen months of government. Clements for example, welcomed the Social Contract because it rejected a wage-push theory of inflation, thereby strengthening the solidarity between the Party and the unions: 'We have seen the revival of the Labour movement since it turned its back on the divisive policies which wrecked the chances of the last Labour Government. For the future, the links between the trade unions and the party must be made even stronger. For it is in this alliance that the only real chance of social progress exists in Britain.'[56] The conviction that 'the trade union, Labour link (was the) best guarantee for a socialist future'[57] was strengthened by the TUC's *Economic Review*, which advocated economic and social policies broadly coinciding with those of *Tribune*,[58] and by Jack Jones, then the most influential trade union leader, who wrote several articles suggesting full support for *Tribune* strategy.[59] The internal balance of power within the movement still sustained a left majority on the NEC. And, the first year of the government produced various pieces of legislation which were sincerely welcomed.

The end came in May 1975 with the referendum over continued membership of the EEC. Labour's promise, in the October 1974 Manifesto, to hold a referendum on the renegotiated terms for British membership was itself a significant victory for the left. Throughout 1974—75 *Tribune* campaigned for British withdrawal on the grounds that membership was largely responsible for the economic crisis and that it hampered adequate, corrective measures. When a majority of the Cabinet came out in favour of the new terms the left made the issue one of confrontation within the movement. A substantial defeat in the referendum was a major set-back for the left; the balance of power within the Party swung back in favour of the parliamentary leadership and resulted in Benn, an anti-marketeer, being removed from the key post of Minister for Industry.

Tribunites campaigned for the 'alternative economic strategy' — a much more sophisticated version of the economic measures recommended between 1967 and 1969 - which had matured within the Home and Industrial policy committees of the NEC.[60] The details of the alternative economic strategy varied: *Labour's Programme 1973* gave an abbreviated outline; the columns of *Tribune* and TUC *Economic Reviews* after 1974 elaborated on the Programme, and Holland's *The Socialist Challenge* presented the most comprehensive theoretical justification for it. One major premise of the government's diagnosis of the deep causes of inflation was accepted, that insufficient investment in British manufacturing industry prevented economic growth, but the government's solution was rejected.

The primary objective of the alternative strategy was to revive economic growth through asserting effective public control over the economy. While other segments of the Party began to proclaim that all governments were congenitally incapable of managing the economy, the Tribunites pressed for more rigorous planning and control. They argued that the current problems merely demonstrated the limitations of Keynesian techniques and that more comprehensive controls were required to counteract the long-term structural weakness of British manufacturing industry. The main defect of Keynesian thinking was that it obscured the importance of controlling production: as one Tribune Group statement on the economy put it:

> Such thinking challenged the socialist claim that only the public management of the production and supply of goods and services could ensure economic efficiency and social justice. It implied that, subject to a general role as spender, umpire and planner and within a general framework of progressive taxation, the state could achieve the ends of socialism with only a limited degree of direct intervention in industry.[61]

Such analysis was mistaken, it was argued, because it failed to grasp the implication of the concentration of private capital in large, monopolistic, multi-national companies: 'we live in a society dominated by multi-national monopolistic companies where less than 100 are leaders or potential leaders in terms of prices, investment, job creation, trade and so on'.[62] Tribunites, at last, began to confront directly the problems posed by multi-national corporations. They argued that such companies had established a 'new domination' over the British economy because, not being subject to market constraints, they were immune to the effects of Keynesian intervention. It was imperative, therefore, to develop distinctive ways of controlling their activities. The most favoured instrument was the NEB which, provided with very substantial funds to invest across a wide range of profitable industries, could 'gain the power to carry out its function of breaking the monopoly power of the multi-nationals, encouraging import substitution, bringing jobs to the regions and helping the Government with its planning in each sector'.[63] In effect Tribunites endorsed the initial conception of the NEB as it was presented in *Labour's Programme 1973,* despite its ambiguities. They also pressed for Planning Agreements as instruments for controlling multi-nationals, though these were advocated as much for their capacity to increase the flow of inform-ation to workers and the state as for their directive capacity *vis-a-vis* private capital.[64] Their proposals implied a considerable expansion of the public sector, though more for reasons of enhanced public control than as a matter of general principle regarding ownership. Demands for nation-alization were selective, mostly restricted to bestowing upon the NEB a 'controlling interest' in one profitable privately-owned company in the most important industrial sectors in order to break oligopolistic prac-tices.[65] Of the specific candidates for public ownership two, the aircraft and ship-building industries, were chosen on the orthodox grounds that they were only viable on the strength of public finance, and the other, pharmaceuticals, was selected because it had only one major consumer, the National Health Service, from which it was deriving unacceptably high profits.[66] The main exception to this selectivity was the require-ment that banks, pension funds and insurance companies should be taken into public ownership to secure the finance for industrial invest-ment. Universally, Tribunites condemned the City and finance capital for employing potential sources of increased funds for industrial devel-opment in foreign investment and property speculation.[67]

The primary rationale of the alternative economic strategy was to stimulate investment in manufacturing industry, it being believed that that was the only way to revive economic growth and substantially reduce unemployment: investment control, import controls and the re-patriation of capital were primarily means to that end. But behind the detail of economic and industrial policy lay a series of social object-ives, primary among which were the protection of the living standards of the working class, the reduction of levels of unemployment, and the maintenance of public spending.

In the 1970s the left became the principal defenders of public expend-iture on both social and economic services. The early budgets of Healey were received with only mild criticism, mainly on the grounds that they failed to reflate the economy fast enough. After 1975, however, as deflationary budgets came to include cut-backs in public expenditures, the imposition of the cash-limits system on public agencies, the aband-onment of some commitments in the field of social reform, and a gradual move towards substituting income tax relief for social benefits, *Tribune* became increasingly hostile. Partly this derived from a conviction that raising public expenditure was one way of reflating the economy in a period when capital investment was not forthcoming;[68] the growing influence and application of monetarist theory actually brought forth cryptic accolades of Keynesian wisdom in the columns of *Tribune* in 1978.[69] But it also derived from the belief that raising public expenditure on community services was a distinctive and essential part of a Labour or socialist programme; as Orme put it, 'the Labour Movement must not turn away from its commitment to increasing public expenditure as a fundamental socialist policy'.[70] In this respect the Tribunites sought to occupy the ground vacated by the Social Reformists; preserving the progressive achievements of the post-war settlement and seeking the restoration of full employment became, singularly, the terrain of the left.

The Tribunite determination to maintain levels of social expenditure was highly dependent upon the success of their policies to reflate the economy because even with severe defence cuts and a stringent wealth tax the problem of raising sufficient revenue remained. In this respect the alternative strategy bore some striking resemblances to the Technocratic-Collectivist project of 1964 which, I argued earlier, was necessarily unfeasible in the crisis conditions of the late 1960s and early 1970s. As it was never implemented one can only speculate as to whether the addition of much stricter controls over capital would be sufficient for the alternative strategy to succeed where Technocratic-Collectivism failed. Perhaps protectionist import controls would have led to retaliation from Britain's trading partners; and, more probably, the strategy would have led to a flight of foreign capital and a rapid decline in the value of sterling. On the other hand Britain was in no sense a poor country; as *Tribune* frequently pointed out,[71] and the government implicitly recognized, the problem was the use of resources. It is quite conceivable that sensitively directed investment in industry, protected from foreign competition, would have restructured the economy and averted many of the consequences of the government's anti-inflation policies. Less a matter of speculation is the character of the alternative strategy through which the echoes of Technocratic-Collectivism reverberated. The logic was very similar: stimulate growth through modernising and increasing the efficiency of British industry so as to provide the funds for extending social provision. Plan for growth. This is not to deny that the Tribunite strategy of 1974 was more radical than that of Wilson in 1964. The technical apparatus for controlling private capital, the determination that capital should be forced to act in accordance with state planning, the egalitarian ethos of plans for social spending and, indeed, the social logic of the alternative strategy were quite distinct. The ultimate priority was not to reinvigorate capital but to protect the interests of the working class, in particular those employed in productive industry.

The demand for the development of industrial democracy, which figured universally in policy-packages, was another indicator of Tribunite concern with working-class interests. The precise form of acceptable schemes of industrial democracy was a source of considerable uncertainty and disagreement. *Labour's Programme 1973* was enthusiastic but agnostic;[72] Benn put great emphasis on the accessibility of information to workers;[73] Holland analysed various schemes and came to the conclusion that workers should decide for themselves;[74] and Sedgemore opted for extended information through planning agreements, 50–50 representation on boards, and the extension of collective bargaining into new spheres.[75] Promoting the cause of industrial democracy, in public as well as private enterprise, was probably the major contribution of Benn to the left strategy. Benn was a powerful advocate of Wilson's policy for scientific and technological revolution in the early 1960s until he became aware that it co-existed awkwardly with popular, democratic control. From the late 1960s onwards he began to campaign for wider democratic control, recognizing that expert planning and the technocratic ethos were anti-democratic even if state control were informed by working-class, rather than capitalist, interests. Hence he raised issues of government secrecy, the power of the media, the social consequences of technological change, democracy in the Labour Party and the absence of worker control in industry.[76] Later, as a Cabinet minister, between 1974 and 1979, he encouraged the creation of worker co-operatives, tried to facilitate disclosure of information through planning agreements, and also became closely associated with the Institute for Workers Control. Despite their differences, all these schemes went beyond those token-forms of profit-sharing and minority representation on company boards which are consistent with managerial autonomy and the pecuniary interests of shareholders. Others among the Tribune Group were, however, more sanguine about industrial democracy. Notably, Heffer registered scepticism in an article which was as much concerned to defend the traditional, independent functions of the unions as to encourage experiments in industrial democracy, workers control or self-management. He avowed 'I believe that the role of the trade unions is one of protecting and extending the rights of working people by negotiating wages and conditions, of being a shield against management and governments, whatever form society takes'.[77]

He continued:

trade unions must remain independent and that means they must escape the en tanglements of management as well — no matter where that management is draw from. It may well be essential, even in a self-management form of society, for the unions to be a check and balance against the actions of the workers they have elected.[78]

This scepticism was partly shared by the trade unions, for in some ways industrial democracy threatened to shift power away from the leadership towards the rank-and-file. Certainly the cause of industrial democracy was granted little space in TUC Economic Reviews. The issue was potentially divisive to the left, signifying the rather different priorities of Heffer and Benn; and it also indicated one of the problems associated with the close identification of the left and the trade union interest.

Somewhat similar problems occured over the Social Contract. The left interpreted the Social Contract as the basis of working-class solidarity against capital. While absolutely committed to it, they found the Social Contract something of a mixed blessing. On the positive side it provided a way of circumventing the issue of incomes policy. Tribunite economic policy statements made only occasional reference to incomes policies, tending usually to imply that restraint would be necessary for a short while, until the beneficent effects of the alternative strategy blossomed forth. In exchange, tight price controls and food subsidies would operate to offset the effects of such restraint. The Social Contract also represented a formal acknowledgement of trade union support for the left policies adopted by Conference. On the negative side, though, the TUC was committed to an accommodation with the government rather than the Tribune Group. When the government ignored the policies of Conference, and the trade union leaders continued to collaborate, the Tribunites were presented with an awkward dilemma. While in other circumstances they might have protested vehemently that the Contract was actually operating as a mode of wage control and that union members were getting no real returns because of the very unsatisfactory bargains being struck by their leaders, in the event they could not, for fear of endangering the alignment with the unions. Their embarrassment was multiplied by the retreat of Jack Jones from leading advocate of the alternative strategy to major defender of the government's policies.[79] By late 1977 *Tribune* began to berate the government for not keeping its side of the bargain,[80] but still felt constrained to uphold the principle of the Social Contract and to remain silent about the part played by the trade union leadership in its continued operation. *Tribune* was thus rather relieved when the TUC refused to accede to a fourth round of incomes policy covering the period 1978–9, for it was then able to revert to the stance of defending trade union interests against the government.

The other major campaign fought by the Tribunites concerned intra-party democracy. The period 1975–9 forced the left to re-evaluate its long-sustained position on the political channels through which socialism might emerge in Britain. The Fundamentalists had thought that winning majority support within the Party for left-wing policies would be a sufficient condition. Their theory of political process and social change was based on the notion of the mass party — that parliamentary elections were the means for choosing between the programmes of parties, and that a party with a parliamentary majority was effectively mandated to implement that programme. Since Labour Party policy was authorized in Conference the main task was to get left-wing policies accepted there. The illusory nature of this theory was exposed when government policies after 1975 diverged completely from those of Conference and the NEC. The situation was different from 1964—70, for then Conference had supported the Government's avowed objectives and was thus limited to *ad hoc* expressions of discontent. After 1975 it was clear that the government was flouting the traditional understanding of the authority structure of the Party. For the left this confirmed a growing suspicion that acceptance by the Party of a socialist programme was no guarantee of its implementation by a Labour government. This realization motivated their various campaigns to re-organize the structure of the Party: the Campaign for Labour Party Democracy;[81] the prolonged and bitter disputes about re-selection of sitting MPs; and the more recent proposals for making Labour governments more accountable to Conference, through direct election of the leader and the Cabinet, and the transference of responsibility for writing the election manifesto to the NEC. The necessity of fighting these issues was undeniable, for if the formal prerogatives of Conference were rescinded the chances for democratic socialism would become extremely slim, since Conference was the only locus of power which the left was likely to command in the foreseeable future.

Tribunism and the balance of power

The strategy of the left between 1964 and 1978 eludes simply summary Its changing character derived from the crisis tendencies of British society and economy, and their effects on the labour movement. Continuities in left strategy in this period emanate primarily from discontents with the practices of Labour governments. Whereas the precipitating factor behind changes in strategy among the dominant segments in the Party has tended to be their concerns to create a formula for the harmonization of the interests of capital and labour, the drive behind left strategic reconceptualization has been to ensure that Labour governments act in favour of labour. The left devoted most attention to the apparent unwillingness of Labour governments to promote the interests of the working class, especially of union-organized labour. Tribunite positions on incomes policy, increasing state control over the economy, industrial relations legislation and intra-party democracy, derived from that central rationale.

With this objective in mind, key aspects of Fundamentalism were discarded. Some impulses were retained, of course: particularly there were continuities in foreign policy, in the determination to extend public ownership and control of the economy, and in basic sympathies with the working class. But three important differences can be detected; ethical socialism was abandoned, the potentiality of trade unionism was completely re-evaluated, and the strategic priorities of Fundamentalism were inverted.

Transformative concerns, expressed as arguments based on socialist ethics, diminished, being replaced by practical calculations as to the effect of policy measures on the standards of living of the working class. As these latter concerns grew after 1966, the left at first did little more than react against the consequences of Technocratic-Collectivism. *Tribune* became absorbed in the technical arguments about programmes for growth, incomes policies and devaluation, which became the *lingua franca* of British political debate in the late 1960s. The left retained its initial optimism that scientific and technological revolution could provide the basis for rapid socialist change if only the government were more determined. The growing discontents of the period between 1967 and 1970 expressed themselves primarily in terms of the failure to achieve the programme of 1964, yet without ever developing a critique of the basic logic of Technocratic-Collectivism. In such circumstances the left was primarily rebelling against the consequences of government strategy, particularly for the organized working class.

The immediate result of this was that the left re-introduced the concept of class into its discourse. The Labour Party had dispensed with the concept of class in the early 1960s, but changes in economic fortunes, and the critical response to government after 1966, revived it. Class lay at the centre of the left's social analysis, it being taken for granted both that class antagonism was an ineradicable characteristic of capitalist society, and that the Labour Party should take working-class interests as the root of its policies. Nowhere was this more clearly expressed than in Heffer's *The Class Struggle in Parliament*.

Heffer's book, addressed to the history of industrial relations legislation in the period 1965–73, was the most elaborate formulation of a class-corporatist orientation. The position expressed was a relatively 'natural' working-class response to economic recession: it was not sectional-corporatist, for it relied on an analytic frame of reference in which the concept of class, and the identity of interests of the working class as a whole, was central. A conception of class struggle entered the theoretical scheme. Heffer said,

I have to answer those in the Labour Movement who mistakenly believe that the class struggle is dead. It is the acceptance of this idea that has led to immense problems within the Labour Movement and at one time during Labour's period in office 1964–70 almost caused the trade unions to split away from the political party it formed.[82]

Heffer professed,

I begin from the premise that because we live in a class society, based on private ownership, there is a fundamental struggle between those who own and control industry, and those who do not. In other words, the class struggle is a reality.[83]

Such premises had quite distinct corollaries: a refusal to accept that either the state or the law was neutral in its intervention in class relations,[84] an awareness that 'the post-war days of consensus politics have largely been destroyed',[85] and a general support for industrial militancy so long as it united rather than divided the working class. As Heffer said, 'I am in favour of strikes that unite the workers for better conditions, or pay, or security of employment. I am not in favour of strikes that divide, setting one group of unions against another.'[86]

The gist of the position was that class conflict was endemic to capitalist society, that industrial disputes were but one manifestation of that conflict, and that the Labour Party existed to advance the interests of the working class in the political arena.

But though the concept of class was used more frequently and critically by the Tribunites than by any other segment since the war, there was little clarification of the character of the class or the nature of its interests. In fact the concept of working-class interest appeared confused, and was conflated with the interests of the trade unions. The conflation of class and union interests was fostered by events between 1967 and 1974: both in the struggle for dominance within the Party, and in projects for intervention in social conflict, it served the Tribune Group well to identify itself with the union interests. But the validity of such an identity of interest is dubious. The class-corporatist concentration on protecting the economistic interests of male, unionized wage-labourers necessarily restricted the Tribunites' potential support and the range of their social criticism. *Tribune* showed limited concern with student issues in 1968, almost no cognizance of the fact that half of the working class was female, and an ignorance of the fact that a large proportion of male workers were not union members.

The postulate of a common interest among trade unionists was itself suspect. The history of British trade unionism has led to systematic structured divisions between unions and their respective memberships. The existence of craft rather than industrial unionism continues to create as many problems for working-class politics as for industrial management.

The craft unions of the aristocracy of labour retain a concern with differentials of income and prestige, which hinders any attempt to rationalize or reconstruct a national wage structure independent of conventional or market constraints. The traditional sectionalism of British trade unions also makes it extremely difficult to talk simply of working-class interests, or to equate union and class interest. It was not accidental that it was over *In Place of Strife* and the Industrial Relations Act that the TUC was able to act in the most concerted fashion in defence of the legal rights and privileges of unions, for this was one of the few topics on which an immediate, common interest among unions was recognized.

In some ways the difficulties of defining exactly what constituted working-class interests were circumvented by simply endorsing the prevailing TUC definition of the collective interests of the unions. This depended largely on the economic conditions pertaining at any particular time and the stance of government towards the trade unions. Thus, while the economy, though facing balance of payments difficulties, was still expanding during the late 1960s the segment's task was conceived as increasing the working-class's share of rewards; when governments were attempting to introduce industrial relations legislation the task was to defend the established legal status of the unions; and when the economy was contracting and real wages falling in the mid-1970s, the task was to try to maintain existing standards of living and reduce unemployment. Such strategic orientations were defensive in the sense that they did not challenge the fundamental structures of the existing social order: the primary concern was with the corporate interests of the class rather than the framework of relations which encompassed them. The absence of an independent and extensive criterion of what constituted working-class interests led to situations where the left was subject to permanent ambivalence, rapid reversals, or embarrassing silence on issues of principle. One illustration of this was the incapacity of Tribunites to resolve internal disagreements over the status of incomes policies. Both positions, one advocating free collective bargaining, the other commending wage control as an element of socialist planning, made coherent sense, but were mutually incompatible. Though submerged during the period of the Conservative government, because the Industrial Relations Act was far more threatening to the unions than wage restraint, the disagreement was never resolved. *Tribune* vacillated. Initially supporting planning, it later came round to the defence of free collective bargaining when that became overwhelmingly popular with rank-and-file and official unionists. While never totally committed to a return to free collective bargaining, and despite some awareness that the immediate satisfaction of union demands and the pursuit of a transformatory socialist programme were not necessarily compatible, the Tribunites remained undecided. One reason for them welcoming the Social Contract was that this basic inconsistency was, in theory, removed by prior and 'voluntary' agreement with the TUC. However, when the trade unions appeared satisfied by collaboration with the Labour government in 1975—8, the left was temporarily disarmed.

The great advantage of representing the trade union interest in parliament was that it improved the left's position in the balance of power within the Party. The Tribunites' capacity and willingness to act as representative of the union interest derived partly from the character of the new personnel of the Labour left after 1964 whose composition, as Heffer pointed out, was considerably different from Bevanite days:

> The Tribune Group of today is very different from the Bevanite group of yesteryear. The Bevanites were mainly academics with a few trade unionists. They had slender links with the trade union movement. Today, the reverse is the case. The Tribune Group is largely made up of trade union MPs, many of them past and present National Executive Officers of their unions or ex-shop stewards, branch officials, etc. They retain close personal links with some of the trade union leaders. They understand industry and have participated in class struggle at the factory level. It is this close association of trade unionists with the Left in Parliament which holds out great hope for the future of the Labour Party. Even if the Party as a whole has not got the balance correct, the Tribune Group of MPs has. When the Tribune Group is even more firmly linked with the Trade Union Group (a process continually developing), it is clear that we shall see a major advance on the socialist front in Britain.[87]

The implications of this observation were clear; the more experienced trade unionists there were in the PLP, and the closer the alliance between the Tribune Group and the Trade Union Group, the more likely was the Labour Party to represent faithfully its true social constituency. This was the basis of left strategy and tactics in the late 1960s and early 1970s which, for a few years at least, succeeded in changing the balance of power in the Party in their favour. Changes in the political awareness of the unions themselves, the introduction of legislation which threatened the traditional rights of the unions, and the new situation of labour in the era after affluence, all strengthened class-corporatist appeals.

Realizing that they were increasingly affected by political decisions some unions changed their attitudes to sponsorship in the 1960s. The AEU, for example, began a campaign to improve the quality of their sponsored MPs;[88] and the TGWU considered censuring those of their sponsored members who voted in parliament against union policy on incomes in 1967.[89] While the direct power of unions over their sponsored members remained slight, the Trade Union Group, of its own accord, was always likely to share prevalent views of the nature of the union interest. Additionally, a shift in perspective among trade union leaders[90] and an increase in social demands by the unions[91] fuelled Tribunite optimism. They were able to maintain that they had the support of key figures in the powerful unions and that their policies corresponded most closely to those espoused by the TUC. None of the other segments, neither Social Reformists who were advocating the abandonment of formal links between the Party and the unions, nor the technocrats, who, prior to the arrangement of the Social Contract, were still in disgrace over *In Place of Strife*, were able to provide a basis for the satisfaction of union interests or to promise any future workable agreement. The Tribunite opposition to the EEC, concern for full employment, growth and an improvement of working-class living standards, and basic sympathy with the plight of the unions and their members, increased the sense of identification.

The zenith of the alliance between unions and the left came in the years 1971–73, articulated in hostility to governmental encroachment upon the traditional rights of trade unions. The trade unions were forced to produce something of a united front against the Conservative government; even those union leaders who believed that co-operation with the government was necessary realized that co-ordinated TUC action had, at least temporarily, to take precedence over the traditional sectionalism of union activity. The policies of the Heath government created a degree of political unrest unknown since the 1930s. Confrontation with the unions, imposed incomes restraint, and the desperate and ineffective rush for growth, provided ideal conditions for a renewal of class politics. Whereas the Fundamentalists had struggled in most unfavourable circumstances, the Tribunites were presented with conditions of industrial militancy and nascent political discontent. As social consensus gave way to social conflict, political apathy to political disillusionment, and economic growth to economic contraction, the unions became central institutions in the emergent class conflict.

In the struggle against the Industrial Relations Act the Tribunites were in an ideal position to represent the interests of the trade unions. Whereas other segments of the Party might be expected to suffer some embarrassment at opposing industrial relations legislation, the Tribunites, having opposed *In Place of Strife*, could make out a strong case for having always rejected any infringement of the traditional legal rights of the trade unions. As Heffer's account illustrated, the Tribunites did all that was in their power as a parliamentary group to obstruct the Act.[92] The existence of the Act also provided them with grounds for supporting trade union militancy in all its manifestations; they opposed the National Industrial Relations Court for being a political court, and they proclaimed the unacceptability of 'class law'. The trade unions themselves, fighting both over their legal position and the fall in their members' real living standards, could hardly spurn whatever legitimacy for their actions they could derive from the Tribune Group. It might be said that this period witnessed the return of the Labour Party to its trade union origins. For the period of the

Conservative government defensive class corporatism and a defence of trade union interests coincided.

The election of a Labour government in 1974 re-posed the problem of the relationship between the left, the union interest, and the Party leadership-in-government. Initially the Tribunites saw the Social Contract as a progressive form guaranteeing union support for a radical strategy: they believed that the unions would use the *quid pro quo* to press for structural change in accordance with the radical objectives of the Party Programme and the Liaison Committee document. When, later, the Social Contract proved to be a means to restore social cohesion and induce the union leadership to collaborate in the tripartite compromise, the Tribunites faced a major dilemma. They wanted the Social Contract in principle, and they needed the sympathy and support of the unions, but the outcome appeared neither radical nor in the interests of the working class. All that they were in fact able to do was to wait until the compromise broke down of its own accord — in the sense that the terms of the compromise, rather than the compromise itself, became unacceptable to trade union leaders pressed by their own memberships to counter declining standards of living in the winter of 1978—9. One reason for hesitancy was the ambiguity of the Tribunite conception of class struggle. Sections of the Parliamentary left often seemed to want such struggle to be waged only within Parliament. The paradox of this was not so much that the Labour left sought a peaceful and consensual transition to a socialist society, but that despite its influence in this period being founded upon industrial militancy at the first opportunity it supported measures designed to contain conflict. Indeed even those Tribunites who considered that extensive mobilization outside conventional party political channels was necessary for a transition to socialism failed to resist the stultifying effects of the Social Contract. A second reason, equally basic, for acquiescence was their undue optimism about trade unionism as an agency of radical social change. The problem was one of presenting a transitional strategy to convert defensive, class-corporatist solidarity into an autonomous movement for social change but, not for the first time, the economistic protest of the unions was mis-identified as socialist opposition. Saville coined a useful phrase, 'fractured consciousness', to describe similar orientations among trade union leaders of the late nineteenth century.[93] He pointed out that the union leaders of that time were highly militant in industrial disputes but at the same time were staunch supporters of the Liberal Party; their industrial concerns seemed divorced from their political aspirations. The danger inherent in the left's preparedness simply to follow the line of the trade union interest was that economistic opposition might never translate itself into a political impetus for change. The task of forming such a bridge was given to the programme associated with the alternative economic strategy.

Socialism, class corporatism and contradictions

The pervasive orientation of left strategy after 1964 was its class corporatism, but at the same time there remained an explicit attachment to a socialism predicated upon altering patterns of both property ownership and industrial authority. Until the early 1970s the left had no coherent conception of how these two elements of its strategy could be integrated. Rather like Fundamentalism, though with its priorities inverted, there was little connection between the two objectives of defending the interests of the working class and promoting a socialist transformation. Increasingly this disjuncture was confronted as a problem of mobilizing union support for the transcendent project of creating a socialist Britain. The early, reactive critique of Technocratic-Collectivism was gradually transposed into a programme designed to harness class-corporatist impulses to transitional reforms towards socialism. The question which arose, however, was whether the alternative economic strategy and its supplementary proposals actually contained such potential.

The alternative strategy was without doubt the most coherent, persuasive and constructive programme developed by the left since 1945. It grew organically out of the disappointments with the 1964–70 governments: the rather blind, defensive criticisms of Wilson's administrations were drawn together in *Tribune*, in Tribune Group statements, in NEC committees and, with Benn as political catalyst and figurehead, were finally formulated as a unified programme in the writings of Sedgemore and Holland. The strategy was important because it spoke directly to identified social and economic problems – stagnation, inflation and unemployment – and did so in a way which simultaneously articulated a critical position *vis-a-vis* Government policy and generated policies compatible with the economistic interests of the trade unions. As a programme for a transition to socialism, though, it contained certain ambiguities and contradictions which were recognized, though not resolved, by its most perceptive advocates. First there was the question of whether the alternative economic strategy represented a rational programme for renovating, rather than undermining, interventionist capitalism. Second, there was a sense in which the transformative impulse of the programme lay in its supplementary measures, like the implementation of industrial democracy, about which there was less clarity and agreement than on the economic and industrial strategy *per se*. And finally there was the problem of whether, even with a resolute Labour government, dominant social institutions might not be able to withstand the pressures of a strategy with a relatively narrow focus.

The outcome of implementing the alternative economic strategy was uncertain. Holland, who anticipated many of the possible lines of criticism against his proposals,[94] acknowledged that they might be construed as a mode of strengthening state capitalism rather than laying the grounds for a socialist transition.[95] For several reasons it is possible to think that the implementation of the economic strategy might have had a similar structural effect to that of the Attlee governments, that is to direct economic change in such a way as to re-structure economic arrangements and strengthen private capital within the framework of the mixed economy. Its immediate proposals might simply have changed the proportions of public and private economic enterprise within the mixed economy. Demands for competitive public enterprise were hardly revolutionary in themselves, particularly as it seemed that private capital bought out by the NEB would then be free to invest in other companies. And while Planning Agreements with other major corporations might enforce greater state control, the criterion of profitability would still underpin major economic institutions. Moreover, the major instruments of control advocated in the strategy were directly modelled on institutions developed by continental, capitalist, states: the NEB was a replica of the Italian IRI (Industrial Reconstruction Institute) and Planning, Agreements were already operated in France, Belgium and Italy.[96] In such respects the objectives and rationale of the strategy bore signs of an intellectual origin in Technocratic-Collectivism, which sought to do no more than revive economic growth so as to sustain full employment and finance social provision.

The economic proposals entailed intervention, accountability and access to information at the level of the individual enterprise, the state acquisition of profitable private companies, a substantial change in the balance between the private and the public in the mixed economy, and a commitment to progressive social objectives which were being abandoned by other groupings on the parliamentary stage. *Prima facie* such proposals were unlikely to satisfy capital and its representatives. Contradictions inherent in the strategy could only become apparent in practice. The objective condition of fiscal crisis was just as real an obstacle to the alternative economic strategy as it had been to Social Reformism. There were no contingency plans for a situation where growth lagged and strategic decisions had to be taken regarding the immediate distribution of resources between policies to support industrial investment and social expenditures. Also the strategy depended upon the continued support of the trade union interest which was forthcoming on the promise of growth and effective state economic management but, as union engagement with the Labour government's version of the Social Contract indicated, was liable to alter in line with calculations about their more immediate interests. Like the Technocratic-Collectivist project much depended on success in economic management: if the economic strategy worked then class-corporatist motivations could be consistent with the transformative impulse, while if it failed there was a strong possibility that the problems faced by the Labour government after 1964 would recur in yet more virulent forms.

The socialist potential of the Tribunite programme depended to a large extent on measures taken to supplement the economic policy, a fact recognized by some of its advocates. Stuart Holland made it quite clear that the transformative potential of the economic policies could only be realized if there was both a radical change in the distribution of income and wealth and an effective system of industrial democracy. The former received little attention beyond the call for a strong wealth tax, which was vital because the economic proposals themselves contained nothing more than a long term prospect of gradually reducing the ratio of private to total wealth through competition. Yet it is inconsistent to suggest heavy taxation of wealth (as opposed to income) and at the same time to rely to a considerable extent upon increasing private capital investment in order to re-industrialize Britain. Thorny dilemmas about the mode of distributing income — free collective bargaining or a wages policy, differentials or greater equalisation — were avoided by consigning them, in the event of the strategy being implemented, to negotiations with the TUC. The really radical edge of the strategy, and probably the principal reason for Benn becoming capital's principal demon, was the suggestion that managerial prerogatives should be strictly contained and that workers should have a substantial role in the running of individual enterprises. Despite limited agreement about the form that industrial democracy should take, all the proposals violated territory sacrosanct to capital. The clauses for disclosure of information, included in the Planning Agreement system, caused the most strenuous opposition by capital to proposals in the Labour Party manifesto; and the haste with which the Bullock Report was shelved by the government also testified to the sense in which business felt threatened by proposals for industrial democracy. Attachment to industrial democracy was, however, a source of some difficulty in the Tribunite strategy for it co-existed uncomfortably with the faith in centralized state control over the economy through a National Plan. Though aware of a discrepancy they were without a solution other than an assumption that a socialist national plan and worker control of enterprise would converge because both were founded upon working-class interests. But in the absence of explicit criteria of working-class interest this remained ambiguous, to say the least.

The final problem of the overall strategy lay in its orientation towards vested interest and established institutions. In one sense this is simply to note the recurrence of the primary difficulty of democratic socialism, of how to secure the interests of the living generation of the working class whilst transforming the social system from within its institutional forms.

The Tribunite attitude to the Social Contract illustrated the dilemma: when the TUC General Council between 1975 and 1978 defined the interests of union members in terms of collaboration with the Labour government, the left was disarmed both because, for reasons of *Realpolitik*, it could not attack the TUC, and because it could not present any transcendent criteria of working-class interest against which to criticise the Contract. The limited definition of working-class interest, the simple identification of the interests of class, union and Party, hampered the socialist project and attenuated left social criticism. The renewed theoretical vigour, important though it was, concentrated almost entirely on economic organization — on multi-national corporations, the City, the Treasury and managerial authority. The conservative functions of institutions and elites which did not directly impede their economic strategy were largely ignored. The question of whether there would be conscious obstruction to the left's policies, a question which was in fact posed by the Labour Party left in the 1930s, was never introduced. Holland's observation, conceding some ground to revolutionary left critiques of the Labour Party, that the alternative strategy, even fully implemented, was nothing more than a 'framework' for socialism because without extensive popular mobilization legislation would be insufficient, fell on stony ground.[97] Some Tribunites rejected the argument altogether, and those who saw its force failed to act upon it. Understandably from their point of view, they concentrated on securing majority support within the Party rather than on gaining mass popular support, but that ignored the problem of generating the mass consent necessary for a socialist transformation. In essence the left strategy failed to bridge the gap between class corporatist and socialist consciousness and action. The most likely structural effect of their strategy would be similar to that of the Attlee governments, transformist without being socialist, anti-capitalist without abolishing capitalism. As such the Tribunites continued within the Labour Party tradition, providing oppositional expression of working-class discontent without transgressing the bounds of prevailing hegemonic forces.

Conclusion

Socialism, a single word for several irreconcilable visions, has persisted less as utopian projection, and more as a practical means for managing the contrary social constraints experienced by the Labour Party. Within the Party, socialism is a balm, a soothing symbol of unity to which it is obligatory to pay homage. Externally, as a practical strategy, it is just another way of attenuating or combatting social contradictions. Yet, although the Party offers no revolutionary solutions, cleavages within it do reflect substantively different alternative futures for Britain.

Intra-party division is a complex phenomenon, as complex as the social contradictions which encompass it. It is impossible to predict the outcome of intra-party conflict; its very nature precludes authoritative forecasting of the results of internal mobilization. But conflict is not random. The contradictions of society generate regular constraints upon the Party, which account for the logic of those patterns of conflict and alliance revealed by the analysis of strategy.

In the framing of alliances in the post-war period, the union interest has proved decisive. The structure of the balance of power in the Party has passed through several phases. In the 1950s the union interest was aligned with the Social Reformists around an amalgamated programme of free collective bargaining, democratic planning, a mixed economy and complementary reform. As the economic climate deteriorated in the next decade, the dominant alliance was between the unions and the Technocratic-Collectivists, founded on planned rises of income, increased system efficiency and some measures of social reform. When the Wilson governments failed to solve the basic problems of modernizing and expanding the economy, the left increased its influence, constructing an alliance with the union interest. This survived, predominantly as defensive and reactive opposition, until the creation of the Social Contract re-formed a leadership—union front. However, the accommodation of the unions with the

Labour government after 1974 proved unstable so that by the end of the 1970s the balance of power in the Party was again in a state of flux.

The trade unions, though predominantly economistic and sectional institutions, preferring where possible to avoid entanglement in the party-political arena, have considerable potential power. The union interest exercises a negative veto power over the trajectory of the Party; it determines certain parameters which the Party cannot transgress. Such negative power has, in the past, enabled the union interest to avoid accusations of illegitimate or unconstitutional domination while still ensuring that their basic rights, privileges and interests are not infringed by legislation.

There is little information about the political beliefs of union leaderships but, despite a lack of homogeneity, it still makes sense to understand their activities principally in terms of trade union consciousness or sectional-corporatism. The main rationale of their practice is to protect the interests of their members, whether through free collective bargaining or negotiated agreements with government. It is significant that the issues which have caused crises of confidence in the party leadership have been generally ones where the trade union interest has combined in opposition with the left — Clause IV, In Place of Strife, the Conservative Industrial Relations Act, and the EEC, are the most obvious examples. Consequently, the only period in which the left of the Party gained real influence since the war was between 1968 and 1975 when it was able to project a strategy corresponding with the interests of the unions, although that was not very propitious for its socialist aspirations. Contrary to the theory which maintains that it is the middle-class intellectuals who hold back the Party from a socialist path, the principal cause of the Party's moderation has been the sectional-corporatist tendencies of the unions. At the same time, however, it would seem that the incorporation of the unions into national politics, even if primarily at the behest of Labour governments, indicates that the Labour Party is felt to be increasingly inept at protecting the central, economistic interests of the subordinate classes in Britain.

It was, ultimately, the onset of the social crises of the Welfare State which altered the trajectory of the Labour Party in the 1970s. The crisis of profitability and the contraction of British industry, the fiscal crisis of the state, and legitimation problems, re-ordered the Party. The consensus of the post-war settlement, expressed most coherently in the political formula of Social Reformism, disintegrated. From its ruins came the Social Contract, a temporarily successful mode of class collaboration which appeared capable of attenuating the crisis tendencies by providing formal channels for reaching a tripartite compromise between capital, labour and the state. But union acquiescence could not be unconditional: the absence of success in regenerating the economy put the Government—

TUC concordat under severe strain. The fundamental antinomies of the Labour Party asserted themselves yet again.

What, perhaps, is theoretically most interesting about the study of intra-party conflict is the light it sheds on the ways in which social-democratic parties are beset by the general contradictions of capitalist society. Recurrent issues of dispute, repeated political dilemmas and regular differences in strategic orientation derive from those contradictions of which two, posing problems for all segments equally, are particularly important.

That minority control over economic production and gross inequalities in distribution are both in contradiction with dominant legitimations in terms of civic or 'politico-juridical' equality, is widely recognized as a determinant of political management in capitalism. Liberals and marxists observe that the class differences generated by economic processes render fraudulent claims that all citizens are equal, their interests sufficiently compatible for each to live in harmony with one another. The contradiction takes many forms. Opaque in the Welfare State, the fiscal crisis rendered it transparent again as governments of the 1970s reneged upon newly accepted rights to social provision where they interfered with the requirements of capital accumulation. Yet, even during the era of the consensus the contradiction was not eliminated, as was shown by the range of political solutions to the contrary imperatives of production and legitimate distribution which were canvassed within the Party. Social Reformism advocated the preservation of market mechanisms and free collective bargaining, on the grounds that consumer freedom, equal opportunity and equal access to welfare would eliminate resentments generated by material inequality. Technocratic solutions relied, instead, on expert direction of production to increase quantitatively the share of every social group on the assumption that improved material standards were sufficient to divert attention away from inequalities without disrupting the accumulation process. Left solutions, Fundamentalist and Tribunite, shared a faith in planning, but declared that erosion of the logic of accumulation, through common ownership, was necessary in order to achieve a distribution of wealth and power capable of justification. None of these solutions proved viable. As the continuing confusion over incomes policies demonstrates, no permanent agreement can overcome the contradictions between processes of production, distribution and social cohesion.

Less frequently appreciated, though more apparent after the debate on corporatism, are certain contradictions of political representation. The Labour Party is, on the one hand, subject to the electoral logic of a plebiscitarian, liberal-democratic, political system in which, *de facto*, MPs must be responsive to individual voters in constituencies. On the other hand, the Party, as a group of active political persons, derives its *raison d'être* from a concern to promote particular social interests, primarily functional interests of class, unions, occupational groupings and welfare recipients. The two logics, of plebiscitarian and functional representation, derive, respectively, from the legal and political framework of bourgeois individualism and from the class relations of economic production. Not easily reconciled, they are responsible for a series of strategic ambiguities and disputes across the Party.

The responsibilities of the Party for popular representation are strenuously contested. There is the question of whether the Party should promote sectional-occupational, class, or community interests, three types which cannot all be promoted simultaneously, but none of which can be neglected because of the immense institutional forces which lie behind each. There is also the related problem of which groups of people legitimize Party programmes, whether it be Party members, Labour voters, functional interest groups, experts or the nation. Attempts decisively to resolve these issues of representation have produced a variety of untenable positions since the war. The Tribunites, for example, were caught between their support for working class interests and their deep attachment to parliament, the liberal-democratic integument of plebiscitarian principles. One aspect of the left's dilemma of gradualism is that since parliament does not mirror directly the functional divisions of class, hopes of socialist transformation depend upon strong, party government, with compatible internal procedures, to circumvent the difficulty. The same contradiction appeared, inverted, in Social Reformism. Crosland, one of the clearest of thinkers, was reduced to profound inconsistency in trying to reconcile his desire for community solidarity with the Party's class base. The class character of society runs counter to civic equality, the foundation of plebiscitarianism and consensus politics. Tripartism, explicitly recognizing the dual imperatives of plebiscitarian and functional representation, sought an alternative solution in the construction of parallel channels of representation. The Social Contract was a way of removing class conflict from parliament into a special forum for state-sponsored negotiations between capital and labour. A possible consequence might have been the withering away of effective parliamentary representation, precisely the fear associated with the coming of the corporate state. In practice class opposition was stifled by securing the collaboration of the leaders of organized labour, thereby neutralising class solidarity within the Party.

A permanent resolution of the representational contradiction would require its transcendence, through institutional transformations not contemplated within the Party. Consensual, plebiscitarian politics, the vision of Social Reformism, would require either the supersession of capitalist economic relations or the disavowal of the support for the

Party which comes from class solidarity. A Tribunite resolution would appear to demand either the overthrow of those hegemonic ideologies which dissuade electors from the belief that their class interests are more important than any other, or the renunciation of plebiscitarian principles, or else the abandonment of the Labour left view of the relation between party, class and socialism.

Some contradictions cannot be resolved by the Labour Party. The effort expended by dominant segments since 1950 to establish a solely affirmative role for the Party was to no avail. The various integrative strategies from Social Reformism to Tripartism, despite favourable conditions for a relatively long period, could not eradicate oppositional impulses from the Party. It is necessary, therefore, to be suspicious of the popular thesis, particularly seductive after the experience of the Labour Government 1974—79, that the trajectory of the Labour Party. is a steady evolution towards total affirmation of capitalist society. It is worth remembering that although modern social-democratic parties are nowhere agents of revolutionary socialism, labour movements have never disappeared from capitalist societies except as a result of forcible suppression. The Labour Party is engulfed within the contradictory imperatives of its affirmative and oppositional roles. Even while, as Nairn argued, it frequently spares society the implications of class struggle by containing it within its own organization, it continues to give political expression to working class interests.

Despite defections, it is unlikely that the Party will change substantially in the foreseeable future. In the short term it will remain attached to Tripartism: the leadership of 1981 can envisage no alternative, and the left continues to believe that the union alliance is the prime impetus for radical change. Above all, the policies of the Conservative government elected in 1979 will ensure the survival of Tripartism. The entire experience of twentieth-century capitalism suggests that Conservative policies will exacerbate the crisis tendencies of Britain. Minimizing economic intervention, increasing unemployment, reducing social provision, and antagonizing the union interest, must cause further economic contraction and wider social conflict. If the Labour Party is returned to office it will be in circumstances similar to 1974, in which a programme of regeneration of the mixed economy and restoration of public services might be such a relief that union support would readily be given. The government would then face the same problems as before, and the left the same awkward dilemmas as after 1975. Even if there was a significant shift in the balance of power within the Party, which is the only way that it might, of its own accord, avoid a replication of the problems of 1975—79, it is difficult to imagine that it could transcend the dual contradictions of the social-democratic predicament. The history of the Party since the second world war has been one of unavailing attempts to find a *modus operandi* within those contradictions, with, as yet, no viable strategy for escaping or transcending them.

INTRODUCTION

1 E.g. D. Owen, *et al.*, 'Open letter', *Guardian*, 1 August 1980.
2 Middlemas attributes the 'trivial, personalised view of political activity, which since the 1930s has been the bane of British journalism' to the cult of secrecy surrounding the British state; see K. Middlemas, *Politics in Industrial Society*, p. 364.
3 C. Offe, 'Political Authority and Class Structures'.
4 see P.H. Partridge, *Consent and Consensus*, pp. 71–95.
5 I say 'imputed' to the citizenry as recent evidence casts doubt upon assumptions that the consent of the governed implies any positive support; see Chapter 2, below. For useful distinctions between general support, specific support, legitimation and mass loyalty, etc. see R. Mayntz, 'Legitimacy and the Directive Capacity of the Political System'.
6 L.V. Panitch, *Social Democracy and Industrial Militancy*, p. 1.

CHAPTER 1

1 Quoted in M. Harrison, *Trade Unions and the Labour Party*, p. 11.
2 E.g. H. Pelling, *The Origins of the Labour Party*, and S. Pierson, *Marxism and the Origins of British Socialism*.
3 S. Beer, *Modern British Politics*, pp. 126–87.
4 E.g. J. Hinton, *The First Shop Stewards' Movement*; W. Kendall, *The Revolutionary Movement in Britain, 1900–21*; R. Dowse, *Left in the Centre*.
5 R. Miliband, 'Socialism and the Myth of the Golden Past'; but, cf. B. Pimlott, *Labour and the Left in the 1930s*.
6 E.g. L.D. Epstein, 'The Cohesion of British Parliamentary Parties'; J.B. Christoph, 'Consensus and Cleavage in British Political Ideology'.
7 G. Loewenberg, 'The Transformation of British Labour Party Policy since 1945'.
8 R. Miliband, *Parliamentary Socialism*, postscript to second edition, pp. 350–77; but see also K. Coates, 'Socialists and the Labour Party'.
9 R. Miliband, *Parliamentary Socialism*; S. Haseler, *The Gaitskellites*. The same dichotomy appears, labelled Fundamentalist–Revisionist, in Beer, *Modern British Politics*, p. 219.
10 See R.T. McKenzie, *British Political Parties*.

11 E.g. S.E. Finer, *et al.*, *Backbench Opinion*.
12 This was a division examined for reasons of internal Party polemic, but it was elaborated by K. Hindell & P. Williams, 'Scarborough and Blackpool'.
13 R. Rose, 'Parties, Factions and Tendencies in Britain'; also Rose, *The Problem of Party Government*, pp. 319—35.
14 Rose, 'Parties, Factions and Tendencies in Britain', pp. 33—5.
15 *Ibid.*, p. 46.
16 H. Valen, 'Factional Activities and Nominations in Political Parties'.
17 Rose, 'Parties, Factions and Tendencies in Britain'.
18 Valen, 'Factional Activities and Nominations in Political Parties'.
19 R. Zariski, 'Party Factions and Comparative Politics'.
20 E.g. Finer *et al.*, *Backbench Opinion in the House of Commons, 1959—63*; H.B. Berrington, *Backbench Opinion in the House of Commons, 1945—55*; J.R. Piper, 'Backbench Rebellion, Party Government and Consensus Politics'.
21 For a summary see S. Lukes, *Power: A Radical View*.
22 See Finer, *et al.*, *Backbench Opinion*; W.D. Muller, 'Trade Union MPs and Parliamentary Specialisation'; W.D. Muller, *The 'Kept Men'?*.
23 E.g. R. Miliband, *Parliamentary Socialism*.
24 Finer, *et al.*, *Backbench Opinion*, p. 67.
25 V. Feather, *The Essence of Trade Unionism*, pp. 38—9.
26 I. Richter, *Political Purpose in Trade Unions*, p. 17.
27 *Ibid.*
28 Important among the expanding literature on this are: V.L. Allen, *Trade Unions and the Government*; G.A. Dorfman, *Wage Politics in Britain, 1945—67*; L.V. Panitch, *Social Democracy and Industrial Militancy*; and C. Crouch, *Class Conflict and the Industrial Relations Crisis*.
29 The relationship between the political orientations of particular unions and their industrial activities is more or less uncharted. The pioneering work of M. Harrison, *Trade Unions and the Labour Party since 1945*, analysed the varying stances of unions in Conference between 1945 and 1958 and showed that they were less monolithic than had usually been thought, although without explaining the processes which produce them. There are also very useful case studies in Richter, *Political Purpose in Trade Unions*, and in L. Minkin, *The Labour Party Conference*. But it is still necessary to rely on theoretical assumptions, admittedly well-established assumptions, that the political aspirations of trade unions are generally subordinated to an economistic rationale. The changing character of TUC demands, and the campaign of the TGWU for increased pensions in 1973—74, etc., do, however, provide potentially disconfirming evidence.
30 On changes in the role of the Trade Union Group of MPs see J. Ellis & R.W. Johnson, *Members from the Unions*.
31 see L.V. Panitch, 'Ideology and Integration', and *Social Democracy and Industrial Militancy*, pp. 235—59; T. Nairn, 'The Nature of the Labour Party', and 'The Left Against Europe?'; also R. Miliband, *Parliamentary Socialism*.
32 See Pierson, *Marxism and the Origins of British Socialism*.
33 For example, Lukacs attempted to solve the problem by positing that working-class interests are *universal*, but that the attainment of that universality could only be the result of a *class*-based strategy. More recently commentators, the Frankfurt School for example, have questioned whether the working class is capable of transmuting its class interest into a universal interest either practically, given its growing assimilation into consumer society, or ethically, given its tendency to pursue its own material preferment.

34 This method was applied, classically, by Miliband, *Parliamentary Socialism. Qua* critical theory it is perfectly legitimate, but it may be misleading if what is sought is an understanding of what the actors in the events intended to do. The use of a basic theoretical distinction between reformist and revolutionary socialism, typical of this method, is not very useful in the case of British Labour because the latter category is entirely vacuous.

35 H. Valen, 'Factional Activities and Nominations in Political Parties'.

36 A. Gramsci, *Prison Notebooks*, p. 181.

37 The concept of defensive class corporatism derives from Gramsci's useful distinction between three levels of 'homogeneity, self awareness and organization attained by the various social classes':

> The second moment is that in which consciousness is reached of the solidarity among all the members of a social class — but still in the purely economic field. Already at this juncture the problem of the State is posed — but only in terms of winning politico-juridical equality with the ruling groups: the right is claimed to participate in legislation and administration, even to reform these — but within the existing fundamental structures.' (*Prison Notebooks*, p. 181).

For useful exegetical and critical comments on Gramsci's concepts as employed here see G. Williams, 'The Concept of "Egemonia"'; J. Merrington, 'Theory and Practice in Gramsci's Marxism'; P. Anderson, 'The Antinomies of Antonio Gramsci'.

38 See, for example, R. Bendix, *Nation-Building and Citizenship*; also N. Young, 'Prometheans or Troglodytes?'.

39 Gramsci, *Prison Notebooks*, p. 182.

40 See G. Williams, 'The Concept of "Egemonia"', also P. Anderson, 'Problems of a Socialist Strategy', in Anderson, ed., *Towards Socialism*.

41 See Chapter 2, below.

42 See Chapter 9, below.

CHAPTER 2

1 C.A.R. Crosland, *The Future of Socialism*, held a very strong version of this thesis. He argued that it was wrong of critics to ascribe the social changes instituted by the Attlee governments to the war because:

> Wars are only permanently revolutionary if followed by Left-Wing Governments which dig in, consolidate the changes, and use them as a basis for further advance.
> This was the historic task of Mr. Attlee's Government. Just how successfully it was accomplished, people perhaps scarcely realize today. Memories are feeble; the changes are quickly taken for granted and accepted as part of the status quo. (p. 58.)

2 See R. Brady, *Crisis in Britain*; A.A. Rogow & P. Shore, *The Labour Government and British Industry*; D.N. Pritt, *The Labour Government*; S. Beer, *Modern British Politics*.

3 This was the dominant theme of the accounts of R. Miliband, *Parliamentary Socialism*, and D. Coates, *The Labour Party and the Struggle for Socialism*; see also G. Loewenberg, 'The British Constitution and the Structure of the Labour Party': cf. H. Laski, *Parliamentary Government in England*, who contended that the emergence of the Labour Party with a different ideology threatened the stability of the system.

4 R.H.S. Crossman, 'Towards a Philosophy of Socialism', in Crossman ed., *New Fabian Essays,* p.1.

5   Rogow & Shore, *The Labour Government and British Industry*, p. 9.
6   D. Thompson, Discussion, *New Reasoner*, 4, (1958), p. 127, said, 'The import-
    ant thing is that these benefits are provided purely on the basis of *need*, and
    not of cash payment, or even of any abstract conception of *social value*. This
    conception is a profoundly anti-capitalist one'.
7   N. Harris, *Competition and the Corporate Society*, pp. 77–80.
8   E.g. the optimism of G.D.H. Cole in 1948, *History of the Labour Party since
    1914*.
9   R.H.S. Crossman, *Socialist Values in a Changing Civilisation*, p. 9.
10 A. Bevan, *Democratic Values*, p. 10.
11 J. Strachey, *Labour's Task*, p. 5.
12 *Ibid*. p. 6.
13 K. Martin, *Socialism and the Welfare State*, p. 10; Crossman, *Socialist Values
    in a Changing Civilisation*, p. 10.
14 Crossman, *ibid*, p. 10., 'These moral values are the real achievements of social-
    ism in the last five years': and Bevan, *Democratic Values*, p. 11.
15 Bevan, *Democratic Values*, p. 14.
16 Crossman, *Socialist Values in a Changing Civilisation*, p. 11.
17 See Rogow & Shore, *The Labour Government and British Industry*, p. 103ff.
18 It was not really until the 1960s that it was established that poverty still existed
    in the 'affluent society'; see P. Townsend & B. Abel Smith, *The Poor and the
    Poorest*: nor was it realized that the proportional distribution of wealth remained
    similar; see R. Titmuss, *Income Distribution and Social Change*. Again the case for
    the conservative nature of the system of social provision has been strengthened by
    research in the 1960s, see J. Kincaid, *Poverty and Inequality in Britain*.
19 See M.R. Gordon, *Conflict and Consensus in Labour's Foreign Policy*, pp. 103–
    221.
20 Note Morrison and Shinwell, considered the reactionary elements in the Attlee
    government, coming forward to criticize the moderation of the Labour Party in
    the 1950s: *LPCR*, 1957, pp. 135 & 139.
21 For details of what policies were implemented see the monographs on the Labour
    governments referred to in note 2, above. Useful shorter accounts can be found
    in D. Coates, *The Labour Party and the Struggle for Socialism*, pp. 42–74; and
    D. Howell, *British Social Democracy*, pp. 135–77.
22 See N. Harris, *Competition and the Corporate Society*, pp. 77–84.
23 On the significance of state intervention in the steel industry see D. McEachern,
    A Class Against Itself.
24 S. Beer, *Modern British Politics*, p. 208.
25 These principles were characteristic of educational reform, social security legis-
    lation and the National Health Service, respectively.
26 see M.R. Gordon, *Conflict and Consensus*, pp. 209–12; also D. Howell, *British
    Social Democracy*, pp. 144–9.
27 Attlee, *in retrospect*, said of the 1945 manifesto:

Its ultimate objective was the creation of a society based on social justice, and, in our view,
this could only be attained by bringing under public ownership and control the main factors
in the economic system.
Nationalisation was not an end in itself but an essential element in achieving the ends which
we sought. Controls were desirable not for their own sake but because they were necessary
in order to gain freedom from the economic power of the owners of capital. A juster distribution of wealth was not a policy designed to soak the rich or to take revenge but because
a society with gross inequalities of wealth and opportunity is fundamentally unhealthy.

C.R. Attlee, *As It Happened*, (London, 1954), p. 189. (see also pp. 164–6).

28 The phrase is M. Barratt-Brown's, see *From Labourism to Socialism.*

29 see A. Gramsci, *Prison Notebooks*, p. 58 & pp. 109—20.

30 E.g. A. Briggs, 'The Welfare State in Historical Persepective'; D. Fraser, *The Evolution of the British Welfare State.*

31 F.F. Piven & R. Cloward, *Regulating the Poor.*

32 A. Gamble & P. Walton, *Capitalism in Crisis.*

33 On the economic motivations behind American war-time diplomacy see G. Kolko, *The Politics of War.*

34 See R. Miliband, *The State in Capitalist Society.*

35 See R. Dow, *The Management of the British Economy 1945—60*, pp. 214—322.

36 See J. Hughes, 'Nationalization and the Private Sector', in J. Urry & J. Wakeford, eds., *Power in Britain*, p. 152.

37 For a survey of the types of planning used since the 1930s see A. Budd, *The Politics of Economic Planning.*

38 For the concentration of capital see M. Barratt-Brown, 'The Controllers of British Industry', in J. Urry & J. Wakeford, *Power in Britain*: on the density of trade union membership see P. Abrams, ed., *Work, Urbanism and Inequality*, p. 130.

39 See M. Barratt-Brown, *From Labourism to Socialism*, p. 78; also, for an alternative computation, Gamble & Walton, *Capitalism in Crisis*, pp. 165—7.

40 See I. Gough, 'State Expenditure in Advanced Capitalism'. For a comparative and theoretical analysis of the development of welfare states see Gough, *The Political Economy of the Welfare State*, an important recent contribution in this area.

41 J. O'Connor, *The Fiscal Crisis of the State*, pp. 6—7.

42 M. Barratt-Brown, *From Labourism to Socialism*, p. 78.

43 See R. Dow, *The Management of the British Economy*, pp. 214—221.

44 M. Barratt-Brown, *From Labourism to Socialism*, p. 78.

45 See J. Weinstein, *The Corporate Ideal in the Liberal State.*

46 O'Connor, *The Fiscal Crisis of the State*, pp. 13—19.

47 See M. Mann, 'The Social Cohesion of Liberal Democracy'; also R.M. Blackburn & M. Mann, 'Ideology in the Non-Skilled Working Class', in M. Bulmer, ed., *Working Class Images of Society.*

48 J. O'Connor, *The Fiscal Crisis of the State*, p.7.

49 See F.F. Piven & R. Cloward, *Regulating the Poor*, showing that welfare payments are expanded in periods of high unemployment in order to maintain social order, and contracted at other times in order to reinforce the incentive to work.

50 See for example, T.H. Marshall, *Citizenship and Social Class*, pp. 10—27.

51 *Ibid.*, pp. 28—9.

52 J. Habermas, *Legitimation Crisis*, pp. 68—75.

53 Class differences are clearly not the only pivot. Religious and ethnic differences remain important in many European societies as theories of 'consociational democracy' indicate: see, for example, K. McRae, ed., *Consociational Democracy.*

54 This distinction was made in the influential article of D. Lockwood, 'Sources of Variation in Working-Class Images of Society'.

55 See the debate surrounding S. Mallet, *The New Working Class.*

56 See for example, K. Roberts *et al.*, *The Fragmentary Class Structure.*

57 E.g. L. Comer, 'The Question of Women and Class'; S. Castles & G. Kosack, *Immigrant Workers and Class Structure.*

58 See the analysis of N. Poulantzas, *Political Power and Social Classes.*

59 See B. Hindess, *The Decline of Working Class Politics*; but also see the criticisms of that work in T. Forrester, *The Labour Party and the Working Class.*

60 M. Barratt-Brown, *From Labourism to Socialism*, p. 68.

61 See the summary of inter-war social policies in S. Glynn & J. Oxborrow, *Inter-war Britain* pp. 245—69. 'Contingency' or 'uncovenanted' benefits, those outside the confines of insurance schemes, while paid in considerable amounts throughout the period, were obviously granted with the greatest degree of reluctance. The predominant reason for their existence was the requirement of maintaining public order; any sense of social obligation or social justice was marginal.

62 See M.J. Cowling, *The Impact of Labour 1920—24.*

63 See C.A. Cline, *Recruits to Labour.*

64 See H. Marcuse, *One-Dimensional Man*; and D. Bell, *The End of Ideology.*

65 See P. Addison, *The Road to 1945.* Addison argued that a 'consensus' on social policy and national reconstruction emerged *during* the war and that the reforms of the Attlee governments were simply the expression of political agreement established between 1940 and 1944. While it is true that many of the reports on which subsequent legislation was based emanated from war-time commissions, Beveridge, Uthwatt, etc., and that one major piece of legislation — the 1944 Education Act — was introduced by Butler on behalf of the coalition government with a Conservative majority, Addison is not entirely convincing. He shows that public opinion (as indicated by Opinion Polls, Home Intelligence reports and by-elections) was moving to the left, favouring radical social change and guarantees of a 'national minimum'. But he does not establish that the Conservative Party as a whole, or key sections of the ruling class, followed public opinion or genuinely shared the tenets of the consensus. Despite the importance of the 'middle ground' reformers, Macmillan, Butler, Keynes, Beveridge, etc., who were influential opponents of socialism, the evidence presented by Addison suggests that the bulk of the Conservative establishment was opposed to many of the measures put forward for post-war reconstruction, and was keen to dilute those other measures which they felt *pressured* to support. Addison exaggerated the degree of consensus fostered within the coalition government and thus over-stressed continuities from 1940 forwards. He entirely discounted the possibility that the recommendations of the various war-time commissions might not have been implemented by a Conservative government after 1945, a possibility which seems to have been very real on the evidence of N. Harris in *Competition and the Corporate Society*, pp. 77—84. The post-war settlement was more the result of Labour government actions, and the subsequent reformulation of Party policy and philosophy, than Addison conceives.

CHAPTER 3

1 R.H.S. Crossman, 'Towards a Philosophy of Socialism', in Crossman, ed., *New Fabian Essays*, p. 1.

2 See G. Loewenberg, 'Transformation of the British Labour Party Policy since 1945'.

3 S. Beer, *Modern British Politics*; V. Bogdanor, 'The Labour Party in Opposition', in V. Bogdanor & R. Skidelski, eds., *The Age of Affluence*; D. Howell, 'The Restatement of Socialism'.

4 V. Bogdanor, 'The Labour Party in Opposition'.

5 D. Coates, *The Labour Party and the Struggle for Socialism*; E. Burns, *Right-Wing Labour.*

6 H. Dalton, *Practical Socialism for Britain*; D.P.T. Jay, *The Socialist Case*; E.F.M. Durbin, *The Politics of Democratic Socialism.*

7 C.A.R. Crosland, *The Future of Socialism*; J. Strachey, *Contemporary Capitalism*; H. Gaitskell, *Socialism and Nationalisation*; Socialist Union, *20th Century Socialism*. Of course they did not accidentally and independently arrive at a common position; there is ample evidence of a long history of personal communication and intellectual debate among the central characters of the segment: see M. Postan, 'Political and Intellectual Progress' in W.T. Rodgers, ed., *For Hugh Gaitskell*, pp. 49–66.

8 C.A.R. Crosland, 'The Transition from Capitalism', in *New Fabian Essays*.

9 See K.J.W. Alexander & A. Hobbs, 'What influences Labour MPs?', *New Society*, 11th December 1962.

10 Indeed, marxist though has had little impact on the British labour movement at any time. The notion that it flourished in the 1930s is questionable; see R. Miliband, 'Socialism and the Myth of the Golden Past'; for a contrasting view see E.P. Thompson, 'The Peculiarities of the English', though even he did not argue that marxist contributions were significant in the development of the Labour Party.

11 E.F.M. Durbin, *The Politics of Democratic Socialism*; D.P.T. Jay, *The Socialist Case*; C.A.R. Crosland, *The Future of Socialism*.

12 Strachey was the only exception to this tendency, in that he appreciated marxism more and chose to derive his reformulation of socialism partially from marxism; see his *Contemporary Capitalism*.

13 *The Future of Socialism*, pp. 79–96; *20th Century Socialism*, pp. 19–20.

14 *The Future of Socialism*, p. 216.

15 *Ibid.*, p. 97.

16 *20th Century Socialism*, p. 56.

17 C.A.R. Crosland, *The Future of Socialism*, pp. 62–3.

18 See C.A.R. Crosland, *The Future of Socialism*, pp. 466–82; H. Gaitskell, *Socialism and Nationalisation*.

19 A. Albu, 'The Organization of Industry', in R.H.S. Crossman, ed., *New Fabian Essays*, p. 217.

20 C.A.R. Crosland, *The Future of Socialism*, p. 40.

21 *Ibid.*, p. 40.

22 A. Albu, 'The Organization of Industry', pp. 141–2.

23 *Industry and Society*, (Labour Party, 1957).

24 Cf. N. Harris, *Competition and the Corporate Society*. The Social Reformists were fond of saying 'we are all planners now'.

25 Crosland introduced so many qualifications to his argument that he undermined his own position: for instance, that making a profit was still an essential condition of successful management; that managers and shareholders can for many purposes be seen as a socially homogeneous group; and that diversification in shareholding can result in a minority of shareholders wielding effective control.

26 'It is clear, then, that within any given framework greater or lesser harmony is largely a function of the quality of management', Crosland, *The Future of Socialism*, p. 338.

27 *Ibid.*, p. 346.

28 Note the explicit position of Douglas Jay:

where manpower is concerned we should normally prefer the uncontrolled price process to any positive compulsion. That is to say, we should, in general, allow wages to be determined by the strength of demand for manpower in different industries as reflected in the collective bargaining process ... the 'wage policy' problem is, in fact, a problem not of Socialism but of inflation. Remove the inflation, and free bargaining over wages, without the limitation on personal freedom and with the minimum provided by the social services, will give us the best practical solution.

D.P.T. Jay, in *The Road to Recovery* (Fabian Society Lectures, Autumn 1947) quoted by L.V. Panitch, *Social Democracy and Industrial Militancy*, p. 14.

29   Lord Williamson, 'Winning the Trade Unions', in W.T. Rodgers, ed., *For Hugh Gaitskell*, p. 109.

30   A. Albu, 'The Organization of Industry', in *New Fabian Essays*; C.A.R. Crosland, *The Future of Socialism*, p. 340.

31   R. Hattersley, 'New Blood', in G. Kaufman, ed., *The Left*, p. 160.

32   C.A.R. Crosland, *The Future of Socialism*, pp. 169—89.

33   *Ibid.*, p. 170.

34   *Ibid.*, p. 170.

35   *Ibid.*, pp. 173—8. Education was most important: 'This interacting triad, at the top of the social scale, of education, style of life, and occupational status is unquestionably a more important cause of social inequality than income.' (p. 178.)

36   *Ibid.*, p. 202 and p. 200.

37   D.P.T. Jay, *Socialism in the New Society*, p. 9.

38   Cf. Crosland, *The Future of Socialism*, p. 237: 'in Britain equality of opportunity and social mobility, though they lead to the most admirable distribution of intelligence, are not enough.'; R. Jenkins, 'Equality', in *New Fabian Essays*, pp. 84—6; also D.P.T. Jay, *Socialism in the New Society*, p. 16.

39   See F. Parkin, *Class, Inequality and Political Order*, pp. 18—22.

40   Debate on 'subjective' theories of class and the theory of *embourgeoisement* became popular largely due to Social Reformist explanations of the 'new' society and, later, Labour's declining vote. The Social Reformist position had some affinities with the analysis advanced by American stratification theorists: see the seminal article of K. Davis & W.E. Moore, 'Some Principles of Stratification'.

41   H. Gaitskell, *Socialism and Nationalisation*, p. 29.

42   *Ibid.*, pp. 26—7.

43   Crosland proposed the capital gains tax which the Wilson government implemented in 1965.

44   *The Future of Socialism*, p. 499.

45   *Ibid.*, p. 505.

46   R. Jenkins, *The Pursuit of Progress*, p. 136.

47   *20th Century Socialism*, p. 134.

48   *Ibid.*, p. 134.

49   *The Pursuit of Progress*, p. 139.

50   *The Future of Socialism*, p. 247.

51   J. Strachey, 'Tasks and Achievements of British Labour', in *New Fabian Essays*, pp. 182—9.

52   L.V. Panitch, 'Ideology and Integration'.

53   See R.H.S. Crossman, *Labour in the Affluent Society*.

54   W.J.M. MacKenzie, 'Models of English Politics', in R. Rose, ed., *Studies in British Politics*, p. 53.

55   C.A.R. Crosland, *Socialism Now*, pp. 98—102.

56   See J.J. Rousseau, *The Social Contract*. Crosland in fact used the term the 'general will', *Future of Socialism*, e.g. p. 291.

57   Haseler, *The Gaitskellites*, in particular saw Strachey's work as wholly consonant with the thought of Social Reformism. It seems that Strachey's allegiance to the

Social Reformists derived from his concerns with defence policy rather than from his social analysis. Strachey tends to use different concepts, inequality playing a lesser, and struggles for power a greater role than was usual in Social Reformist thought. See the chapter, 'Democracy and the Last Stage of Capitalism', in *Contemporary Capitalism*, which is much closer to Bevan's position in *In Place of Fear*.

58 *Socialist Commentary* became an organ of Social Reformism around 1950, see Haseler, *The Gaitskellites*, pp. 68–75. Previously it had been the journal of the Socialist Vanguard Group, the 'Organ of the British Section of the Militant Socialist International'. (P. Sedgwick, 'The Origins of *Socialist Commentary*: British Section of the International Sozialistischer Kampf-Bund ("Nelson Bund")'; (unpublished paper).)

59 *20th Century Socialism*, p. 7.

60 *Ibid.*, p. 20.

61 R. Jenkins, *The Pursuit of Progress*, p. 87 'it is now possible to see that the general case for nationalisation should not have been allowed to go so much by default'.

62 Socialist Union, *20th Century Socialism, Part II, passim.*

63 *Ibid.*, pp. 52–3.

64 *Ibid.*, p. 54.

65 Socialist Union, *Socialism and Foreign Policy*, p. 11.

66 *Ibid.*, pp. 38–9.

67 E.g. Healey, Younger, Prentice, Mayhew and Strachey: see Haseler, *The Gaitskellites*, pp. 65–72 and pp. 112–36.

68 D. Healey, 'Power Politics and the Labour Party', in *New Fabian Essays*, p. 168.

69 See D. Healey, *A Neutral Belt in Europe*; M. Stewart, *Policy and Weapons in the Nuclear Age*, p. 14; Socialist Union, *Socialism and Foreign Policy*, pp. 53–55.

70 Of the 1956 official publications of the Party, *Towards Equality* was the one most clearly bearing the stamp of Social Reformist thought.

71 *Parliamentary Socialism*, p. 333.

72 *Britain Belongs to You*, reprinted in F.W.S. Craig, *British General Election Manifestos*, p. 202.

73 R.H.S. Crossman, *Labour in the Affluent Society.*

74 *LPCR*, 1959, p. 86.

75 P. Gay, *The Dilemma of Democratic Socialism.*

76 'The Lessons for Labour', in M. Abrams & R. Rose, *Must Labour Lose?*, p. 104.

77 See also 'More or Less Socialism', *Socialist Commentary*, editorial, (November, 1959).

78 D. Jay, article in *Forward*, 16th October, 1959, quoted by Haseler, *The Gaitskellites*, p. 163.

79 Quoted by D. Butler and R. Rose, *The British General Election of 1959*, p. 197.

80 R. Hinden, 'The Lessons for Labour', in M. Abrams, *Must Labour Lose?*, p. 100.

81 C.A.R. Crosland, 'Can Labour Win?', in Crosland, *The Conservative Enemy*, p. 153.

82 *Ibid.*, p. 154.

83 *Ibid.*, p. 157.

84 *Ibid.*, p. 160: see also 'More or Less Socialism?', *Socialist Commentary*, (November 1959), which awoved that, 'The essence of the socialist creed is a concern with the common good of all. It is precisely because we appear to be lacking in this concern that our image has become unattractive.' (p. 3).

85 *Ibid.*, p. 149: see also 'Ends and Means', *Socialist Commentary*, editorial, (January 1960).

86   *Ibid.*, p. 154.
87   In M. Abrams, *Must Labour Lose?*, p. 111.
88   See S. Haseler, *The Gaitskellites*, pp. 158—77; R.T. McKenzie, *British Political Parties*, pp. 606—11.
89   See *LPCR*, 1957, pp. 135 & 139.
90   Both *New Statesman* and *Tribune* came out in favour of unilateralism in 1958 and the Campaign for Nuclear Disarmament was already mobilizing support.
91   See Lord Windlesham, *Communication and Political Power*; S. Haseler, *The Gaitskellites*; and P. Seyd, *Factionalism with the Labour Party*. One London group consisted of Jenkins, Crosland, Jay and Gordon Walker, though they never allowed this to be publicly known and they did not attach their signatures to *A Manifesto: addressed to the Labour Party* (the initial communique of CDS). The other groups consisted of professional men of various descriptions, significant among them Will Rodgers, Denis Howell, Dick Taverne, Michael Shanks and Philip Williams.
92   Haseler, *The Gaitskellites*; Windlesham, *Communication and Political Power*; CDS started out as 'Victory for Sanity', in direct opposition to 'Victory for Socialism'. It received very sympathetic press coverage and produced its own broadsheet *Campaign*. Realizing that for success at Blackpool one or more unions would have to be persuaded to reallocate their votes, it carefully planned its tactics so that it was well under way when the first two, most important, trade union conferences of 1961, USDAW and AEU took place. The organizers of CDS seem to have been proficient at their task of concentrating on key workers within the CLPs and the trade unions, and of getting favourable reports in the press, etc. CDS wound up in 1964 after Labour won the election, towards which most of its later activity was directed.
93   In M. Abrams, *Must Labour Lose?*, p. 102.
94   This is a phrase of A. Gamble, *The Conservative Nation*, e.g. p. 6.
95   See C.A.R. Crosland, *Can Labour Win?*.
96   J. Gyford & S. Haseler, *Social Democracy*.
97   C.A.R. Crosland, *The New Socialism*, p. 13.
98   See C.A.R. Crosland, *Socialism Now*, pp. 98—108: and see below, Chapter 7.
99   See R.T. McKenzie, *British Political Parties*.
100   D. Rawson, 'The Life-Span of Labour Parties'.
101   For 'sectarian doctrinaires' who 'still live in the misery and murk of the nineteen-thirties' see *Socialist Commentary*, (December 1960): for attacks on the trade unions see *Socialist Commentary* (October 1960), (January 1960; Fox pp. 16—19), and 'Ballotting the Members', (February 1961).
102   'Unions and the Party' editorial, *Socialist Commentary*, (October, 1960).
103   'Ballotting the Members', editorial, *Socialist Commentary*, (February 1961).
104   H. Spencer, *Man Versus the State*, editor's introduction by D. MacRae, p. 7.
105   See R. Skidelski, *Oswald Mosley*, p. 154.
106   See N. Harris, *Competition and the Corporate Society*; and A. Gamble, *The Conservative Nation*.
107   See T.H. Green, *Lectures on the Principles of Political Obligation*; and M. Richter, *The Politics of Conscience*.
108   Richter argued that T.H. Green was closer to Bright than is usually assumed: *The Politics of Conscience*, pp. 267—73.
109   L.T. Hobhouse, *Liberalism*, p. 110; and see P. Weiler, 'The New Liberalism of L.T. Hobhouse', p. 157.
110   L.T. Hobhouse, *Liberalism*, p. 70.

111   T.H. Marshall, *Citizenship and Social Class*, pp. 28—9.
112   *Ibid.*, p. 47.
113   C.A.R. Crosland, *Socialism Now*, p. 194: (part of a speech given in 1966).
114   Socialist Union, *Socialism*, p. 47.
115   See T. Nairn, *The Break-Up of Britain*; cf. P. Anderson, 'Components of the National Culture', in R. Blackburn & A. Cockburn, eds., *Student Power.*
116   *The Future of Socialism*, pp. 196—7.
117   *Ibid.*, p. 115.
118   For a recent summary of the voluntarist component in union ideology see A. Fenley, 'Labour and the Trade Unions', in C. Cook & I. Taylor, eds., *The Labour Party*, pp. 50—53.
119   See Haseler, *The Gaitskellites*; Beer, *Modern British Politics*; and Howell, *British Social Democracy.*
120   See Chapter 4, below.
121   For analysis of this antagonism see L. Minkin, 'The British Labour Party and the Trade Unions'.
122   See Z. Bauman, 'Officialdom and Class', in F. Parkin, ed., *The Social Analysis of Class Structure.*
123   M. Ziff, 'The Myth of the Myth of Classlessness', (unpublished paper, Leeds University, 1975).
124   See L.V. Panitch, *Social Democracy and Industrial Militancy*, pp. 47—52.

CHAPTER 4

1   The sole exponent of the opposite position is M. Jenkins, *Bevanism, Labour's High Tide.* He argues, on the strength of CLP membership figures, levels of union affiliation, and voting at union and Party conferences, that the Bevanites were attracting very substantial working class support within the movement (pp. 113—45). This demonstration appears to me to be founded on a spurious interpretation of the statistics. His other main argument, that the Bevanites were unable to develop a consistent attitude towards the USSR and Eastern Europe, is true; but to claim that it was their 'greatest single deficiency' is to exaggerate.
2   The debate was relatively quiescent during the early 1950s. The split in the Communist Party over Hungary in 1956 revived it. The emergence of the New Left and the revival of Trotskyism ensured its further development. The Bevanites themselves largely ignored it. All contemporary analyses of the Labour left are, however, coloured by the dispute.
3   D. Coates, *The Labour Party and the Struggle for Socialism*, pp. 177—217.
4   *Ibid.*; R. Miliband, *Parliamentary Socialism*, pp. 13—16.
5   C. Harman, 'Tribune of the People, II'.
6   *Ibid.*, p. 16.
7   Cf. Miliband, *Parliamentary Socialism*, p. 327, who rather surprisingly implied that the left foreign policy of the period was not distinctive.
8   S. Beer, *Modern British Politics*, p. 219ff.
9   *Tribune*, 2 January, 1948. See also Jennie Lee, *Tribune*, 9 March, 1956, for a later reflection:

> In the immediate post-war years, while the Labour Government elected in 1945 still retained its socialist vigour, Britain's standing in the world was very different. We had authority. We had moral status. We were champions of ordinary men and women. We had fought Hitler. We had begun to build a new society on the ruins of the old. For a time Britain held out the hope that our gentler, more democratic approach was winning the day ...

It was not our bombs or bank balance that impressed. It was the free national health service, the nationalisation of steel, our insistence on planning priorities.

10 *Keeping Left*, Preface.
11 *Ibid.*, p. 3.
12 *Ibid.*, p. 28.
13 *Ibid.*, p. 32.
14 See I. Mikardo, *The Second Five Years*.
15 *Keeping Left*, p. 42.
16 *Ibid.*, p. 4.
17 A. Bevan, *Democratic Values*, p. 11.
18 *Keeping Left*, p. 39.
19 *Ibid.*, p. 40.
20 Cf. J. O'Connor, *The Fiscal Crisis of the State*, pp. 13–22, who distinguished competitive, monopoly and state sectors of the economy and showed how each embodied a different rationale with respect to the determination of levels of wages and profits.
21 R.H.S. Crossman, *Socialist Values in a Changing Civilisation*, thought a solution to the wages and profits question the most important facing the Labour government.
22 A. Bevan, *In Place of Fear*, p. 2.
23 *Ibid.*, pp. 10–11; see also M. Foot, *Parliament in Danger!*, for an even more conventional account of parliamentary practice and its value.
24 Bevan, *In Place of Fear*, p. 29.
25 *Ibid.*, p. 47.
26 Bevan was most effective at criticism of capitalist culture and *mores*.
27 *One Way Only*, (Tribune pamphlet).
28 *Ibid.*
29 M.R. Gordon, *Conflict and Consensus*, p. 240.
30 *One Way Only*, p. 2.
31 Foreword to H. Jenkins & W. Wolfgang, *Tho' Cowards Flinch*.
32 *Ibid.*, p. 3.
33 K. Hindell & P. Williams, 'Scarborough and Blackpool'.
34 Victory for Socialism, *The Red Sixties*, p. 8.
35 *Ibid.*, p. 11.
36 *Tribune*, 4 May 1956, and *Tribune*, 3 August 1956.
37 *Ibid.*, 16 March 1956.
38 See *Tribune*, 29 June 1956, 19 July 1957, 23 August 1957, 6 September 1957.
39 *Tribune*, 16 August 1957, p. 5.
40 See I. Mikardo, *Tribune*, 12 December 1958.
41 *Tribune*, 15 November 1957.
42 *Ibid.*, 20 February 1959, and 6 March 1959.
43 *Ibid.*, 7 September 1962, and 16 February 1962.
44 *Ibid.*, 6 September 1963.
45 *Ibid.*, 9 January 1959.
46 I. Mikardo, 'Present Day Problems of Great Britain's Labour Movement', p. 128.
47 *Tribune*, 14 December, 1956.
48 Ted Bedford, (Secretary of the Political Committee of the London Co-operative Society), *Tribune*, 16 October 1959.
49 See Judith Hart, 'What we need is basic political education', *Tribune*, 16 October 1959; also 'The Age for Socialism', Victory for Socialism Manifesto, *Tribune*, 13 November 1959.

50 *Ibid.*
51 *Tribune*, 11 December 1959.
52 *Ibid.*, 3 January 1958.
53 *Ibid.*, 21 April 1962.
54 *Ibid.*, 30 November 1962.
55 *New Statesman*, 12 March 1955, p. 345.
56 Victory for Socialism, *Policy for Summit Talks*, p. 10.
57 *Ibid.*
58 *Ibid.*
59 Victory for Socialism, *Why NATO?*, p. 15.
60 *LPCR*, 1957, pp. 179—82.
61 See M.M. Foot, *Aneurin Bevan, 1945—60*, Volume II, pp. 547—83.
62 *Tribune*, 19 January 1962.
63 VFS Statement, *Tribune*, 19 January 1962.
64 *Ibid.*
65 *Tribune*, 11 May 1962.
66 T. Nairn, 'The Left Against Europe'.
67 E.g. Harman, 'Tribune of the People'; and D. Coates, *The Labour Party and the Struggle for Socialism*, p. 205.
68 See G. Lichtheim, *Marxism*; and R. Jacoby, 'The Politics of the Crisis Theory'.
69 *The Red Sixties*, p. 14.
70 S. Perlman, *A Theory of the Labor Movement*; and I. Richter, *Political Purpose in Trade Unions*.
71 'The Injured Party', *Socialist Commentary*, (April, 1955).
72 F. Parkin, *Middle Class Radicalism*, pp. 174—92.
73 D. Widgery, *The Left in Britain, 1956—68*, p. 114.
74 See P. Anderson, 'The Left in the 50s'; and F. Parkin, *Middle Class Radicalism*.

CHAPTER 5

1   E.g. P. Anderson, 'Critique of Wilsonism'.
2   The Labour Party frequently produces people who seek to procure a compromise between various segments in the Party. For example, Wilson was aligned with Crossman and Wigg among others in the unilateralist dispute, trying to get the Party to cover over its differences. However the term 'centrism' avoids any question of what the content of such a compromise might be. It is particularly misleading in this case.
3   M. Shanks, *The Stagnant Society*; also the symposium, 'Suicide of a Nation?' *Encounter*, July, 1963.
4   E.g. P. Einzig, *Decline and Fall?*
5   *Let's Go with Labour for the New Britain*.
6   *LPCR* 1963, p. 272.
7   *LPCR* 1963, p. 140.
8   'The New Britain', speech made at Town Hall, Birmingham, 19th January, 1964, in *The New Britain: Labour's Plan Outlined by Harold Wilson*.
9   A. Wedgwood Benn, *The Regeneration of Britain*, p. 31.
10 *Ibid.*, p. 13.
11 P. Shore, *Entitled to Know*, p. 150.
12 In *The New Britain*, p. 14.
13 *Ibid.*, pp. 14—15.
14 H. Wilson, *The Relevance of British Socialism*, p. 55.

15 Labour and the Scientific Revolution, *LPCR* 1963, p. 275.
16 *Let's Go With Labour.*
17 For a discussion of some of the reasons for the failure of indicative planning in Britain between 1964 and 1970 see S. Holland, *The Socialist Challenge*, pp. 120—28.
18 See *One Way Only*, (Tribune Pamphlet, 1951).
19 H. Wilson, 'A Four-Year Plan for Britain', *New Statesman*, 24 March 1961, p. 463.
20 *The Relevance of British Socialism*, p. 22.
21 'A Four-Year Plan for Britain', p. 468.
22 *The Relevance of British Socialism*, p. 98.
23 T. Nairn, *The Left Against Europe.*
24 See L.V. Panitch, 'Ideology and Integration'.
25 *The Relevance of British Socialism*, p. 22.
26 J. Habermas, *Towards a Rational Society*, pp. 62—80.
27 C. Mueller, *The Politics of Communication.*
28 P. Shore, *Entitled to Know*, pp. 152—3.
29 *Ibid.*, p. 152.
30 See A. Wedgwood Benn, *The New Politics.*
31 G. Fanti, 'The Resurgence of the Labour Party'; see also P. Anderson, 'Critique of Wilsonism', which was rather less effusive but still quite impressed by the potential of the new Labour government.
32 G. Fanti, 'The Resurgence of the Labour Party', p. 34.
33 *The Regeneration of Britain*, p. 143.
34 Wilson in early times, and to some extent at the beginning of the 1964—70 administration, did make significant and concrete references to social problems which predominantly affected the working class. See his speech, made when moving the 1956 NEC statement 'Towards Equality' at Conference, quoted by P. Foot, *The Politics of Harold Wilson*, pp. 143—4. Wilson seemed gradually to forget about this element of the Labourist tradition as he became more involved in solving technical problems. His penchant for such problem-solving is of course apparent in his pronouncements as a Bevanite, and in his seeming relish of administration in the civil service during the war: see L. Smith, *Harold Wilson.*
35 See J. Northcott, *Why Labour?*
36 This represented a change in Houghton's position since 1960: see his 'One Nation or Two?', *Socialist Commentary*, (June, 1960), where he opposed any decline in universalism in social provision.
37 *Paying for the Social Services*, p. 11.
38 *Ibid.*, p. 23.
39 Both B. Abel-Smith and P. Townsend, who were important figures inspiring the social policies of Technocratic-Collectivism, began to write critical essays on Labour's performance as early as 1966: B. Abel-Smith, *Labour's Social Plans*; P. Townsend, *Poverty, Socialism and Labour in Power*. For a critical assessment after the government had left office see P. Townsend & N. Bosanquet, eds., *Labour and Inequality.*
40 See, for example, B. Whitaker, ed., *A. Radical Future*; J. Saville, 'Labourism and the Labour Government'; R. Williams, ed., *May Day Manifesto*; T. Burgess *et al.*, *Matters of Principle*; W. Beckerman, ed., *The Economic Record of the Labour Government*; D. Coates, *The Labour Party and the Struggle for Socialism*, pp. 97—129.
41 See H. Wilson, *The Labour Government.*

42 W. Beckerman, 'Objectives and performance: an overall view', in Beckerman, *The Economic Record.*

43 See P. Foot, *The Politics of Harold Wilson*, pp. 155—98, amassing a catalogue of statements by Wilson, and some by Callaghan, proclaiming the end of the immediate crisis and the imminent departure on the journey to the New Britain. These were repeatedly confounded by further adverse turns in the course of economic events.

44 *The Relevance of Socialism*, p. 56.

45 B. Lapping, *The Labour Government 1964—70*, p. 36.

46 *Ibid.*, p. 54.

47 See M. Shanks, *Planning and Politics*, pp. 35—9 (esp. p. 37).

48 See S. Holland, *Socialist Challenge*, esp. p. 134.

49 A. Budd, *The Politics of Economic Planning*, pp. 111—14.

50 M. Shanks, *Planning and Politics*, pp. 34—5.

51 B. Lapping, *The Labour Government 1964—70*, p. 42.

52 H. Wilson, *The Labour Government*, pp. 61—6.

53 See P. Foot, *The Politics of Harold Wilson*, p. 185, who says that Wilson did not make any important statement about the economy between 27 June 1966 and 31 May 1967.

54 Although those people relying on public benefits might have been better off in 1969 than in 1964, see M. Stewart, 'The Distribution of Income', in W. Beckerman, ed., *The Economic Record*, pp. 98—103.

55 The Minister of Education was Crosland, who was more concerned with equal opportunity and status than with real social equality. Equal opportunity was an integral part of the Wilson strategy in that the removal of well-connected amateurs from key occupational positions implied that more capable beings existed elsewhere and could be nurtured through education.

56 One of Wilson's principal electoral jibes against the Conservatives was that they would replace the Welfare State with the Means Test State.

57 Within Crossman's proposals for a graduated pensions scheme there was a certain redistributive mechanism; those of the lower end of the contribution scale were to receive proportionally greater benefits in return.

58 'The 1969 National Superannuation and Social Insurance Bill involved *some* degree of income redistribution', J. Kincaid, *Poverty and Inequality in England*, p. 138. Stewart also shows that there was some redistribution through social benefits accruing to the very poor. The proportional tax contributions of those with incomes above £1,000 p.a. remained more or less the same: M. Stewart, 'The Distribution of Income'.

59 See P. Kellner & C. Hitchens, *Callaghan*, pp. 75—86.

60 Cf. W. Beckerman, *The Economic Record*, pp. 48—52.

61 See A. Shonfield, *Modern Capitalism.*

62 B. Catley & B. McFarlane, 'Labour's Plans'.

63 *Ibid.*; also their, *From Tweedledum to Tweedledee.*

64 See E. Hobsbawm, 'The Fabians Re-considered', in *Labouring Men*, pp. 250—71.

65 One of the ironies about this was that Wilson in his memoirs constantly extols his Civil Servants despite the fact that he made no significant changes in personnel.

66 A.M. McBriar, *Fabian Socialism and English Politics 1884—1914*, p. 65.

67 B. Semmel, *Imperialism and Social Reform.*

68 See G. Searle, *The Quest for National Efficiency.*

69 It should be remembered that Wilson's main criticism of Gaitskell was that he tended unnecessarily to promote discord in the Party.

70   See L.V. Panitch, *Social Democracy and Industrial Militancy*, pp. 52—62. George Woodcock, General Secretary of the TUC, was an important figure in establishing support for the idea: for an expression of his approach to voluntary agreement between the TUC and government see his *The Trade Union Movement and the Government.*

71   Fanti, 'The Resurgence of the Labour Party'.

72   Though see Roger Williams, *Politics and Technology*, pp. 52—7, for reservations about the extent of a techno-stratum in Britain.

73   P. Foot, *The Politics of Harold Wilson*, pp. 153—4.

74   A. Wedgwood Benn, *The New Politics*, p. 11.

75   *Ibid.*, p. 23.

76   See B. Barry, *Political Argument*, pp. 207—36; also S. Lukes, *Power.*

77   *Entitled to Know*, pp. 152—3.

CHAPTER 6

1   On the escalation of industrial militancy in the 1970s see C. Crouch, 'The Intensification of Industrial Conflict in the United Kingdom', in C. Crouch & A. Pizzorno, eds. *The Resurgence of Class Conflict.*

2   P. Mattick, *Marx and Keynes.*

3   For a discussion of this point see F. Hirsch, *The Social Limits to Growth*, pp. 173—8.

4   J. O'Connor, *The Fiscal Crisis of the State.*

5   For the concept of collective consumption see M. Castells, *The Urban Question*, pp. 460—2.

6   C. Mueller, *The Politics of Communication*, p. 136.

7   See J. Habermas, *Legitimation Crisis.*

8   *Ibid.*, pp. 80—9.

9   Mueller, *Politics of Communication*, p. 136.

10   *Ibid.*, p. 167.

CHAPTER 7

1   E.g. 'Misleaders of Opinion', *Socialist Commentary*, (January, 1969); 'Let's Keep Our Heads', *Socialist Commentary* (May, 1969); C.A.R. Crosland, *Socialism Now, passim.*

2   *Socialist Commentary*, editorial, (June, 1970).

3   R. Jenkins, 'Labour in the Seventies — "Retrospect and Prospect"', *Socialist Commentary*, (November, 1970), p. 4.

4   *Socialism Now*, pp. 18—22.

5   'Labour and "Populism"', originally published in *Sunday Times*, 4 April, 1971, re-printed in *Socialism Now*, pp. 97—8.

6   *Socialist Commentary*, editorial, (July, 1970).

7   *Socialist Commentary*, editorial, (February, 1970): see also R. Prentice, 'What Kind of Labour Party?', *Socialist Commentary*, (April 1973).

8   *Socialism Now*, p. 26.

9   *Ibid.*, p. 57.

10   *Ibid.*, p. 63.

11   R. Jenkins, *What Matters Now*, p. 15.

12   Cf. Tribune's amazement and disbelief in reviewing the book — *Tribune*, 21 July 1972.

13 *What Matters Now*, p. 41.
14 'injustice between the regions cannot be dealt with except by a significant expansion of the public sector', (*ibid.*, p. 36).
15 *Ibid.*, p. 25.
16 *Ibid.*, p. 30.
17 *Ibid.*, p. 19.
18 *Ibid.*, p. 17—18.
19 *Ibid.*, p. 57.
20 *Ibid.*, pp. 36—7.
21 *Ibid.*, pp. 83—4.
22 *Socialist Commentary*, editorial (December, 1970).
23 R. Prentice, 'What Kind of a Labour Party?'. *Socialist Commentary* (April, 1973).
24 Cf. 'Parting of the Ways', *Socialist Commentary* (March 1971); also the article by A. Day, *Socialist Commentary* (February, 1971), pp. 9—10.
25 For a discussion of Britain as a corporate state, see the editorial of *Socialist Commentary* (December, 1972).
26 Gyford & Haseler, *Social Democracy*.
27 *Socialism Now*, p. 104—5.
28 *Ibid.*, p. 105.
29 See P. Norton, *Dissension in the House of Commons*, pp. 395—8.
30 See Haseler, *The Gaitskellites*, pp. 227—36. For a Social Reformist argument against entry see D. Jay, *After the Common Market*. For a history of pro-Market activity in the Labour Party see U. Kitzinger, *Diplomacy and Persuasion*.
31 See *Socialist Commentary*, editorial, (October, 1971).
32 The Werner Plan was given great accolades: see D. Taverne, *Monetary and Economic Union in Europe*.
33 See A. Day, *Socialist Commentary* (June, 1972) on the buoyancy of European social democracy. Social Reformists, and *Socialist Commentary*, were loyal supporters of the Socialist International.
34 A common European defence policy was one hope of the Social Reformists, a way of getting out of the embarrassment of the link with the USA in NATO.
35 For a summary of the arguments used in the debate of October 1971, see Norton, *Dissension in the House of Commons*, pp. 396—7.
36 See, for example, the debate on 'the end of the democratic era' in *Socialist Commentary*, Feb. 1974; note also M. Meacher, 'Is Britain Governable Any More?', *Socialist Commentary*, March 1974.
37 The theme of equality still recurred in Social Reformist thought, but its ambience was much more limited. For a rather unconvincing regurgitation of the juxtaposition of 'liberty' and 'equality' and the desirability of gradual, *piecemeal* change see R. Hattersley, 'The Radical Alternative', *New Statesman*, 31 Oct. 1975. It is interesting to compare C.A.R. Crosland, *Social Democracy in Europe*, with the Manifesto Group of Labour MPs, *What We Must Do*: whereas Crosland appeared fairly unrepentant about his advocacy of egalitarianism despite economic problems, the Manifesto Group were far more circumspect and hesitant about their commitment to equality.
38 As a statement of the Manifesto Group, 'Keep On Course', *Socialist Commentary*, Dec. 1976, p. 3, put it: 'For the past two years the Government has pursued an economic strategy with two overriding aims: to reduce inflation and to regenerate industry. That strategy has had, and will continue to have, our complete support.'
39 'Profit and Socialism', *Socialist Commentary*, June 1974.

40   For various definitions of democratic socialism see 'A Year for the Party', *Socialist Commentary*, Jan. 1977; 'Phase III for Socialism', *Socialist Commentary*, May 1977; R. Jenkins, 'Europe' (Hinden Memorial Lecture), *Socialist Commentary*, March 1978; M. Stewart, 'Strivings of Democratic Socialism', *Socialist Commentary*, Nov. 1978. For some particularly spurious uses of the term 'socialism', see 'A Year for Realities', *Socialist Commentary*, Jan. 1975.

41   'Phase III for the Party', *Socialist Commentary*, May 1977.

42   Manifesto Group, *What We Must Do*, p. 12.

43   *Ibid.*, p. 18.

44   *Ibid.*, p. 15.

45   *Ibid.*, p. 14.

46   See, for example, 'Language of Priorities', *Socialist Commentary*, November 1975; and *What We Must Do*, p. 23.

47   W. Rodgers, 'Socialism Without Abundance' (Hinden Memorial Lecture), *Socialist Commentary*, July 1977.

48   The terms are those of J. Habermas, *Legitimation Crisis*, p. 75. 'Civil privatism' denotes 'little participation in the legitimising process' and 'corresponds to the structures of a depoliticised public realm'. 'Familial–vocational privatism ... consists in a family orientation with developed interests in consumption and leisure on the one hand, and in a career orientation suitable to status competition on the other.'

49   *What We Must Do*, p. 16.

50   *Ibid.*, p. 16.

51   See 'Taking and Paying', *Socialist Commentary*, July/August 1975.

52   See 'Who is for Socialism', *Socialist Commentary*, January 1974; 'Frankness for Victory', *Socialist Commentary*, July/August 1974; 'Taking and Paying', *Socialist Commentary*, July/August 1975; 'Phase III for Socialism', *Socialist Commentary*, May 1977.

53   'Consent — or What?', *Socialist Commentary*, September 1975.

54   'Consensus? Nonsense!', *Socialist Commentary*, May 1975.

55   'Two Oppositions', *Socialist Commentary*, November 1976.

56   'Conference, Party and Government', *Socialist Commentary*, December 1974.

57   'Party and the Politicians', *Socialist Commentary*, October 1975.

58   For a brief account of these, and other, intra-party organizations in the 1970s see P. Seyd, 'Fighting for the soul of the Labour Party', *New Society*, 20 April 1978.

59   Social Democratic Alliance, 'A Manifesto', *Socialist Commentary*, July/August 1975, p. 20.

60   'Government and Party', *Socialist Commentary*, July/August 1975.

61   P. Seyd, 'Fighting for the Soul of the Labour Party'.

62   'Two Oppositions', *Socialist Commentary*, November 1976, p. 3.

63   See, for example, F. Mulley, 'The Imperatives of Defence', *Socialist Commentary*, November 1977.

64   '*Bundeskanzler* Callaghan', *Socialist Commentary*, May 1976.

65   'Must Socialism Wait?', *Socialist Commentary*, April 1977.

CHAPTER 8

1   T. Nairn, *The Left Against Europe*, p. 63.

2   See M. Hastings, *The House the Left Built*, pp. 151–6.

3   On Holland's role in the formation of policy see M. Hastings, *The House the Left Built*, pp. 87–90: see also Chapter 9 below.

4   M. Hastings, *The House the Left Built*, esp. pp. 237–44.
5   *The Regeneration of British Industry*, (HMSO, Cmnd. 5710, August 1974).
6   *Ibid.*, p. 2.
7   See A. Shonfield, *Modern Capitalism*; also S. Holland, *The Socialist Challenge*.
8   *The Regeneration of British Industry*, p. 6.
9   Reported in *Guardian*, 28 November, 1974.
10 *The Regeneration of British Industry*, p. 7.
11 *Economic Policy and the Cost of Living*, p. 3.
12 *Ibid.*, pp. 3–4.
13 *Ibid.*, p. 6.
14 *Ibid.*, p. 8.
15 *Ibid.*
16 *Ibid.*
17 In the mid 1960s Beer was speculting about the possibility that increased involve-
    ment in government by functional interest groups would produce a 'highly statist
    form of corporatism', S. Beer, *Modern British Politics*, p. 428. For an indication
    of an analysis which likens corporatism to fascism see R. Huntford, *The New
    Totalitarians*.
18 See D. Marsh & W. Grant, 'Tripartism: Reality or Myth', pp. 207–8.
19 B. Jessop, 'Corporatism, Fascism and Social Democracy', (mimeo, paper presented
    at Leeds University, April 1978).
20 *Ibid.*, p. 6.
21 E.g., G. Lehmbruch, 'Liberal Corporatism and Party Government'.
22 Marsh and Grant, 'Tripartism: Reality or Myth', make just such an error. They
    define tripartism in such a way that it includes a basic consensus and 'similar
    degrees of influence' among its adherents. Consequently they argue that tri-
    partism is mythical and dismiss the most significant development in British
    politics in the last decade as unimportant.
23 For an account of the Lib–Lab pact see A. Michie & S. Hoggart, *The Pact*.
24 For a summary of the Party's proposals see *Labour's Programme: Campaign
    Document* 1974, p. 15.
25 For a convenient summary of statistical information on the government's econ-
    omic policies see D. McKie, C. Cook & M. Phillips, *The Guardian Quartet Election
    Guide*. For the Labour Party's own account see *The Economy*, (Labour Party
    Campaign Handbook, 1978). The information in this section derives from mis-
    cellaneous newspaper, periodical and pamphlet sources. David Coates, *Labour
    in Power?*, contains a detailed analysis of the Governments' economic policies,
    but was, unfortunately, published too late for me to make full use of.
26 M. Shanks, *Planning and Politics*, pp. 78–84.
27 *Ibid.*, p. 81.
28 *Ibid.*, p. 13.
29 R. Bacon & W. Eltis, *Britain's Economic Problem*.
30 R. Taylor, *Labour and the Social Contract*, concluded that the unions had had
    very little influence on general economic strategy (except between the two elect-
    ions in 1974), industrial strategy, or even industrial relations legislation. (p. 13).
31 D. Marsh & W. Grant, 'Tripartism: Reality or Myth'.
32 T. Nairn, 'The Left Against Europe'; and *The Break-Up of Britain,* esp. Ch. 1.
33 See R. Bacon & W. Eltis, *Britain's Economic Problem*, pp. 27–32. For a critique
    of these categories see B. Sedgemore, *The How and Why of Socialism*, pp. 52–3.
34 For a brief treatment of this idea of Saint-Simon, see A. Gray, *The Socialist
    Tradition*, pp. 150–54.

35 J. Habermas, *Legitimation Crisis*, pp. 70—5.
36 See *Comparative Political Studies*, 10(1), (1977).

CHAPTER 9

1   The Tribune Group was formed in September 1966.
2   Even Left-wing commentators outside the Labour Party shared this belief. See for example, Fanti, 'The resurgence of the Labour Party', for an extremely optimistic view of the socialist potential of the Wilson strategy; and P. Anderson, 'Critique of Wilsonism', for a more ambivalent but still optimistic appraisal.
3   E.g. *Tribune*, 11 September 1964.
4   M. Foot, *Tribune*, 25 September 1964, who said that though the Labour programme was not as socialist as he would like, it was a far remove from the defeatism of 1959 and was promising.
5   'The Labour Government and Home Affairs', *Tribune*, 23 October 1964, p. 5.
6   *Tribune*, 11 November 1964, p. 4.
7   *Ibid.*, p. 5. Mikardo was still making the same provisional excuses in April 1965 (see *Tribune*, 16 April 1965, p. 5.), namely that the majority small and that Labour had inherited an economic mess. However he argued that though there had been some lively activity, this represented an 'improvement in means rather than re-casting of ends'. He expressed dissatisfaction at the nature of foreign policy over East of Suez, Vietnam, the defence budget, and East—West tension. And concerning domestic policy he argued that 'the two key factors in our economic structure remain virtually unchanged. These key features are (i) the relative size of the public and private sectors; and (ii) the relations between the Government and the private sector.'
8   *Tribune*, 26 February, 1965, p. 1.
9   Quoted by L. Panitch, *The Labour Party and the Trade Unions*, p. 111.
10 *Tribune*, 11 February, 1966.
11 *Ibid.*, 14 May, 1965, p. 7.
12 *Ibid.*, 17 December, 1965, p. 9.
13 *Ibid.*, 30 April, 1965. p. 4.
14 *Ibid.*, 7 May, 1965, p. 4.
15 *Ibid.*, 17 December, 1965, p. 4.
16 *Ibid.*, 17 September, 1964, p. 5.
17 *Ibid.*, 1 April, 1966, p. 1.
18 *Ibid.*, 22 June, 1967.
19 E.g. I. Mikardo, *Tribune*, 2 August 1968, (on incomes policy): 'We (*Tribune*) have not opposed the policy or the Acts, because we are in principle against an incomes policy. Our opposition is to this particular policy within the particular circumstances of the present time, and particularly within the general framework of non-Socialist economic and social policies, i.e. of a failure to extend public ownership, to use selective economic controls and to narrow the gap between rich and poor'. See also S. Orme, *Tribune*, 15 March, 1968.
20 *Tribune*, 8 December, 1967.
21 *Ibid.*, editorials, 3 January, 1969, and 17 January, 1969.
22 Panitch, *Social Democracy and Industrial Militancy*, p. 182.
23 *Tribune*, editorials, 3 January, 1969, 10 January, 1969, 7 March, 1969; and H. Collins, 'Strategy for the Left', 24 January, 1969.
24 *Tribune*, 21 July, 1967.
25 *Ibid.*, 7 June, 1968, p. 5.

26 *Ibid.*, 8 January, 1970. p. 3.

27 See *Tribune*, 22 April, 1966, 6 May, 1966, 13 May, 1966, and 27 May, 1966.

28 See Heffer, *Tribune*, 6 May, 1966, and H. Jenkins, *Tribune*, 27 May, 1966.

29 M. Foot, 'Credo of the Labour Left — Interview', *New Left Review*, 49, (1968), p. 32.

30 *Tribune*, 1 May, 1970; see also Scanlon, *Tribune*, 10 April 1970.

31 *Ibid.*, 12 June, 1970.

32 *Ibid.*, 26 June, 1970.

33 *Ibid.*, 31 July, 1970.

34 *Ibid.*, 3 July, 1970.

35 *Ibid.*, 28 May, 1971.

36 P. Shore, *Tribune*, 7 January, 1972; see also P. Shore, *Europe: the way back*, (Fabian Tract 425, 1973).

37 See Tribune Group statement on Labour and the Common Market, *Tribune*, 4 February, 1972, p. 6.

38 *Tribune*, 15 October, 1971.

39 *Ibid.*, 3 September, 1971.

40 *Ibid.*

41 *Ibid.*

42 F. Allaun, *No Place Like Home: Britain's Housing Tragedy*, (London, 1972).

43 *Tribune*, 10 September, 1971.

44 'Miners' Victory', editorial, *Voice of the Unions*, (March, 1972).

45 See e.g. *Labour's Programme for Britain: The Red Paper*, (Nottingham, n.d.), signed by Barratt-Brown, Ken Coates, Stan Newens, Joan Maynard and others which concluded 'Socialism will consist of a self-managing society, democratically constituted at every level, or it will not exist at all.' (pp. 19–20).

46 R. Fletcher, *Tribune*, 16 March 1973.

47 *Ibid.*, 10 August 1973.

48 *Ibid.*, 4 September 1970.

49 *Ibid.*, 11 September 1970.

50 See Hastings, *The House the Left Built*, pp. 171–90.

51 This was the principal theme of Judith Hart's commendation of the NEB, see *Tribune*, 25 May 1973; see also *Tribune*, 4 May 1973.

52 'We've kept the Red Flag flying here', *Tribune*, 6 October 1973; and *Tribune*, 9 November 1973.

53 *Tribune*, 2 March 1973; see also Jack Jones endorsement, 27 April, 1973.

54 See L. Minkin, 'The British Labour Party and the Trade Unions', for evidence of changing political complexion of the TUC General Council.

55 See *Tribune*, 23 August 1974, p. 5.; and *Tribune*, 7 February 1975, editorial, 'The People's Bill'.

56 *Tribune*, 1 March 1974, p. 8.

57 *Tribune*, 1 March 1974, p. 1.

58 TUC, *Economic Review*, 1974. *Tribune* welcomed it in an article 'TUC strategy sets course for Britain', 22 March 1974.

59 E.g. *Tribune*, 26 April 1974 and 4 October 1974.

60 See M. Hatfield, *The House the Left Built*, *passim*.

61 See 'The Crisis — and the only way in which the Labour Government can solve it!' Tribune Group Statement, *Tribune*, 31 January 1975, p. 1.

62 *Ibid.*

63 *Ibid.*, p. 5.

64 *Ibid.*; see also S. Holland's article, *Tribune*, 29 September 1978.

65 See *Labour's Programme 1973*, p. 34; also S. Holland *The Socialist Challenge*, pp. 159—62, and 177—211, and especially 24—30.

66 See *Labour's Programme 1973*, pp. 30—36.

67 Brian Sedgemore was the most trenchant critic of the City: see *The How and Why of Socialism*, pp. 46—9; also his articles in *Tribune*, 21 June 1974, 17 January 1975, and 8 October 1976.

68 See B. Sedgemore, 'Public Expenditure', *Tribune*, 20 February 1976; B. Castle, 'Reducing Growth — not making room for it!', *Tribune*, 30 July 1976.

69 E.g. *Tribune*, 20 January 1978, p. 2, and 24 February 1978.

70 S. Orme, *Tribune*, 16 September 1977, see also B. Dix, *Tribune*, 27 February 1976, p. 1., and B. Sedgemore, 'The City and CBI can now vote Labour', *Tribune*, 1 April 1977.

71 See, for example, R. Clements, 'Is Britain Bankrupt?', *Tribune*, 20 September 1974.

72 *Labour's Programme 1973*, pp. 26—8.

73 E.g., T. Benn, F. Morrell & F. Cripps, *A Ten-Year Industrial Strategy for Britain*.

74 S. Holland, *The Socialist Challenge*, pp. 255—69.

75 B. Sedgemore, *The How and Why of Socialism*, pp. 41—4.

76 See T. Benn, *Speeches by Tony Benn*.

77 *Tribune*, 17 June 1977, p. 5.

78 *Ibid.*. But note that Heffer's *ideal* form of self-management was probably the most radical of all.

79 Jones in 1974 and early 1975 was a staunch supporter of *Tribune* policies. By late 1975, however, he began to write articles which appealed for 'unity' rather than specific radical policies. An article in *Tribune*, 19 December 1975, indicated that he accepted the government's equation between inflation and unemployment; another article, *Tribune*, 5 March 1976, signified his acceptance of public expenditure cuts; and a further joint article with Scanlon and Basnett, *Tribune*, 19 March 1976, pleaded for unity behind the Labour government. It is not insignificant that it was in 1976 that the national press proclaimed that the left offensive had finally been contained. Later articles of Jones, see *Tribune*, 9 December 1977, became, once again, more sympathetic to left policies. The impression given is that Jones believed that maintaining a Labour government in power was the most important of all concerns.

80 E.g. editorial, *Tribune*, 9 September 1977.

81 The Campaign for Labour Party Democracy was founded in 1973 and was an extra-parliamentary campaign to increase the power of CLPs and Conference *vis-a-vis* the PLP. Its basic aim was 'the translation of the Labour Party programme into Labour government policies'. For its initial statement of aims see its 'Newsletter', June, 1973.

82 E. Heffer, *The Class Struggle in Parliament*, p. 17.

83 *Ibid.*, p. 280.

84 *Ibid.*, p. 281 and p. 17.

85 *Ibid.*, p. 20.

86 *Ibid.*, p. 67.

87 Heffer, *The Class Struggle in Parliament*, p. 102. This development was welcomed by Mikardo as early as 1965: 'Some of the most militant voices heard at Blackpool (Conference, 1965) were those of the 1964 intake into the Trade Union Group of the PLP. That Group, too, is losing its monolithic, universally conformist character it had a few years ago.' (*Tribune*, 8 October, 1965). In 1972, 24 out of 48 members of the Tribune Group were union-sponsored. There was a much

greater propensity for MPs sponsored by white-collar unions to be members of the Tribune Group, 33 per cent, cf. 15 per cent: see *Political Companion*, July–September, 1972, pp. 76–9 and 91.

88   See I. Richter, *Political Purpose in Trade Unions*, pp. 52–9.

89   See D. Houghton, 'Trade Union MPs'; also W.D. Muller, 'Union-MP Conflict'.

90   See L. Minkin, 'The British Labour Party and the Trade Unions'.

91   E.g. J. Jones, *What about the Pensioners?*

92   E. Heffer, *The Class Struggle in Parliament*.

93   J. Saville, 'The Ideology of Labourism'.

94   S. Holland, *The Socialist Challenge*, pp. 142–74.

95   *Ibid.*, pp. 149–56.

96   *Ibid.*, p. 179.

97   *Ibid.*, p. 144 and 154–62.

Select bibliography

The bibliography is divided into three sections: Official Party Publications, Primary Sources, and Secondary Sources. The decision as to whether a text should go into the second and third sections was sometimes difficult. In order to find the full references to works mentioned in the footnotes, where short titles are given, it may be necessary sometimes to look through sections 2 and 3.

1 OFFICIAL LABOUR PARTY PUBLICATIONS

Report of the Annual Conference of the Labour Party, (*LPCR*), 1956—77.

(a) Election Manifestos
1918—66, see F.W.S. Craig, editor, *British General Election Manifestos, 1918—66*, (Chichester, Political Reference Publications, 1970).
1970, *Now Britain's Strong — Let's make her great to live in.*
1974 (January), *Let Us Work Together — Labour's Way Out of the Crisis.*
1974 (October), *Britain Will Win With Labour.*
1979, *The Labour Way is the Better Way.*

(b) Other official statements
Labour and the New Social Order, 1918.
For Socialism and Peace, 1934.
Labour's Immediate Programme, 1937.
Production: the Bridge to Socialism, 1948.
Labour Believes in Britain, 1949.
Labour and the New Society, 1950.
Challenge to Britain, 1953.
Personal Freedom: Labour's Policy for the Individual and Society, 1956.
Towards Equality: Labour's Policy for Social Justice, 1956.
Industry and Society: Labour's Policy on Future Public Ownership, 1957.
Public Enterprise: Labour's Review of Nationalised Industries, 1957.
Disarmament and Nuclear War, 1958.
The Future Labour Offers You, 1958.
Labour's Foreign Policy, 1958.

Plan for Progress: Labour's Policy for British Economic Expansion, 1958.
Disarmament and Nuclear War: The Next Step, 1959.
The Constitution of the Labour Party, 1960.
Foreign Policy and Defence, 1960.
Labour in the Sixties, 1960.
Labour's Aims, 1960.
Signposts for the Sixties, 1961.
Policy for Peace, 1961.
Labour and the Common Market, 1962.
Labour and the Scientific Revolution, 1963.
Labour and the National Plan, 1965.
Overseas Policy, 1966.
Economic Policy, 1966.
Labour and the Common Market, 1967.
Action: The Economy, 1967.
Labour: Progress and Change, 1968.
Race Relations, 1968.
Labour's Economic Strategy, 1969.
Labour's Social Strategy, 1969.
Labour and the Common Market, 1969.
Agenda for a Generation, 1969.
Economic Strategy, Growth and Unemployment, 1971.
Labour and the Common Market: Report of Special Conference of the Labour Party, 1971.
Labour's Programme for Britain, 1972.
Labour's Programme, 1973.
Capital and Equality, 1973.
Economic Policy and the Cost of Living, 1973.
Labour's Programme: Campaign Document, 1974.
Labour and Industry: The Next Steps, 1975.
The Next Three Years: and the Problem of priorities, 1976.
Labour's Programme, 1976.
Labour Party Campaign Handbooks, 1978.
Into the Eighties: an agreement, 1978.

2   **PRIMARY SOURCES** (Works whose principal significance is in expressing or causing developments in ideologies)

(a) Periodicals
New Left Review
New Statesman
Socialist Commentary
Tribune
Voice of the Unions
Labour Weekly
Militant

(b) Books and articles
Abrams, M. & Rose, R., *Must Labour Lose?* (Harmondsworth, Penguin, 1960).
Albu, A., Prentice, R. & Bray, J. 'Lessons of the Labour Government', *Political Quarterly,* 14, (1970), 141–55.

Allaun, Frank, *No Place Like Home: Britain's Housing Tragedy*, (London, Deutsch, 1972).

Attlee, C.R., *The Labour Party in Perspective*, first published 1937, (London, Gollancz, 1949).

Attlee, C.R., *As It Happened*, (London, Heinemann, 1954).

Bacon, R. & Ellis, W., *Britain's Economic Problem: too few producers*, (2nd edition), (London, Macmillan, 1978).

Balogh, T. *Planning for Progress: A Strategy for Labour*, (Fabian Tract 346, 1963).

Benn, A.W.G., *The Regeneration of Britain*, (London, Gollancz, 1965).

Benn, A.W.G., *The New Politics: A Socialist Reconnaissance*, (Fabian Tract 402, September 1970).

Benn, T., *Speeches by Tony Benn*, (Nottingham, Spokesman, 1974).

Benn, T., Morrell, F. & Cripps, F., *A Ten-Year Industrial Strategy for Britain*, (I.W.C. pamphlet, No. 49).

Bevan, A., *Democratic Values*, (Fabian Tract 282, 1950).

Bevan, A., *In Place of Fear*, (London, Heinemann, 1952).

Bing, Inigo. (ed.), *The Labour Party: an Organizational Study*, (Fabian Tract 407, 1971).

Braddock, J. & B., *The Braddocks*, (London, Macdonald, 1963).

Bray, Jeremy W., *Decision in Government*, (London, Gollancz, 1970).

Brown, G., *In My Way*, (Harmondsworth, Penguin, 1972).

Brown, M. Barratt *et al.*, *The Red Paper: a response to Labour's Programme for Britain*, (Nottingham, Russell Press, 1972).

Burgess, T. *et al.*, *Matters of Principle: Labour's Last Chance*, (Harmondsworth, Penguin, 1968).

Callaghan, James, 'Labour's Plan for Prosperity', *Statist*, 16th February, 1962, pp. 486–7.

Callaghan, James, *A House Divided: the dilemma of Northern Ireland*, (London, Collins, 1973).

Crosland, C.A.R., *The Future of Socialism*, (London, Cape, 1956).

Crosland, C.A.R., *Can Labour Win?*, (Fabian Tract 324, 1960).

Crosland, C.A.R., *The Conservative Enemy*, (London, Cape, 1962).

Crosland, C.A.R., *The New Socialism: (Thomas Memorial Lecture)*, (Melbourne, Dissent Pamphlet No. 1, 1963).

Crosland, C.A.R., *A Social Democratic Britain*, (Fabian Tract 404, 1971).

Crosland, C.A.R., *Socialism Now*, (London, Cape, 1974).

Crosland, C.A.R., *Social Democracy in Europe*, (Fabian Tract 438, 1975).

Crossman, R.H.S., *Socialist Values in a Changing Civilisation*, (Fabian Tract 286, 1950).

Crossman, R.H.S. (editor), *New Fabian Essays*, (London, Turnstile Press, 1953).

Crossman, R.H.S., 'On Political Neuroses', *Encounter*, 2(1) (1954), 65–7.

Crossman, R.H.S., *Socialism and the new despotism*, (Fabian Tract 298, 1956).

Crossman, R.H.S., *Government and the Governed*, (London, Christophers, 1958).

Crossman, R.H.S., *Labour in the Affluent Society*, (Fabian Tract, 325, 1960).

Crossman, R.H.S., *Planning for Freedom*, (London, Hamish Hamilton, 1965).

Crossman, R.H.S., *Paying for the Social Services*, (Fabian Tract 399, 1969).

Crossman, R.H.S., *Inside View*, (London, Cape, 1972).

Crossman, R.H.S., *The Diaries of a Cabinet Minister*, 3 vols, (London, Hamilton, 1975–7).

Dalton, H., *Practical Socialism for Britain*, (London, Routledge, 1935).

Dalton, H., *Memoirs Vol 3. High Tide and After*, (London, Muller, 1962).

Dell, E., *Political Responsibility and Industry*, (London, Allen & Unwin, 1973).

Durbin, E.F.M., *The Politics of Democratic Socialism*, (London, The Labour Book Service, 1940).

Feather, V., *The Essence of Trade Unionism*, third edition, (London, Bodley Head, 1963).

Foot, M.M., *Parliament in Danger!*, (London, Pall Mall, 1959).

Foot, M.M., 'Credo of the Labour Left', *New Left Review* 49, (1968), 19–34.

Gaitskell, H., 'Economic Aims of the Labour Party', *Political Quarterly*, 24 (1) (1953), 5–18.

Gaitskell, H., *The High Cost of Toryism*, (Labour Party pamphlet, January 1953).

Gaitskell, H., *Recent Developments in Socialist Thinking*, (London, Co-operative Union, 1956).

Gaitskell, H., *Socialism and Nationalisation*, (Fabian Tract, 300, 1956).

Galbraith, J.K., *The Affluent Society*, (London, H. Hamilton, 1958).

Griffiths, J., *Pages from Memory*, (London, Dent, 1969).

Hart, Judith, *Aid and Liberation, A Socialist Study of Aid Politics*, (London, Gollancz, 1973).

Healey, D., *A Neutral Belt in Europe*, (Fabian Tract 311, 1958).

Healey, D., *A Labour Britain and the World*, (Fabian Tract 352, 1964).

Heffer, E., 'Labour's Future', *Political Quarterly* 43, (1972), 380–88.

Heffer, E., *The Class Struggle in Parliament*, (London, Gollancz, 1973).

Holland, S., *The Socialist Challenge*, (London, Quartet, 1975).

Houghton, Douglas, *Paying for the Social Services*, (Institute of Economic Affairs, Occasional Paper 16, London, 1967).

Houghton, Douglas, 'Trade Union MPs in the British House of Commons', *Parliamentarian*, (October 1968), 215–21.

Houghton, Douglas, 'The Labour Back-bencher', *Political Quarterly*, 40, (1969), 454–63.

Hughes, E., *Parliament and Mumbo Jumbo*, (London, Allen & Unwin, 1966).

Hughes, E., *Sydney Silverman – Rebel in Parliament*, (London, Skilton, 1969).

Hughes, J., *Socialism in the 1960s*, (Tribune Pamphlet, 1960).

Hughes, J., *Nationalised Industries in the Mixed Economy*, (Fabian Tract 328, 1960).

Hughes, J., *The TUC: a plan for the 70s*, (Fabian Tract 397, October 1969).

Jay, D.P.T., *The Socialist Case*, (London, Faber, 1937).

Jay, D.P.T., *Socialism in the New Society*, (London, Longmans, 1962).

Jay, D.P.T., 'Government Control of the Economy: Defects in the Machinery', *Political Quarterly*, 39, (1968), 134–44.

Jay, D.P.T., *After the Common Market: a Better Alternative for Britain*, (Harmondsworth, Penguin, 1968).

Jay, D.P.T. & Jenkins, R., *The Common Market Debate*, (Fabian Tract 341, 1962).

Jenkins, Clive & Mortimer, Jim, *British Trade Unions Today*, (London, Pergamon Press, 1965).

Jenkins, H. & Wolfgang, W., *Tho' Cowards Flinch: Democracy, Power and Socialism in the Labour Party*, (Future and Victory for Socialism pamphlet, 1956).

Jenkins, R., *Pursuit of Progress: a critical analysis of the achievement and prospect of the Labour Party*, (London, Heinemann, 1953).

Jenkins, R., *The Labour Case*, (Harmondsworth, Penguin, 1959).

Jenkins, R., *Essays and Speeches*, ed. Lester, A., (London, Collins, 1967).

Jenkins, R., *What Matters Now*, (London, Fontana, 1972).

Jones, James L. (Jack), *What About the Pensioners?*, (TGWU. pamphlet, London, 1973).

Kaufman, Gerald (ed.), *The Left: a Symposium*, (London, Anthony Blond, 1966).

Lapping, Brian & Radice, Giles, (eds.), *More Power to the People*, (London, Longmans, 1968).

MacDonald, J.R., *Ramsey MacDonald's Political Writings*, B. Barker ed., (London, Allen Lane, 1973).

Mackenzie, Norman (ed.), *Conviction*, (London, MacGibbon & Kee, 1958).

Mackintosh, J.P., '40 years on?', *Political Quarterly*, **41** (1970), 42—55.

Mackintosh, J.P., 'The House of Commons and Taxation', *Political Quarterly*, **42** (1971), 75—86.

Mackintosh, J.P., 'The problem of the Labour Party', *Political Quarterly*, **43** (1972), 2—19.

Mackintosh, J.P., 'Socialism or Social Democracy? The Choice for the Labour Party', *Political Quarterly*, **43** (4) (1972), 470—84.

Magee, Bryan, *The New Radicalism*, (London, Secker & Warburg, 1962).

Manifesto Group, *What We Must Do: a Democratic Socialist Approach to Britain's Crisis*, (London, 1977).

Mann, Jean, *Woman in Parliament*, (London, Odhams, 1962).

Martin, K., *Socialism and the Welfare State*, (Fabian Tract 291, 1951).

Mayhew, C.P., *Britain's role tomorrow*, (London, Hutchinson, 1967).

Mayhew, C.P., *Party Games*, (London, Hutchinson, 1969).

Mikardo, Ian, *The Second 5 years: A Labour Programme for 1950*. (Fabian Research Series, 124, 1948).

Mikardo, Ian, 'Present Day Problems of Great Britain's Labour Movement', in H.F. Infield (ed.), *Essays in Jewish Sociology, Labour and Co-operation: in memory of Dr. Noah Baron, 1889—1955*, (London, Thomas Yoseloff, 1962).

Morrison, H., *Government and Parliament: a survey from the inside*, (London, Oxford University Press, 1954).

Morrison, H., *Herbert Morrison: An Autobiography*, (London, Odhams, 1960).

Mulley, F.W., *The Politics of Western Defence*, (London, Thames & Hudson, 1962).

New Statesman & Nation, Keep Left, (pamphlet, 1947).

New Statesman & Nation, Keeping Left, (pamphlet, 1950).

Northcott, Jim F., *Why Labour?*, (Harmondsworth, Penguin, 1964).

Owen, D., Rodgers, W. & Williams, S., 'Open letter to fellow members of the Labour Party', *Guardian*, 1 August 1980.

Prentice, R., 'Lessons of the Labour Government: not socialist enough', *Political Quarterly*, **41** (1970), 146—50.

Rees, Merlyn, 'The Social Setting', *Political Quarterly*, **31** (1960), 285—99.

Rodgers, W.T. (ed.), *For Hugh Gaitskell, 1906—1963*, (London, Thames & Hudson, 1964).

Sedgemore, B., *The How and Why of Socialism*, (Nottingham, Spokesman, 1977).

Shanks, Michael, 'Labour Philosophy and the Current Position', *Political Quarterly*, **31** (1960), 241—54.

Shanks, Michael, *The Stagnant Society: A warning*, (Harmondsworth, Penguin, 1961).

Shinwell, E., *The Labour Story*, (London, Macdonald, 1963).

Shinwell, E., *I've Lived through it All*, (London, Gollancz, 1973).

Shore, Peter, *Entitled to Know*, (London, McGibbon & Kee, 1966).

Shore, Peter, 'The case against entry ... reply to the White Paper', (London, New Statesman, 1971).

Shore, Peter, *Europe: the way back*, (Fabian Tract 425, 1973).

Short, Edward, *Education in a Changing World*, (London, Pitman, 1971).

Simpson, Bill, *Labour: the Unions and the Party. A Study of the Trade Unions and the British Labour Movement*, (London, Allen & Unwin, 1973).

Socialist Union, *Socialism: A New Statement of Principles*, (London, Lincolns-Prager, 1952).

Socialist Union, *Socialism and Foreign Policy*, (London, Book House, 1953).

Socialist Union, *20th Century Socialism: the Economy of Tomorrow*, (Harmonds-worth, Penguin, 1956).

Stewart, M., *Policy and Weapons in the Nuclear Age*, (Fabian Tract 296, 1955).

Stewart, M. & Winsbury, R., *An Incomes Policy for Labour*, (Fabian Tract 350, 1963).

Strachey, John, *The Coming Struggle for Power*, seventh impression, (London, Gollancz, 1937).

Strachey, John, *Labour's Task*, (Fabian Tract 290, 1951).

Strachey, John, *Contemporary Capitalism*, (London, Gollancz, 1956).

Strachey, John, *End of Empire*, (London, Gollancz, 1959).

Strachey, John, *On the Prevention of War*, (London, Macmillan, 1962).

Taverne, D., *Monetary and Economic Union in Europe*, (London, Labour Committee for Europe, 1971).

Taverne, D., *The Future of the Left*, (London, Cape, 1974).

Tawney, R.H., *Equality*, first published 1931, new edition, with an introduction by R.M. Titmuss, (London, Unwin, 1964).

Titmuss, R.M., *The Irresponsible Society*, (Fabian Tract 323, 1960).

Tribune, Full Speed Ahead (pamphlet, 1950).

Tribune, One Way Only (pamphlet, 1951).

Tribune, Going Our Way (pamphlet, 1951).

Tribune, Tribune 21, E. Thomas, editor, (London, MacGibbon & Kee, 1958).

Tribune Group, *Labour — Party or Puppet?*, (pamphlet, 1972).

Tribune Group, *The Block Vote*, (pamphlet, 1973).

Victory for Socialism, *Equality in Education*, (1958).

Victory for Socialism, *A Roof over your Head?*, (1958).

Victory for Socialism, *Industry Your Servant*, (1958).

Victory for Socialism, *Policy for Summit Talks: How to End the Cold War*, (1958).

Victory for Socialism, *The Red Sixties*, by H. Jenkins, R. Lewis, G. Southgate and W. Wolfgang, (1959).

Victory for Socialism, *Why NATO?*, by H. Davies, (1960).

Walker, P.C. Gordon, *The Restatement of Liberty*, (London, Hutchinson, 1951).

Whitaker, B. (ed.), *A Radical Future*, (London, Cape, 1967).

Wigg, Lord, *George Wigg*, (London, Joseph, 1972).

Williams, Shirley, 'The External Setting', *Political Quarterly*, **31** (1960), 272—84.

Wilson, H., *In Place of Dollars*, (Tribune pamphlet, London, 1952).

Wilson, H., *The War on World Poverty*, (London, Gollancz, 1953).

Wilson, H., *Remedies for Inflation*, (Labour Party, 1957).

Wilson, H., *The New Britain: Labour's Plan Outlined*, (Harmondsworth, Penguin, 1964).

Wilson, H., *Purpose in Politics*, (London, Weidenfeld & Nicolson, 1964).

Wilson, H., *The Relevance of British Socialism*, (London, Weidenfeld & Nicolson, 1964).

Wilson, H., *Purpose in power: selected speeches*, (London, Weidenfeld & Nicolson, 1966).

Wilson, H., *The Labour Government 1964—70: a Personal Record*, (London, Weiden-feld & Nicolson & Michael Joseph, 1971).

Woodcock, G., *The Trade Union Movement and the Government*, (Leicester, University Press, 1968).

Young, E. & Young, W., *The Socialist Imagination*, (Fabian Tract 326, 1960).

Younger, K., 'Britain and the Outside World', *Political Quarterly*, 35 (1964), 212–21.

Younger, K., 'British Interests and British Foreign Policy', *Political Quarterly*, 38 (1967), 339–50.

Younger, K. & Beswick, F., *German Rearmament – For and Against*, (Fabian Tract, 1954).

3   OTHER WORKS, (theory, analysis and commentary)

Abel-Smith, B., *Labour's Social Plans*, (Fabian Tract 369, 1966).

Abrams, P. (ed.), *Work, Urbanism and Inequality: U.K. society today*, (London, Weidenfeld, 1978).

Addison, P., *The Road to 1945: British Politics and the Second World War*, (London, 1975).

Adler-Karlsson, G., *Functional Socialism: A Swedish Theory of Democratic Socialization*, (Stockholm, Bokforlaget Prisma, 1967).

Allen, V.L., *Trade Unions and the Government*, (London, Longmans, 1960).

Anderson, P., 'Origins of the Present Crisis', *New Left Review*, 23 (1964), 26–53.

Anderson, P., 'Critique of Wilsonism', *New Left Review*, 27 (1964), 3–27.

Anderson, P., 'The Left in the 50s', *New Left Review*, 29 (1965), 3–18.

Anderson, P. (ed.), *Towards Socialism*, (London, Fontana, 1966).

Anderson, P., 'The Antinomies of Antonio Gramsci', *New Left Review*, 100 (1976–7), 5–78.

Bachrach, P., *The Theory of Democratic Elitism: a critique.* (London, London U.P., 1969).

Barker, Rodney, *Education and Politics 1900–51: A Study of the Labour Party*, (Oxford, Clarendon Press, 1972).

Barratt-Brown, Michael, *From Labourism to Socialism: The Political Economy of Labour in the 1970s*, (Nottingham, Spokesman Books, 1972).

Barry, B., *Political Argument*, (London, Routledge, 1965).

Barry, E.E., *Nationalisation in British Politics*, (London, Cape, 1965).

Bauman, Z., *Between Class and Elite: the Evolution of the British Labour Movement*, (Manchester, University Press, 1972).

Bauman, Z., *Socialism: The Active Utopia*, (London, Allen & Unwin, 1976).

Baxter, R., 'The working class and Labour Politics', *Political Studies*, 20 (1972), 97–107.

Bealey, F., *The Social and Political Thought of the British Labour Party*, (London, Weidenfeld & Nicolson, 1970).

Beckerman, Wilfred (ed.), *The Economic Record of the Labour Government, 1964–70*, (London, Duckworth, 1972).

Beer, S., 'Democratic One-Party Government for Britain', *Political Quarterly*, 32 (1961), 114–23.

Beer, S., *Modern British Politics*, (London, Faber, 1965).

Bell, D., *The End of Ideology: (On the Exhaustion of political ideas in the fifties)*, (Glencoe, Illinois, Free Press, 1960).

Bendix, R., *Nation-Building and Citizenship. Studies on Changing Social Order*, (London, Wiley, 1964).

Berrington, H., *Backbench Opinion in the House of Commons, 1945–55*, (Oxford, Pergamon, 1973).

Bilski R., 'The Common Market and the Growing Strength of Labour's Left Wing', *Government and Opposition*, **12(3)** (1977), 306—331.

Birnbaum, Norman, 'Great Britain: the Reactive Revolt', in Morton A. Kaplan, (ed) *The Revolution in World Politics*, (New York, Wiley, 1962).

Blackburn R. & Cockburn, A. (eds.), *The Incompatibles: trade union militancy and the consensus*, (Harmondsworth, Penguin, 1967).

Blackburn, R. & Cockburn, A. (eds.), *Student Power: Problems, Diagnosis, Action*. (Hardmondsworth, Penguin, 1969).

Bogdanor, V. & Skidelski, R. (eds.), *The Age of Affluence*, (London, Macmillan, 1970).

Brady, R., *Crisis in Britain: Plans and Achievements of the Labour Government*, (Cambridge, University Press, 1950).

Briggs, A., 'The Welfare State in Historical Perspective', *European Journal of Sociology*, 2 (1961), 221—58.

Brittan, S., *Left or Right: the Bogus Dilemma*. (London, Secker & Warburg, 1968).

Brittan, S., *Steering the Economy: the role of the Treasury*, (London, Secker & Warburg, 1969).

Budd, A., *The Politics of Economic Planning*, (Manchester, Manchester University Press, 1978).

Bulmer, M. (ed.), *Working Class Images of Society*. (London, Routledge, 1975).

Burns, E., *Right Wing Labour: its Theory and Practice*, (London, Lawrence and Wishart, 1961).

Butler, D. & Freeman, J., *British Political Facts, 1900—68*, 3rd edition, (London, Macmillan, 1969).

Butler, D. & Kavanagh, D.A., *The British General Election of February, 1974*, (London/Basingstoke, Macmillan, 1974).

Butler, D. & Kavanagh, D.A., *The British General Election of October, 1974*, (London, Macmillan, 1975).

Butler, D.E. & King, Anthony, *The British General Election of 1964*, (London, Macmillan, 1965).

Butler, D.E. & King, Anthony, *The British General Election of 1966*, (London, Macmillan, 1966).

Butler, D.E. & Stokes, Donald, *Political Change in Britain: Forces Shaping Electoral Choice*, (London, Macmillan, 1969).

Butler, D.E. & Pinto-Duschinsky, M., *The British General Election of 1970*, (London/Basingstoke, Macmillan, 1971).

Butler, D.E. & Rose, R., *The British General Election of 1959*, (London, Macmillan, 1960).

Castells, M., *The Urban Question: a Marxist Approach*, (London, Edward Arnold, 1977).

Castles, S. & Kosack, G., *Immigrant Workers and Class Structure in Western Europe*, (London, OUP, 1973).

Catley, B. & McFarlane, B., 'Labour's Plans: neo-Capitalism comes to Australia', *Intervention*, 3 (1973).

Catley, B. & McFarlane, B., *From Tweedledum to Tweedledee: the New Labour Government in Australia*, (Sydney, Australia and New Zealand Book Co., 1974).

Christoph, J.B., 'Consensus and Cleavage in British Political Ideology', *American Political Science Review*, **59(3)** (1965), 629—42.

Cliff, T., *The Crisis: Social Contract or Socialism*. (London, Pluto, 1975).

Cline, A., *Recruits to Labour*, (New York, Syracuse, 1963).

Coates, D., *The Labour Party and the Struggle for Socialism*, (Cambridge, University Press, 1975).

Coates, K., *The Crisis of British Socialism*, (Nottingham, Spokesman Books, 1971).

Coates, K., 'Socialists and the Labour Party', in R. Miliband & J. Saville, (editors), *Socialist Register 1973*, (London, Merlin, 1974), pp. 158–78.

Coates, K. & Topham, T., *The New Unionism: the case for workers control*, (London, Peter Owen, 1972).

Cole, G.D.H., *History of the Labour Party from 1914*, (London, Routledge & Paul, 1948).

Cole, G.D.H., *A Short History of the British Working Class Movement*, new edition, (London, Allen & Unwin, 1948).

Cole, G.D.H., 'The Labour Party and the Trade Unions', *Political Quarterly*, **24**(1), (1953), pp. 18–27.

Comer, L., The Question of Women and Class, *Women's Studies International Quarterly*, **1** (1978), 165–73.

Cook, C. & Taylor, I. (eds.), *The Labour Party: an introduction to its history, structure and politics*, (London, Longman, 1980).

Cowling, M.J., *The impact of Labour 1920–24: the beginning of modern British Politics*, (Cambridge, University Press, 1971).

Craig, F.W.S. (ed.), *British General Election Manifestos, 1918–66*, (Chichester, Political Reference Publications, 1970).

Crewe, I., Sarlvik, B. & Alt, J., 'Partisan De-alignment in Britain 1964–74', *British Journal of Political Science*, **7** (1977), 129–90.

Crouch, C., *Class Conflict and the Industrial Relations Crisis: Compromise and Corporatism in the Policies of the British State*, (London, Humanities Press, 1977).

Crouch, C. & Pizzorno, A. (eds.), *The Resurgence of Class Conflict in Western Europe since 1968*, vol. 1, (London, Macmillan, 1978).

Dahl, R., 'Workers' control of industry and the British Labour Party', *American Political Science Review*, **41** (1947), pp. 875–900.

Dahrendorf, R., *Class and Class Conflict in Industrial Society*, (London, Routledge & Kegan Paul, 1959).

Davis, K. & Moore, W.E., 'Some Principles of Stratification', *American Sociological Review*, **10** (1945), 242–9.

De'Ath, W., *Barbara Castle: a portrait from life*, (London/Bristol, Clifton Books, 1970).

Donoughue, R. & Jones, G.W., *Herbert Morrison: Portrait of a Politician*, (London, Weidenfeld & Nicolson, 1973).

Dorfman, G.A., *Wage Politics in Britain, 1945–1967: Government v. the TUC*. (Ames, Iowa, Iowa State University Press, 1973).

Dow, R., *The Management of the British Economy, 1945–60*, (Cambridge, CUP, 1964).

Dowse, R.E., *Left in the Centre*, (London, Longmans, 1966).

Driver, C.P., *The Disarmers: A Study in Protest*, (London, Hodder & Stoughton, 1964).

Drucker, H.M., *Doctrine and Ethos in the Labour Party*, (London, George Allen & Unwin, 1979).

Duverger, M., *Political Parties*, third edition, (London, Methuen, 1964).

Eatwell, R., *The 1945–51 Labour Governments*, (London, Batsford, 1979).

Edelman, Murray & Fleming, R.W., *The Politics of Wage-Price Decisions*, (Urbana, University of Illinois Press, 1965).

Einzig, P., *Decline and Fall?: Britain's Crisis in the Sixties*. (London, Macmillan, 1960).

Ellis, John & Johnson, R.W., *Members from the Unions*, (Fabian Research Series **316**, July 1974).

Epstein, Leon D., 'Socialism and the British Labour Party', *Political Science Quarterly*, **66** (1951), 556–75.

Epstein, Leon D., 'The Cohesion of British Parliamentary Parties', *American Political Science Review*, **50** (1956), 360–77.

Epstein, Leon D., 'British class consciousness and the Labour Party', *Journal of British Studies*, **3** (1962), 136–150.

Epstein, Leon D., 'New MPs and the Politics of the Parliamentary Labour Party', *Political Studies*, **10** (1962), 121–9.

Epstein, Leon D., 'Who makes party policy: British Labour 1960–61', *Midwest Journal of Political Science*, (1962), 165–182.

Fanti, G., 'The resurgence of the Labour Party', *New Left Review*, **30** (1965), 27–44.

Finer, S.E., Berrington, H.B. & Bartholomew, D.J., *Backbench Opinion in the House of Commons, 1955–59*, (London, Pergamon Press, 1961).

Foot, M.M., *Aneurin Bevan Volume I*, (London, McGibbon & Key, 1962): *Volume 2*, (London, Davies-Poynter, 1973).

Foot, Paul, *The Politics of Harold Wilson*, (Harmondsworth, Penguin, 1968).

Foot, Paul, 'Harold Wilson and the Labour Left', *International Socialism*, **33** (Summer 1968).

Forrester, T., *The Labour Party and the Working Class*, (London, Heinemann, 1976).

Fraser, D., *The Evolution of the British Welfare State*, (London, Macmillan, 1973).

Galenson, W. (ed.), *Comparative Labour Movements*, (New York, Russell, 1968).

Gamble, A., *The Conservative Nation*, (London, Routledge, 1974).

Gamble, A. & Walton, P., *Capitalism in Crisis: inflation and the state*, (London, Macmillan, 1976).

Gay, P., *The Dilemma of Democratic Socialism: Eduard Bernstein's Challenge to Marx*, second impression, (London, Collier-Macmillan, 1970).

Glyn, A. & Sutcliffe, B., *British Capitalism, Workers and the Profit Squeeze*, (Harmondsworth, Penguin, 1972).

Glynn, S. & Oxborrow, J., *Inter-war Britain: a social and economic history*, (London, George Allen & Unwin, 1976).

Gordon, M.R., *Conflict and Consensus in Labour's Foreign Policy 1914–65*, (Stanford, Stanford University Press, 1969).

Gough, I., 'State Expenditure in Advanced Capitalism', *N.L.R.*, **92** (1975), 53–92.

Gough, I., *The Political Economy of the Welfare State*, (London, Macmillan, 1979).

Gramsci, A., *Selections from the Prison Notebooks of Antonio Gramsci*, edited and translated by Q. Hoare & G. Nowell Smith, (London, 1973).

Gray, A., *The Socialist Tradition: Moses to Lenin*, (London, Longmans, 1947).

Green, T.H., *Lectures on the Principles of Political Obligation*, new impression, (London, Longmans, 1901).

Guttsman, W.L., *The British Political Elite*, (London, MacGibbon & Kee, 1964).

Gwyn, W.B., 'The Labour Party and the Threat of Bureaucracy', *Political Studies*, **19** (1971), 383–402.

Gyford, John & Haseler, Stephen, *Social Democracy: Beyond Revisionism*, (Fabian Research Series 292, 1971).

Habermas, J., *Towards a Rational Society: Student protest, Science and Politics*, (London, Heinemann, 1971).

Habermas, J., *Legitimation Crisis*, (London, Heinemann, 1976).

Hall, Peter G. (ed.), *Labour's New Frontiers*, (London, Deutsch, 1964).

Harman, C., 'Tribune of the People', *International Socialism*, 21 and 24.

Harris, N., *Competition and the Corporate Society: British Conservatives, The State and Industry, 1945–64*. (London, Macmillan, 1972).

Harrison, M., *Trade Unions and the Labour Party since 1945*. (London, Allen & Unwin, 1960).

Harrison, R., 'Labour Government: then and now', *Political Quarterly*, 41, (1970), pp. 67–82.

Haseler, Stephen, *The Gaitskellites: Revisionism in the British Labour Party, 1951–64*, (London, Macmillan, 1969).

Hatfield, M., *The House the Left Built: Inside Labour Policy-Making 1970–75*, (London, Gollancz, 1978).

Helenius, Ralph, *The Profile of Party Ideologies*, (Helsingfors, Svenska Bokforlaget, 1969).

Hindell, K. & Williams, P., 'Scarborough and Blackpool: Analysis of Conferences 1960 and 1961', *Political Quarterly*, **33** (1962), 306–30.

Hindess, B., *The Decline of Working Class Politics*. (London, MacGibbon & Key, 1971).

Hinton, J., *The First Shop Stewards' Movement*, (London, Allen & Unwin, 1973).

Hirsch, F., *The Social Limits to Growth*, (London, Routledge & Kegan Paul, 1977).

Hobhouse, L.T., *Liberalism*, first published 1911, new edition, (London, Oxford University Press, 1964).

Hobsbawn, E., *Labouring Men*, (London, Weidenfeld & Nicolson, 1964).

Holt, Robert & Turner, John, 'Great Britain: the Labour Government and the Politics of Party Consensus' in, W.G. Andrews (editor), *European Politics II*, (New York, Van Nostraud, 1968).

Howell, D., *The restatement of socialism in the Labour Party 1947–61*, (unpublished Ph.D. Thesis, Manchester University, 1972).

Howell, D., *British Social Democracy: a study in Development and Decay*, (London, Croom Helm, 1976).

Hunter, L., *The Road to Brighton Pier*, (London, Arthur Barker, 1959).

Huntford, R., *The New Totalitarians*, revised edition, (Allen Lane, London, 1975).

Hyams, Edward, *The New Statesman: the history of the first fifty years 1913–63*, (London, Longmans, 1963).

Hyman, R., *Marxism and the Sociology of Trade Unionism,* (London, Pluto, 1971).

Hyman, R., 'Industrial Conflict and Political Economy', *Socialist Register*, 1973, pp. 101–52.

Jackson, R.J., *Rebels and Whips*, (London, Macmillan, 1968).

Jacoby, R., 'The Politics of the Crisis Theory: Toward the Critique of Automatic Marxism, II', *Telos, *23 (1975), 3–52.

James, R.R., *Ambitions and Realities: British Politics 1964–70*, (London, Weidenfeld & Nicolson, 1972).

Janosik, G.E., *Constituency Labour Parties in Britain*, (London, Pall Mall, 1968).

Jenkins, M., *Bevanism, Labour's High Tide: the Cold War and the Democratic Mass Movement*, (Nottingham, Spokesman, 1979).

Jenkins, P., *The Battle of Downing Street*, (London, Charles Knight, 1970).

Jessop, B., 'Corporatism, Fascism and Social Democracy', (mimeo, paper presented to Leeds Sociology Department, April, 1978).

Kellner, P. & Hitchens, C., *Callaghan: the road to Number 10*, (London, Cassell, 1976).

Kendall, W., *The Revolutionary Movement in Britain 1900–21*, (London, Weidenfeld & Nicolson, 1969).

Kendall, W., *The Labour Movement in Europe*, (London, Allen Lane, 1975).

Kincaid, J., *Poverty and Inequality in England*, (Harmondsworth, Penguin, 1973).

Kilroy-Silk, Robert, 'Trade Unions and Socialism: The Donovan Report', *Political Studies*, **17** (1969), 95–101.

Kitzinger, U., *Diplomacy and Persuasion: How Britain Joined the Common Market*. (London, Thames & Hudson, 1973).

Kolko, G., *The Politics of War: allied diplomacy & the world crisis of 1943–45*. (London, Weidenfeld, 1969).

Kornberg, A. & Frasure, R.C., 'Policy Differences in British Parliamentary Parties', *American Political Science Review*, **65** (3) (1971), 694–703.

Krug, Mark M., *Aneurin Bevan: Cautious Rebel*, (New York, 1961).

Labedz, L. (ed.), *Revisionism: Essays on the history of Marxist ideas*, (London, Allen & Unwin, 1962).

Lane, Tony, *The Union makes us strong: The British Working Class, Its Trade Unionism and Politics*, (London, Arrow, 1974).

Lapping, B., *The Labour Government 1964–70*, (Harmondsworth, Penguin, 1970).

Laski, H., *Parliamentary Government in England*, (London, Allen & Unwin, 1938).

Lehmbruch, G., 'Liberal Corporatism and Party Government', *Comparative Political Studies*, **10**(1) (1977), 91–126.

Lichtheim, G., *Marxism: an historical and critical study*, (London, Routledge & Kegan Paul, 1965).

Lichtheim, G., *A Short History of Socialism*, (London, Weidenfeld & Nicolson, 1970).

Lockwood, D., 'Sources of Variation in Working-Class Images of Society', *Sociological Review*, **14** (3) (1966), 249–267.

Loewenberg, G., 'The British Constitution and the structure of the Labour Party', *American Political Science Review*, **52**(3) (1958), 771–90.

Loewenberg, G., 'The Transformation of the British Labour Party Policy since 1945', *Journal of Politics*, **21**(1) (1959), 234–57.

Looker, Robert, 'The Future of the Left in Britain', *Studies on the Left*, **7**(2) (1967), 49–69.

Lukes, S., *Power: a Radical View*, (London, Macmillan, 1974).

McBriar, A.M., *Fabian Socialism and English Politics, 1884–1914*, (Cambridge, University Press, 1966).

McEachern, D. 'Party Government and the Class interests of Capital: conflict over the steel industry, 1945–70, *Capital and Class*, **8** (1979), 125–43.

McEachern, D., *A Class Against Itself*, (Cambridge, University Press, 1980).

McKenzie, R.T., 'Policy Decision in Opposition: A Rejoinder', *Political Studies*, **5** (1957), 176–82.

McKenzie, R.T., 'Parties, Pressure Groups, and British Political Process', *Political Quarterly*, **29** (1958), 5–16.

McKenzie, R.T., *British Political Parties*, second edition, (London, Heinemann, 1970).

McKibbin, R., *Evolution of the Labour Party 1910–24*, (London, Oxford University Press, 1975).

McKie, D., Cook, C. & Phillips, M., *The Guardian/Quartet Election Guide*, (London, Quartet, 1978).

McNevin, M., The left-wing in the British Labour Party, (unpublished B. Litt. Thesis, Oxford, 1964).

McRae, K. (ed.), *Consociational Democracy: Political Accommodation in Segmented Societies*, (Toronto, McClelland & Stewart, 1974).

Mallet, S., *The New Working Class*, (Nottingham, Spokesman, 1975).

Mann, M., 'The Social Cohesion of Liberal Democracy', *American Sociological Review*, **35**(3) (1970), 423–39.

Marcuse, H., *One-Dimensional Man: Studies in the ideology of advanced industrial society*, (London, Routledge, 1964).

Marsh, D. & Grant, W., 'Tripartism: Reality or Myth', *Government and Opposition,* **12** (2) (1977), 194—211.

Marshall, T.H., *Citizenship and Social Class: and other essays.* (Cambridge, University Press, 1950).

Mattick, P., *Marx and Keynes: the Limits of the Mixed Economy,* (London, Merlin, 1971).

Mayntz, R., 'Legitimacy and the Directive Capacity of the Political System', in LN. Lindberg, *et al., Stress and Contradiction in Modern Capitalism.* (London, Lexington Books, 1975).

Meehan, E.J., *The British Left Wing and Foreign Policy,* (New Brunswick, Rutgers University Press, 1960).

Merrington, J., 'Theory and Practice in Gramsci's Marxism'. *Socialist Register,* (1968) pp. 145—76.

Michie, A. & Hoggart, S., *The Pact: the inside story of the Lib—Lab Government, 1977—78,* (London, Quartet, 1978).

Middlemas, K., *Politics in Industrial Society: the experience of the British system since 1911,* (London, Deutsch, 1979).

Miliband, R., 'Party Democracy and Parliamentary Government', *Political Studies,* **6** (1958), 170—74.

Miliband, R., 'Socialism and the myth of the Golden Past', *Socialist Register,* (1964) pp. 92—103.

Miliband, R., 'What does the Left want?', *Socialist Register,* (1965) pp. 184—96.

Miliband, R., 'The Labour Government and Beyond, *Socialist Register,* (1966) pp. 11—26.

Miliband, R., 'Vietnam and Western Socialism', *Socialist Register,* (1967).

Miliband, R., *The State in Capitalist Society,* (London, Weidenfeld & Nicolson, 1972).

Miliband, R., *Parliamentary Socialism: A Study in the Politics of Labour,* second edition, (London, Merlin, 1973).

Miliband, R. & Saville, J., 'Labour Policy and the Labour Left', *Socialist Register,* (1964), pp. 149—56.

Minkin, L., The British Labour Party and the Trade Unions: Crisis and Compact, *Industrial and Labor Relations Review,* **28** (1) (1974), pp. 7—37.

Minkin, L., *The Labour Party Conference: a Study in the Politics of Intra-Party Democracy,* (Manchester, University Press, 1980).

Moorhouse, H.F., 'The Political Incorporation of the British working class: an interpretation', *Sociology,* **7** (1973), 341—59.

Mueller, C., *The Politics of Communication: a study in the political sociology of language, socialization and legitimation,* (New York, Oxford University Press, 1973).

Muller, W.D., 'Trade Union MPs and Parliamentary Specialisation', *Political Studies,* **20** (1972), 317—24.

Muller, W.D., Union—MP Conflict: an Overview, *Parliamentary Affairs,* **26** (1972—3), 336—55.

Muller, W.D., *The 'Kept Men'?: the First Century of Trade Union Representation in the British House of Commons, 1874—1975,* (Hassocks, Harvester Press, 1977).

Nairn, T., 'The Nature of the Labour Party', in P. Anderson ed., *Towards Socialism,* (London, Fontana, 1965).

Nairn, T., 'The Fateful Meridian', *New Left Review,* **60** (1970), 3—35.

Nairn, T., 'British Nationalism and the EEC', *New Left Review,* **69** (1971), 3—30.

Nairn, T., 'The Left Against Europe?', *New Left Review,* **75** (1972).

Nairn, T., *The Break-Up of Britain: crisis and neo-nationalism*, (London, NLB, 1977).

Naylor, John F., *Labour's International Policy: the Labour Party in the 1930s*, (London, Weidenfeld & Nicolson, 1969).

Norton, P., *Dissention in the House of Commons, Intra-Party Dissent in the House of Commons' Division Lobbies 1945−74*, (London, Macmillan, 1975).

O'Connor, J., *The Fiscal Crisis of the State*, (New York, St Martin's Press, 1973).

Offe, C., 'Political Authority and Class Structures − an analysis of late capitalist societies', *International Journal of Sociology*, II (1) (1972), 73−105.

Pahl, R.E. & Winkler, J.T., 'Corporatism in Britain: why protecting industry need not mean more bureaucracy', *Times*, 26 March, 1976.

Panitch, Leo V., 'Ideology and Integration: The Case of the British Labour Party', *Political Studies*, 19 (2) (1971), 184−200.

Panitch, Leo V., The Labour Party and the Trade Unions: a study of incomes policy since 1945 with special reference to 1964−70, (Ph.D. thesis, London, 1973−4).

Panitch, Leo V., *Social Democracy and Industrial Militancy: the Labour Party, the Trade Unions and Incomes Policy, 1945−74*, (Cambridge, University Press, 1976).

Panitch, Leo V., 'The Development of Corporatism in Liberal Democracies', *Comparative Political Studies*, 10 (1) (1977), 61−90.

Parkin, F., *Middle Class Radicalism: the social bases of the British Campaign for Nuclear Disarmament*, (Manchester, University Press, 1968).

Parkin, F., *Class, Inequality and Political Order*, (London, Paladin, 1972).

Parkin, F., *The Social Analysis of Class Structure*, (London, Tavistock, 1974).

Parkinson, M., *The Labour Party and the Organization of Secondary Education, 1918−65*, (London, Routledge & Kegan Paul, 1970).

Partridge, P.H., *Consent and Consensus*, (London, Pall Mall, 1971).

Pelling, H., *The British Communist Party: a historical profile*, (London, Black, 1958).

Pelling, H., *A Short History of the Labour Party*, (London, 1965).

Pelling, H., *The Origins of the Labour Party, 1880−1900*, second edition, (Oxford, Clarendon Press, 1965).

Perlman, S., *A Theory of the Labor Movement*, new impression, (New York, Kelley, 1949).

Pierson, Stanley, *Marxism and the Origins of British Socialism: The Struggle for a New Consciousness*, (London, Cornell University Press, 1973).

Pimlott, B., 'The Socialist League: intellectuals and the Labour Left in the 1930s', *Journal of Contemporary History*, 6 (1971), 12−38.

Pimlott, B., *Labour and the Left in the 1930s*, (Cambridge, University Press, 1977).

Piper, J.R., 'Backbench Rebellion, Party Government and Consensus Politics: The Case of the Parliamentary Labour Party, 1966−70, *Parliamentary Affairs*, 27 (1973−4), 384−96.

Piven, F.F. & Cloward, R., *Regulating the Poor: the functions of public welfare*, (London, Tavistock, 1972).

Poulantzas, N., *Political Power and Social Classes*, (London, New Left Books, 1973).

Pritt, D.N., *The Labour Government, 1945−51*, (London, Lawrence and Wishart, 1963).

Prynn, D.L., 'Common Wealth − a British 'third party' of the 1940s', *Journal of Contemporary History*, 7 (1972), 169−79.

Pulzer, Peter, *Political Representation and Elections in Britain*, (London, Allen & Unwin, 1967).

Punnett, R.M., *Front Bench Opposition*, (London, Heinemann, 1973).

Punnett, R.M., 'The Labour Shadow Cabinet 1955−64', *Parliamentary Affairs*, 18 (1964−5), 61−70.

Putnam, R.D., *The Beliefs of Politicians: ideology conflict and democracy in Britain and Italy*, (London, Yale University Press, 1973).

Ranney, A., *Pathways to Parliament: Candidate selection in Britain*, (London, Macmillan, 1965).

Rawson, D.W., 'The Life Span of Labour Parties', *Political Studies*, 17 (1969), 313–33.

Richards, Peter G., *Honourable Members: A Study of the British Backbencher*, (London, Faber & Faber, 1964), second edition.

Richter, I., *Political Purpose in Trade Unions*, (London, Allen & Unwin, 1973).

Richter, M., *The Politics of Conscience — T.H. Green and His Age*, (London, Weidenfeld & Nicolson, 1964).

Roberts, K. *et al.*, *The Fragmentary Class Structure*, (London, Heinemann, 1977).

Robson, W.H., *Nationalisation and Public Ownership*, (London, Allen & Unwin, 1962).

Rogow, A.A. & Shore, P., *The Labour Government and British Industry*, (Oxford, Basil Blackwell, 1955).

Rose, R., 'The Policy Ideas of English Party Activists', *American Political Science Review*, 56 (2) (1962), 360–71.

Rose, R., 'Anatomy of British Political Factions', *New Society*, 1 (2) (11 October, 1962), 29–31.

Rose, R., 'Complexities of Party Leadership', *Parliamentary Affairs*, 16 (3) (1962–3), 257–73.

Rose, R., 'Parties, Factions and Tendencies in Britain', *Political Studies*, 12 (1964), 33–46.

Rose, R., 'Class and Party Divisions: Britain as a Test Case', *Sociology*, 2 (2) (1968), 129–62.

Rose, R., 'The Variability of Party Government — A Theoretical and Empirical Critique', *Political Studies*, 17 (4) (1969), 413–45.

Rose, R. (ed.), *Studies in British Politics*, second edition, (London, Macmillan, 1969).

Rose, R., *The Problem of Party Government*, (London, Macmillan, 1974).

Rose, R. & Unwin, D.W., 'Persistence and Change in Western Party Systems since 1945', *Political Studies*, 18 (3) (1970), 287–319.

Rose, Saul, 'Policy Decision in Opposition', *Political Studies*, 4 (1956), 128–38.

Rose, Saul, 'The Labour Party and German Rearmament: A View from Transport House', *Political Studies*, 14 (2) (1966), 133–44.

Roth, A., *The MPs' Chart*, (London, Parliamentary Profiles, 1971).

Roth, A. & Kerbey, J., *The Business Background of MPs*, (London, Parliamentary Profiles, 1972).

Rothman, S., 'British Labour's New Left', *Political Science Quarterly*, 76 (1961), 393–401.

Rush, M., *The Selection of Parliamentary Candidates*, (London, Nelson, 1969).

Saville, J., 'The Welfare State: A Historical Perspective', *New Reasoner*, 3 (1957–8), 5–25.

Saville, J., 'Labourism and the Labour Government', *Socialist Register*, 1967, pp. 43–72.

Saville, J., 'The Ideology of Labourism', in R. Benewick, R.N. Berki & B. Parekh (eds.), *Knowledge and Belief in Politics*, (London, Allen & Unwin, 1973).

Schmitter, P.C., 'Still the Century of Corporatism?', in F.B. Pike & T. Stritch (eds.), *The New Corporatism: social-political structures in the Iberian world*, (London, University of Notre Dame Press, 1974).

Searle, G.R., *The Quest for National Efficiency, a study in British politics and political thought, 1899–1914*, (Oxford, Blackwell, 1971).

Sedgwick, Peter, 'Varieties of Socialist Thought', in B. Crick & W.A. Robson, (eds.), *Protest and Discontent*, (Harmondsworth, Penguin, 1970), pp. 37—67.

Sedgwick, Peter, 'The End of Labourism', *New Politics*, 8 (3) (1970), 77—86.

Semmel, B., *Imperialism and Social Reform: English social-imperial thought, 1895—1914*, (London, Allen & Unwin, 1960).

Seyd, P., Factionalism within the Labour Party — a case study of the Campaign for Democratic Socialism. (unpublished M. Phil. Thesis, Southampton University, 1968).

Seyd, P., 'Fighting for the soul of the Labour Party', *New Society*, 20 April 1978.

Shanks, M., *Planning and Politics: the British Experience 1960—76*, (London, PEP, 1977).

Shonfield, A., *Modern Capitalism: The Changing Balance of Public and Private Power*, (London, Oxford University Press, 1965).

Silverham, Lawrence, The political sociology of the contemporary Labour Party in Britain, (unpublished Ph.D. Thesis, London University, 1966).

Sissons, Michael & French, Philip, *Age of Austerity*, (London, Hodder & Stoughton, 1963).

Skidelski, R., *Oswald Mosley*, (London, Macmillan, 1974).

Smith, Leslie, *Harold Wilson*, (London, Fontana, 1964).

Spencer, H., *Man Versus the State*, (Harmondsworth, Penguin, 1969).

Stanworth, P. & Giddens, A. (eds.), *Elites and Power in British Society*, (Cambridge, University Press, 1974).

Steck, Henry J., 'The re-emergence of ideological politics in Great Britain', *Western Political Quarterly*, 18 (1965), 87—103.

Steck, Henry J., 'Grass roots militants and ideology: the Bevanite revolt', *Polity*, 2 (4) (1970), 426—42.

Stewart, M., *Protest or Power?: A Study of the Labour Party*, (London, Allen & Unwin, 1974).

Taylor, R., *Labour and the Social Contract*, (Fabian Tract 458, 1978).

Thomas, H., *John Strachey*, (London, Eyre Methuen, 1973).

Thompson, E.P., *Out of Apathy*, (London, New Left Books, 1960).

Thompson, E.P., 'The Peculiarities of the English', *Socialist Register*, 1965, pp. 311—62.

Titmuss, R., *Income Distribution and Social Change*, (London, Allen & Unwin, 1962).

Townsend, P., *Poverty, Socialism and Labour in Power*, (Fabian Tract 371, 1966).

Townsend, P. & Abel-Smith, B., *The Poor and the Poorest*, (London, Bell, 1965).

Townsend, P. & Bosanquet N. (eds.), *Labour and Inequality: sixteen Fabian essays*, (London, Fabian Society, 1972).

Ulam, A., *The Philosophical Foundations of English Socialism*, (New York, Octagon, 1964).

Urry, J. & Wakeford, J. (eds.), *Power in Britain: Sociological Readings*, (London, Heinemann, 1973).

Valen, H., 'Factional Activities and Nominations in Political Parties', *Acta Sociologica*, 3 (1958), 183—99.

Walter, N., 'Damned Fools in Utopia', *New Left Review*, 13—14, (1962), 119—28.

Wedderburn, D., 'Facts and Theories of the Welfare State', *Socialist Register*, 1965, pp. 127—46.

Weiler, P., 'The New Liberalism of L.T. Hobhouse', *Victorian Studies*, 16 (2), (1972).

Weiner, H., *British Labour and Public Ownership*, (London, Stevens & Sons, 1960).

Weinstein, J., *The Corporate Ideal in the Liberal State: 1900—1918*, (Boston, Beacon Press, 1969).

Widgery, D., *The Left in Britain 1956–68*, (Harmondsworth, Penguin, 1976).

Williams, F., *Fifty Years March: the Rise of the Labour Party*, (London, Odhams, 1949).

Williams, G., 'The Concept of "Egemonia" in the thought of Antonio Gramsci: some notes on interpretation', *Journal of the History of Ideas*, **21** (1960), 586–99.

Williams, Raymond, *Culture and Society 1780–1950*, (London, Chatto & Windus, 1958).

Williams, Raymond, *The Long Revolution*, (London, Chatto & Windus, 1961).

Williams, Raymond, 'The British Left', *New Left Review*, **30** (1965), 18–26.

Williams, Raymond (ed.), *May Day Manifesto*, (Harmondsworth, Penguin, 1968).

Williams, Roger, *Politics and Technology*, (London, Macmillan, 1971).

Windlesham, Lord, *Communication and Political Power*, (London, Cape, 1966).

Winkler, J.T., 'Corporatism', *Archives Européen de Sociologie*, **17** (1976), 100–136.

Winter, J.M., *Socialism and the Challenge of War*, (London, Routledge, 1974).

Young, Nigel, 'Prometheans or troglodytes? the English working class and the dialectics of incorporation', *Berkeley Journal of Sociology*, **12** (1967), 1–43.

Zariski, R., 'Party Factions and Comparative Politics: some Preliminary Observations', *Mid-West Journal of Political Science*, **4** (1960), 27–51.

Index